The Need for a Black Bible

THE BLACK MAN'S RELIGION
VOLUME III

The Need for a Black Bible

Yosef ben-Jochannan

Black Classic Press
Baltimore, MD

The Need for a Black Bible

Copyright 1974 by Yosef ben-Jochannan
Published by Alkebu-Ian Book Associates 1974
Published by Black Classic Press 2002

Library of Congress Card Catalog Number: 96-083453

ISBN 13: 978-0-933121-58-4
ISBN 10: 0-933121-58-X

Cover art by Tony Browder, rendered from the original cover design by Yosef ben-Jochannan

FrontCover: TheSun-GOD-Ra; theEver-SeeingEye-GOD-Horus; theHouse of Fire - Pyramid; the Golden Rooster - GOD - Damballah Ouedo and Voodum; the Ankh - original KEY OF LIFE - or Christian Cross of late; the DOG STAR or later Jewish Star of David; the GRAMADON of ancient times, or reverse German Swastika; the CRESCENT STAR or present Moslem Crescent of modern times; 1–11 BASIC MASONIFIED NUMEROLOGY of Mysteries Sytem.

Founded in 1978, Black Classic Press specializes in bringing to light obscure and significant works by and about people of African descent. If our books are not available in your area, ask your local bookseller to order them. Our current list of titles can be obtained by writing:

Black Classic Press
c/o List
P.O. Box 13414
Baltimore, MD 21203

The Black Man's Religion

Volume III

THE NEED FOR A "BLACK BIBLE"

by

Yosef ben-Jochannan

Sir Arthur Evans points to the great antiquity of the worship of the Mother and the Child, declaring: "The worship of a Mother Goddess predominated in later (prehistoric) times generally associated with a divine child—a worship which later survived in a classical guise influenced all later religion." (Report Brit. Assn. for the Adv. of Science, 1916, p. 19.)

The ancient Africans wrote the following thousands of years before there was a <u>Moses</u> to echo one of their theories about the <u>beginning</u> and/or the <u>ending</u>:

...MAN KNOW YOURSELF...

In the light of the above, this work is dedicated to the creators of the "WORD" that became "GOD;" to those that wrote down the "WORD;" to those that gave current meaning to the "WORD;" to those that knew the "WORD;" particularly, to those that know LOVE was, is, and will always be the "WORD." And to those who know that one LOVES with the "MIND," not with the "HEART." Glory be to all who know that:

KNOWLEDGE IS TRULY...THE WORD!

BLESSED BE THE WORD

Godfrey Higgins, who visited the cathedrals of Europe before the destruction of most of the Black Madonnas during the anti-religious period of the French Revolution says: "No person who has considered well the character of the temples in India and Egypt can help being convinced of the identity of their character and of their being the product of the same race of people; and this race evidently Ethiopian. The worship of the Mother and Child is seen in all parts of the Egyptian religion. It prevails everywhere. It is the worship of Isis and the infant Orus or Osiris. It is the religious rite which was so often prohibited at Rome but which prevailed in spite of all opposition, as we find from the remaining ruins of its temples. It was perhaps from this country, Egypt, that the worship of the black Virgin and Child came into Italy and where it still prevails. It was the worship of the mother of God, Jesus, the Saviour; Bacchus in Greece; Adonis in Syria; Cristna in India; coming into Italy through the medium of the two Ethiopias, she was, as the Ethiopians were, black, and such she still remains.

1. J. A. Rogers' SEX AND RACE, p. 279; see following page also.

OFFERINGS OF THE TEXT

---

1. All of the "GODS," or "ONE AND ONLY TRUE GOD," spoke to the world through intermediaries, so far as the "WRITTEN WORDS" show. Thus; why "GOD" could not have spoken through anyone else but a "JEW, CHRISTIAN" or "MOSLEM" [Muslim]? Because the "JEWS, CHRISTIANS" and "MOSLEMS" [Muslims] limited "GOD'S" ability to function only under their own rules they have created for themselves, and of which they expect everyone who does not adhere to their RELIGIOUS DOCTRINE to believe in. Belief is not necessarily proof, nor disproof; it is SOLELY a possibility. A CLOSED BELIEF cannot reason or operate in the presence of any type of "FREE THOUGHT" whatsoever.

The BLACK BIBLE must become the BLACK PEOPLE'S greatest avenue of FREE THOUGHT in which no boundary in MANKIND'S BELIEF is tabooed - RELIGIOUSLY, nor OTHERWISE.

LIST OF ILLUSTRATIONS

[PREFATORY NOTES] In GENESIS, Chapter ii, Verses 8 - 15 we find the following about the LORD and His great works during the period when he was creating everything, and the LAWS thereof. Note that "ETHIOPIA" [Africa, etc., page 108] was part of the Garden of Eden.

8 ¶ And the LORD God planted a garden eastward in E'-dĕn; and there he put the man whom he had formed.

9 And out of the ground made the LORD God to grow every tree that is pleasant to the sight, and good for food; the tree of life also in the midst of the garden, and the tree of knowledge of good and evil.

10 And a river went out of E'-dĕn to water the garden; and from thence it was parted, and became into four heads.

11 The name of the first is Pĭ'-sŏn: that is it which compasseth the whole land of Hăv'-i-läh, where there is gold;

12 And the gold of that land is good: there is bdellium and the onyx stone.

13 And the name of the second river is Gĭ'-hŏn: the same is it that compasseth the whole land of E-thi-ŏ'-pi-â.

14 And the name of the third river is Hid'-dĕ-kĕl: that is it which goeth toward the east of As-sўr'-ĭ-â. And the fourth river is Eu-phrā'-tĕs.

15 And the LORD God took the man, and put him into the garden of E'-dĕn to dress it and to keep it.

But we are reminded to be very careful of the allegories, myths, poetries, historics, etc. about the LORD in the "HOLY SCRIPTURES" as seen through careful scrutiny. Thus:

This brings us to the character of the Creator. We must beg to observe again that we describe not the actual Creator, but the popular idea of the Creator. It is said that the Creator is omnipotent and also that he is benevolent. But one proposition contradicts the other. Again, either sin entered the world against the will of the Creator, in which case he is not omnipotent, or, it entered with his permission, in which case it is his agent, in which case, he selects sin, in which case he has a preference for sin, in which case he is fond of sin, in which case he is sinful. It is certain that the feelings of the created have in no way been considered. If, indeed, there were a judgment day, it would be for man to appear at the bar not as a criminal, but as accuser. What has he done that he should be subjected to a life of torture and temptation? God might have made us all happy and he has made us all miserable. Is that benevolence? God might have made us all pure and he has made us all sinful. Is that the perfection of morality? If I believed in the existence of this man-created God, of this divine Nebuchadnezzar, I would say, "You can make me live in your world, O Creator, but you cannot make me admire it; you can load me with chains, but you cannot make me flatter you; you can send me to hell-fire, but you cannot obtain my esteem. And if you condemn me, you condemn yourself. If I have committed sins, you invented them, which is worse. If the watch you have made does not go well, whose fault is that? Is it rational to damn the wheels and springs?"[1]

Keeping in harmony with the "WORDS" of truth on the previous page Sir Ernest A. Wallis Budge [one of the nineteenth Century C.E.'s most noted European egyptologists] was prompted to observe the following about the earliest of the indigenous Africans that recorded the first principles mankind created and developed with respect to RELIGIOUS LITERATURE. He wrote

---

1. See Winwood Reade's THE MARTYDOM OF MAN; and John G. Jackson's MAN, GOD, AND CIVILIZATION, pp. 155 - 156.

The watery mass of Nu was the prototype of the great World-Ocean which later ancient nations believed to surround the whole world. Out from Nu came the river which flowed through the Ṭuat, or Other World, and divided its valley into two parts, making it to resemble Egypt. From Nu also came the waters which appeared in the two famous caverns in the First Cataract, and which, flowing from their mouths, formed the river Nile. The waters of Nu formed the dwelling place of Tem, and out of them came the sun, which was the result of one of Tem's earliest acts of creation. The early inhabitants of Egypt thought that the sun sailed over the waters of Nu in two magical boats, called Māntchet, or Māṭet, or Āṭet, and Semktet, or Sektet, respectively; in the former the sun set out in the morning on his journey, which he finished in the latter. A very ancient tradition in Egypt asserted that Nu was the head of a divine company, which consisted of four gods and four goddesses. These were :—

Nu, 𓏴	Nut, 𓏴
Ḥeḥu,	Ḥeḥut,
Kekui,	Kekuit,
Ḳerḥ,	Ḳerḥet,

The gods of these pairs were depicted in human form, with the heads of frogs, and the goddesses in the forms of women, with serpents' heads. Nu was the primeval water itself, Ḥeḥu personified its vast and endless extent, Kekui the darkness which brooded over the water, and Ḳerḥ its inert and motionless character. Very little is known about the three last-named gods and their female counterparts, for they belong to a system of cosmogony which was superseded by other systems in which the Sun-god Rā played the most prominent part. The goddess **Nut**, who was in the earliest times a Water-goddess, was depicted under the New Empire in the form of a woman, and also in the form of a cow.

[THE ORIGIN OF THE "WORD" - "GOD"] Historically Magical-Religion has been one of mankind's greatest emotional achievements, equally mankind's gravest creation against peaceful co-existence between socio-political groupings. Thus it is said that: "Each RELIGION is" [supposedly] "handed down by God." But "GOD" is created in the IMAGE of the religionist declaring His, Her and/or It's "DIVINITY." Thus, mankind seems to have forgotten the following historical facts about "RELIGION" [anyone of the past, at present, and apparently for the future] the following pages of this volume reveal.

The first aspect of a THEOSOPHICAL POSITION or CONCEPT to be given consideration is generally the last considered, and that is: What is RELIGION? The second aspect is: Which religion is TRUE or FALSE? The answer to both lies in the fact that the historics of RELIGION and GOD are not taught in SUNDAY nor SATURDAY religious schools. Thus, untold amounts of facts about "GOD" are being suppressed to keep people from knowing that neither JUDAISM, CHRISTIANITY or ISLAM was any where around when evidence of mankind's first recognition of a "GOD-HEAD", and our first justification to honour the same "GOD-HEAD," was being considered and eventually concretized into practise in Alkebu-lan [Africa]; and because of this these three so-called "WESTERN RELIGIONS" have been made by Europeans to relate to an ancient origin among the indigenous peoples of Alkebu-lan and Asia, who were of neither of the three; for neither was in existence until thousands of years following the creation of many hundreds of other African and Asian RELIGIONS, such as the worship of NATURE, SUN, FIRE and FERTILITY, all before the theory about "ADAM AND EVE" was conceived by an African called "Moses" in Ta-Merry [Egypt], Alkebu-lan. This naked TRUTH did not stop certain African-[BLACK]-Americans from making the chronologically impossible claim that:

"ISLAM PRECEDED BOTH JUDAISM AND CHRISTIANITY,"

when in fact the God-Head called "AL'LAH" [the son of the Goddess Al'lat] and the Religion known as "ISLAM"[1] were not known in history until ca. 622 C.E. or 1 A.H. - the year Prophet Mohamet ibn Abdullah introduced both to the world at the Oasis Of Yathrib near the City of Medina, not far from the Red Sea coastline of the Arabian Peninsula in Western Asia. This area is mentioned in the Pentateuch [Torah, Five Books Of Moses or Old Testament] as "MEDIAN" or "MEDIA," as shown on the MAP OF THE EXODUS on page 54 of Volume II. This period in Arab history is called "THE YEAR OF THE HEJIRA" [A.H.] - the year Prophet Mohamet ibn Abdullah fled Mecca for fear of his life.[2] However, the above claim by the orthodox branches of ISLAM, and all of the other types of MOSLEMS, should never fall upon contemptuous ears...; as most "BLACK CHRISTIANS" have equally claimed the following chronologically impossible historical event:

"Jesus Christ was the person Jehovah" [Ywh - the Black Jews or Israelites' God]
"was speaking to"...

---

1. Originally called "Mohametism" and "Mohammedism." The culture and government were jointly called "Islam." An Ethiopian named Hadzart Bilal ibn Rahbad - affectionately known as "BILAL" - headed the nation; Mohamet headed the spiritual life of the nation.
2. See AFRICAN ORIGINS OF THE MAJOR WESTERN RELIGIONS, pp. 195 - 244.

where it is written in <u>Genesis</u> [The First Book Of Moses], Chapter i, Verse 26:

> 26 ¶ And God said, <u>Let us make man in our image, after our likeness</u>: and let them have dominion over the fish of the sea, and over the fowl of the air, and over the cattle, and over all the earth, and over every creeping thing that creepeth upon the earth.. .

We have to remember that neither the <u>New Testament</u> nor the <u>Qur'an</u> supports either claim.

It is equally evident that no one knew about any person who could have been called a "<u>Messiah</u>" until, and/or following, this anouncement by the Hebrew Prophet Isaiah. Thus it is in ISAIAH, Chapter lxvi, Verses 15 - 24 in the <u>King James</u> [Authorized] <u>Version</u> of the <u>Holy Bible</u> we find the following:

> 15 <u>For, behold, the LORD will come with fire, and with his chariots like a whirlwind, to render his anger with fury, and his rebuke with flames of fire.</u>
> 16 For by fire and by his sword will the LORD plead with all flesh: and the slain of the LORD shall be many.
> 17 They that sanctify themselves, and purify themselves in the gardens behind one *tree* in the midst, eating swine's flesh, and the abomination, and the mouse, shall be consumed together, saith the LORD.
> 18 For I *know* their works and their thoughts: it shall come, that I will gather all nations and tongues; and they shall come, and see my glory.
> 19 And I will set a sign among them, and I will send those that escape of them unto the nations, *to* Tär'-shish, Pül, and Lŭd, that draw the bow, *to* Tŭ'-bäl, and Jä'-vän, *to* the isles afar off, that have not heard my fame, neither have seen my glory; and they shall declare my glory among the Gĕn'-tiles.
> 20 And they shall bring all your breth-ren *for* an offering unto the LORD out of all nations upon horses, and in chariots, and in litters, and upon mules, and upon swift beasts, to my holy mountain Jĕ-rŭ'-sä-lĕm, saith the LORD, as the children of Ĭṣ'-rä-ĕl bring an offering in a clean vessel into the house of the LORD.
> 21 And I will also take of them for priests *and* for Lĕ'-vites, saith the LORD.
> 22 For as the new heavens and the new earth, which I will make, shall remain before me, saith the LORD, so shall your seed and your name remain.
> 23 And it shall come to pass, *that* from one new moon to another, and from one sabbath to another, shall all flesh come to worship before me, saith the LORD.
> 24 And they shall go forth, and look upon the carcases of the men that have transgressed against me: for their worm shall not die, neither shall their fire be quenched; and they shall be an abhorring unto all flesh.

Note that there is not a single mention of anyone named "JESUS CHRIST" [Joshua <u>the anoint-ed</u>] in any of the verses above. Yet, there were at least <u>sixteen</u> [16] <u>stories</u> about <u>Gods</u> of "VIRGIN BIRTH" and "CRUCIFIXION" before <u>Jesus Christ</u> did the same, as shown on page 102 of this volume. The so-called "<u>Black Israelites</u>" [Haribus, Hebrews, Jews, or whatever else] are even much more concerned in this than their "<u>Black Christian</u>" and "<u>Black Muslim</u>" bro-thers and sisters of any form of a <u>Judaeo-Christian-Islamic experience</u>; they, knowing too well that their GOD - HEAD   preceded the latter two Gods - "JESUS CHRIST"and "AL'LAH." As such, when the Hebrews [Black and Brown] established their own nation following the PASSOVER or EXODUS, they had to discredit all they learnt about <u>God</u>, ..RA or AMEN-RA... from the Africans of the Nile Valley and Great Lakes region of Central Africa, and from the Asians of the Tigris and Euphrates Valley of Asia; all of this before they adopted one of the minor GODS of Egypt named "YWH" or "JEHOVAH" [in Hieroglyph 𓀁𓂝𓏏𓀀 ; in Hebrew יהוה or יה ; in Greek ΠΑΤΗΣ ; and in Latin DEO]; as their very own...

"THE ONE, AND ONLY, TRUE GOD OF THE UNIVERSE."

It is before this juncture you, as students, should have known that mankind formulated their views about "GODS" and "RELIGIONS" thousands upon thousands of years before they developed their ability to communicate by virtue of writing, mostly through pictoriographical signals.[1] Palaeolithic mankind, particularly, left us limitless evidence through their artifacts of many rituals and incantations depicting the propagation of themselves in terms of their children and food gathering processes, all of which they attributed to "DIVINE PROVIDENCE." Even at this very early stage of mankind's mental development into the esoterical examination of the "ORIGIN OF LIFE" there were attempts to record for future use in said religious ritual and commandment they developed. Yet it is with mankind's first step into the quest for "IMMORTALITY," upon realizing the full meaning of "DEATH" - [particularly lovedones], that the earliest of artifacts and records show that they also began to examine their first step into "LIFE'S ORIGIN" as the prelude to the beginning of a "LIFE-DEATH" realism. In this regards Professor Albert Churchward on pages 454 - 455 of SIGNS AND SYMBOLS OF PRIMORDIAL MAN showed a few indigenous Australians performing a <u>magical-religious</u> "LIFE-DEATH" ritual of "<u>Divine Intervention:</u>"

Here mankind looked for an approach at paying homage to the FERTILITY ORGANS of

---

1. See H.W. Smith's MAN AND HIS GODS; Sir J. Frazier's THE GOLDEN BOUGH [13 vols.]; A. Churchward's THE ORIGIN AND EVOLUTION OF RELIGION; G. Maspero's THE DAWN OF CIVILIZATION; M. Muller's THE SACRED BOOKS OF THE EAST; R. Bell's INTRODUCTION TO THE QUR'AN; A.C. Bouquet's COMPARATIVE RELIGION; E. James' COMPARATIVE RELIGION; B. Malinowski's MAGIC, SCIENCE AND RELIGION AND OTHER ESSAYS; and A. Waley's THE AMALECTS OF CONFUCIUS.

their reproductive tract - the heaven where the "ORIGINAL SOURCE OF LIFE" begins. The
same place that is condemned by the anti-SEX oriented syndrome demonstrated in the Book Of
Genesis about the allegory of the "FORBIDDEN FRUIT" related to the Hebrews' God - YWH;
a story about the "first two chosen people...Adam and Eve;" and the devilish serpent that...
    "TEMPTED ADAM AND EVE IN THE GARDEN OF EDEN."
The articulation of these early African People developed simultaneously with their physical
symbolisms, much of which was demonstrated in their rituals related to the usage of the
physical remains of their ancestors and the non-human animals they had domesticated to provide themselves with food, clothing and shelter. Thus we find among certain archaeological
evidence from these early African ancestors' CROSS-BONE DESIGNS, SKULL DECORATIONS,
HORN ORNAMENTS, and even PRESERVED FEMALE and MALE GENITAL ORGANS in a
state of copulation, that were used in fertility rites. Such RITUALS and their SYMBOLISMS became the foundation of what was later labeled "MAGIC" and "ANIMISM" by bigotted Judaeo-
Christian-Islamic theologians and missionaries. And although some such theologians prefer
to separate "MAGIC" from "RELIGION," this professor found no justification for the distinction except for semantical reason, which is only academic superficiality. Sir Ernest A. Wallis
Budge showed us another aspect of MAGICAL-RELIGION in the following graphical presentation and extract from page 259 of the BOOK OF THE DEAD and PAPYRUS OF ANI:

The mummy of Ani lying on a bier within a funerary
coffer or shrine, to the ends of which are attached coloured
streamers; the bier rests on the roof of a long, low
sepulchral building that is probably intended to represent
Ani's tomb. At the head and foot of the bier is a vulture,
that at the head representing Nephthys ⏀, and that at the
foot Isis ⏀; these birds are the two goddesses in the
character of " nursing mothers," TCHERTI, ⏀ ⏀. Beneath
the bier are two vases of unguents, Ani's palette, the box
containing implements used in writing and painting, and
two wooden or stone vessels painted in imitation of
variegated glass.

The papyri left us by our fellow Africans of the Nile Valley and Great Lakes regions of

Central Africa are further reasons why I cannot agree with E.O. James' conclusion below, which is the most popular on the point. He wrote on pages 2 and 3 of his most outstanding book - HISTORY OF RELIGION, New York, 1957 the following:

> "...The difference between them is in the nature and function of the respective system of ideas and practices. Magic depends upon the way in which certain things are said and done for a particular purpose by those who have the necessary knowledge and power to put the supernatural force into effect. It is tied to its own rites and formulae, and limited by its specific tradition. Whereas religion presupposes the existence of spiritual beings external to man and the world who control mundane affairs, magic is enshrined in man and in the techniques he employs in accordance with the strict rules of magical procedure."

Professor James, obviously, must have been writing from a prefixed conclusion that "MAGIC" is what he deemed it; yet giving no proof to substantiate the reality of those who practice "MAGIC" find in its...

> "EXISTENCE OF SPIRITUAL BEINGS EXTERNAL TO MAN AND THE WORLD WHO CONTROL MUNDANE AFFAIRS...,"

etc. But it was the ancient Africans of Egypt, Meröe, Nubia, Punt, Itiopia, and other northern, western, southern and eastern nations of Africa, philosophical thoughts that created the entire "MAGICAL FOUNDATION" for the "RELIGION" of the Mysteries System, out of which evolved the so-called "JUDAEO-CHRISTIAN-ISLAMIC RELIGIOUS EXPERIENCE." Certainly their spiritual leaders - rabbis, priests and imams are still the "MAGIANS" Professor James and others intentionally overlooked. Some of us are familiar with the same type of conclusion by European and European-American colonialists [most of whom are called "CHRISTIAN MISSION-ARIES"] on the question of "ANIMISM." For they too have decided that there is some kind of an absence of the esoterics of the same magnitude in the...

> "SUPERNATURAL BEINGS EXTERNAL TO MAN AND THE PHYSICAL WORLD THAT CONTROL MUNDANE AFFAIRS...IN ANIMISM...,"

etc. Yet, they cannot point out the difference between "SAINTS" created by their fellow European and European-American theologians and the "ANCESTRAL SPIRITS" created by African and African-Caribbean theologians; African-American theologians having made none, but instead adopted those of the Europeans and European-Americans without exception.

The greatest and most extensive body of "MAGICAL ENCANTATIONS, CONFESSIONS" and "RITES" [all of which amounts to Religion] among the ancient Africans of the Nile Valley High-Cultures dealt with the "MAGIC OF THE DEAD." In one of said scenes the "DECEASED SCRIBE ANI" is being guided past the obstacles to the "NETHER WORLD," according to the teachings and pictures in the BOOK OF THE COMING FORTH BY DAY AND BY NIGHT.[1]

Based upon the archaeological and anthropological findings related to Zinjanthropus boise[2] and other FOSSIL-HUMANS of Central East Africa, as shown on pages 21 - 28 of THE BLACK MAN'S RELIGION: THE MYTH OF GENESIS AND EXODUS, AND THE EXCLUSION OF THEIR AFRICAN ORIGIN, Volume II, we can even note that they had certain religious commonalities with their much later descendants like the "fossil-finds" [men] of Zimbabwe[3] and Broken Hill in southern Africa [Monomotapa],also at Mechta-el-Arbi in northern Africa. The height of this experience is best demonstrated in the 30,000 years old ROCK PAINTINGS and CAVE FRESCOES by the Africans [called "Grimaldis"] of Monomotapa .[4]

The so-called "CULT OF SKULLS" related to the ancient Europeans in the same light as the above, and represented by the Neanderthal FOSSIL-FIND skull arrangements taken from a Monte Circeo grotto in Italy during 1939 C.E., is said to be at least 75,000 to 80,000 years old; thus, an origin of approximately 73,000 B.C.E. at best. But we also found among the Zapotecs of South America, the Twas [the so-called "Pygmees"] of Zaire and Egypt, the Sybenetos of Egypt and Nubia, among many others, GRAMADONS [swastikas] of at least 50,000 years old, also pyramids and temple mounds related thereto. "Neolithic Man" in Africa and Asia continued the development of the so-called "CULT OF THE SKULLS AND HUNTING TOOLS" that penetrated the Sahara from the SOUTH and passed over into Europe from Africa's NORTH. The zenith of these rites was reached by the indigenous Africans in their travels from Central Africa - just around Zaire - to Egypt in North Africa. It became institutionalized at the mouth or Delta Basin of the Nile River in Qamt [Kamt, Kimit, Sais, Ta-Merry, Egypt, etc.]. It had completed a journey of a little more than 4,100 statute miles from its original source at Mwanza Nyanza[5] to the Kimit [Great or Mediterranean] Sea at Alkebu-lan's [Africa's] northern shore.

The "FEAR OF DEATH," the ever - commanding mysterious factor which compels man

---

1. See Sir E. A. Wallis Budge's BOOK OF THE DEAD and PAPYRUS OF ANI, p. 115; and p. xvii of this volume.
2. See Y. ben-Jochannan's BLACK MAN OF THE NILE AND HIS FAMILY, pp. 73 - 113.
3. Formerly called "Southern Rhodesia" by the British colonialists; today's "Rhodesia." Cecil Rhodes, in whose honour the colonialists and slavers renamed this African land, murdered more Africans by genocide than did Adolph Hitler of Nazis Germany exterminated White Jews.
4. Formerly comprised of the areas occupied by Zimbabwe [colonialist "Mozambique"] Monomotapa, Swaziland, Botswana, Malawi, Namibia [colonialist Southwest Africa], and the southern tip of Ngola [Angola]. See MAP OF AFRICA, 1688 C.E. on p.108 of this volume.
5. Called "LAKE VICTORIA" in honour of Queen Victoria of Great Britain; the murderess who committed genocide against Africans to the tune of more than 50,000,000 ruthlessly exterminated in Britain's African slave and colonial empire throughout the continent.

to dream and react by means of "cultic despotism" that expresses itself in religious frenzy also reached its zenith in this regards in ancient Egypt and other Nile Valley High-Cultures among the indigenous Africans. For this reason the ancient Africans concentrated on detailing the travails of the "DEPARTED SOULS" [Spirits] in terms of the "BA" and "KA" - two Human-Headed and Bird-Bodied figures as the following extracted from the BOOK OF THE DEAD and PAPYRUS OF ANI.

 Left: The Ba or Heart-Soul with the symbol of LIFE over its body.
Right: The Ka or Spirit-Soul of the deceased that depends upon the Ba for continuance.

The "Ba" [black] represented the "SOUL IN ITS LIVING STATE;" whereas the "Ka" [white] represented the "SOUL OF THE DECEASED IN ITS DEATH STATE." From this aspect of the "MAGICAL RELIGIOUS RITES" related to the DEATH of any pharaoh or high state official before everyone of the dynastic periods the MAGICIAN-PRIESTS developed the principle of the "DIVINITY OF THE LIVING PHARAOH."[1] And from this juncture the "DIVINE KINGSHIP" principle among the upper-strata Africans of the Nile Valley High-Cultures entered into the area of the "WORSHIP OF THE SUN DISC," which was also known as "Ra" or "God." All of this happened more than three thousand [3,000] years before the first Asian Hebrew[2] named "ABRM"[or Abraham]was born in the City of Ur, Chaldea. This was almost another thousand years before an African Hebrew named "MOSES" [Drawn from water] was born in the City of Succoth in the nation of Ta-Merry [Egypt] - the man that created the story about...

"ADAM AND EVE IN THE GARDEN OF EDEN"

...from extracts out of the BOOK OF THE COMING FORTH BY DAY AND BY NIGHT [Book of the Dead and Papyrus of Ani] he plagiarized. Said plagiarized works have since resulted into what is today called the...

"FIVE BOOKS OF MOSES, PENTATEUCH, OLD TESTAMENT, or HOLY TORAH."

The deification of the "SUN," and the relationship of the "DIVINE PHARAOH" as the...

"SON OF THE SUN...RA,"

...entered mankind into the realm of esoteric MAGICAL-RELIGION as we know it today. All

1. Pharaoh means "HEAD OF THE GREAT HOUSE" or "HEAD OF STATE,"and "KING."
2. See Chronology on p. 7 and compare with the Manethonian Nile List on p. 8 of this volume for comparison between the ancient Jews and the worshipers of Ra.

of this began with the MAGICAL calculations, mythology, dogmas, taboos and science re-
lating the positions and movements of the SUN, MOON and STARS with the "nature of man,"
from which ASTRONOMY and ASTROLOGY developed,in what was later to become the
"MYSTERIES SYSTEM" of the High-Cultures of the indigenous Africans along the Nile River
Valley and Great Lakes regions; and which was later taught in the Grand Lodge of Luxor
[Thebes] and its Subordinate Lodges listed on page 252 of BLACK MAN OF THE NILE AND
HIS FAMILY. By the year ca. 10,000 B.C.E. the Africans' MAGICAL-RELIGION had already
developed the "STELAR CALENDAR" - which was refined much more accurately and scientifi-
cally sometime around ca. 4100 B.C.E. into the "SOLAR CALENDAR,"[1]as shown on page 32
of Volume II.

The entrance of the indigenous Africans of the Nile Valley and Great Lakes regions into
their Dynastic Periods moved "MAGIC" into its esoterical uniqueness dealing with the "resurrection" and "reincarnation" of the deceased by virtue of "rituals" and "encantations."
From this beginning even "VIRGIN BIRTHS" became possible in order to place mankind into
a "DIVINE STATE OF BEING." All of this we find in the MAGICAL-RELIGION of the BOOK
OF THE DEAD and PAPYRUS OF ANI, which indicate an origin to the Dynastic Periods -
from the First Dynasty in ca. 5867 B.C.E. or ca. 3892 B.C.E. [See page 7 of this Volume].[2]

From this origin, or GENESIS, came the worship of the following Gods in chronological
order...,

"RA, YWH, ZEUS, BACCHUS or DIONYSOS"
[also called Zagreus] the Greeks adopted African God with the same "life" and "death" story,
as the following God-Heads...

JESUS CHRIST OF NAZARETH, and AL'LAH.
Since it is impossible to deal with all of the past and present GOD-HEADS of prehistory and
history in this volume, I have elected to use the three most commonly known and worshiped
by Africans, African-Americans, African-Caribbeans and African-Europeans...viz-a-viz
in Judaism, Christianity and Islam - respectively Jehovah, Jesus Christ and Al'lah. However,
because the vast majority of the people of African origin in the so-called "Western World" are
European-American style Christians, it is with this experience in BLACK MAGICAL RE-

---

1.See Y. ben-Jochannan's BLACK MAN OF THE NILE AND HIS FAMILY, p. 32.
2. See Chronology on p. 7 of this volume: 5867 by Champollion-Figeac, 3892 by Lepsius,
4400 by Brugsh, and 5004 B.C.E. by Mariette. The originator of the concept of breaking
down the various periods of Egyptian history into DYNASTIES was the High Priest Manetho,
who used "NILE YEARS" - 9K, 253Y, etc.

LIGION that I will relate my greatest emphasis in the following lecture OFFERINGS. But before you begin, read an "AUTHORITY'S" statement on the "MAGIC" of Judaeo-Christianity today:

THE NEW YORK TIMES, TUESDAY, MAY 29, 1973

A Scholar Infers Jesus Practiced Magic

By ISRAEL SHENKER

In two books scheduled for publication this month, Prof. Morton Smith of Columbia University presents evidence that may alter understanding of the New Testament, of Christianity and of Jesus.

The books deal with a fragment of a purported secret Gospel of Mark, which Professor Smith discovered; a primitive text from which the Gospels of Mark and John may have been drawn; early Christian secret rites and their ties to pagan practices and Professor Smith's conclusion that Jesus practiced magic.

His evidence goes back to his discovery at Mar Saba, an ancient Greek Orthodox monastery near Jerusalem, of a manuscript purportedly the text of a letter from Clement of Alexandria.

Clement was one of the great fathers of the Church, and his writings date back to the end of the second century. This letter, in tiny Greek script on two pages that had been used as the last page and in the binding of a 17th-century book, was to a Theodore (not identified); it referred to what Clement said was a secret Gospel of Mark.

After consulting experts in paleography, Professor Smith announced his discovery in 1960. Since then he has been reaching some startling conclusions about the letter.

Theses Outlined

Harvard University Press is publishing the extended scholarly version of these finds and conclusions, entitled "Clement of Alexandria and a Secret Gospel of Mark." Harper & Row is publishing a layman's account entitled "The Secret Gospel." In an interview at his apartment here, Professor Smith, who has been teaching ancient history at Columbia since 1957, outlined the principal theses.

From the Mar Saba document, Professor Smith concluded that the early church in Alexandria was "a split-level group"; there were initiates privy to secret doctrine and a larger group of faithful who knew only public teaching.

"Everybody knows there were a lot of apocryphal

The New York Times/Meyer Liebowitz
Prof. Morton Smith of the Columbia University faculty

gospels besides the four canonical Gospels—Matthew, Mark, Luke and John," Professor Smith said. "But the notion that an orthodox congregation, such as the church of Clement, had an authoritative secret Gospel is new."

Primitive Source

The secret Gospel recounts a story Professor Smith sees as almost identical with the account that John expanded into the story of the raising of Lazarus from the dead. "It helps us complete a long line of parallels between Mark and John, filling the gap that existed," Professor Smith suggested. "The parallelism now continues from the sixth chapter of both Mark and John until the account of the Crucifixion."

Stylistically, the secret Gospel is close to the Bible's Gospel according to Mark,

and Professor Smith suggests there was a primitive gospel from which the books of Mark and John were both drawn.

"This would take us back well before the year 70," he suggested. "It would give us a notion of the Gospel circulating at or before the time of Paul, who is our earliest source for Christianity, and could thus be much closer to the time of Jesus than the canonical Gospels. This is not an outlandish possibility. Most scholars agree that the Gospels of Matthew and Luke are both taken from Mark."

Professor Smith credits Prof. Cyril C. Richardson, dean of graduate studies at Union Theological Seminary, with the breakthrough leading to the remaining conclusions. What, Professor Rich-

ardson suggested was that Mark 10:13 to 10:45 closely reflects the content of an early baptismal service. (These passages deal with Jesus's blessing children, a rich, young ruler, rewards, Jesus's foretelling death and resurrection and responding to requests of James and John.)

"Professor Richardson's suggestion enables us to understand the nature of the initiation rite that the secret Gospel reports," Professor Smith said. "We now see that 'the mystery of the kingdom of God' is the content of baptism. The canonical Gospel's story [Mark 14:51-52] of a young man apprehended at night alone with Jesus at the time of Jesus's arrest (a story which scholars have puzzled over for 1,800 years), is now understandable as an account of a baptismal rite conducted by Jesus in which the believer united with Jesus and was possessed by his spirit.

"Once we have this report that Jesus administered a nocturnal, secret initiation, we naturally ask, 'Why nocturnal?' 'Why secret? Particularly if this was only a baptism? What was going on?'

Schisms Noted

Professor Smith suggested that the answers could be determined from a consideration of the splits in early Christianity. Some Christians, he said, insisted on strict obedience to Jewish law, others argued for selective obedience, a third group declared itself emancipated from Jewish law and dedicated to guidance by the spirit and a fourth group was blatantly libertine.

Jesus himself violated Jewish law: he did not observe the Sabbath, he consorted with publicans and sinners, he did not fast, or wash his hands before eating. But at times he urged observance of the law.

Some scholars said that Jesus's words should be taken figuratively, others argued the libertine texts were exaggerated or misunderstood and still others maintained that Jesus taught that moral law was binding,

xvii

ritual law not.

Professor Smith argued that Jesus distinguished between levels of his following. For those already in the kingdom of heaven (thanks to secret baptism), the law was not binding. But Jesus urged others to respect the law.

How did Jesus persuade his intimates of his special position and of their membership in the heavenly elect? Professor Smith replied: "I believe the answer is that Jesus had a way with schizophrenics, and that he practiced some sort of hypnotic or suggestive discipline embodied in rituals derived from ancient magic.

"If you take as your task the problem of finding what social type Jesus is, in the gallery of figures provided by the Greco-Roman period, the best answer is the mira-cle-working magician.

Magical Practices

Professor Smith compiled a long list of practices associated with magicians of antiquity and ascribed by the New Testament to Jesus—"the power to make anyone he wanted follow him, exorcism (even at a distance), remote control of spirits, giving disciples power over demons, miraculous cures of hysterical conditions including fever, paralysis, hemorrhage, deafness, blindness, loss of speech, raising the dead, stilling storms, walking on water, miraculously providing food, miraculous escapes, making himself invisible, foreknowledge, mind-reading, claiming to be a god or son of god or in image of god."

"All these claims and stories and rites are those of a magician, not of a rabbi or a Messiah," Professor Smith notes in "The Secret Gospel." "Who ever heard of the Messiah's being an exorcist, let alone being eaten?"

Professor Smith noted that many of the powers claimed are paralleled by practices described in the so-called magical papyri—documents discovered in Egypt that report pagan practices. The magical papyrus most closely associated with a eucharist-like practice deals with erotic magic. And the magical papyri as well as Jewish handbooks purport to explain the hypnotic technique allowing men to enjoy and transmit the illusion of ascent into heaven. "The stories of Jesus's resurrection seem distorted versions of such an illusory ascent," Professor Smith suggested.

A Time of Danger

"The spirit was at first the spirit of Jesus, then gradually became independent of him and was eventually located in the Trinity," he went on, noting: "When the spirit went public, the Apostles lost much of their control of the company and came into danger of displacement."

"If the Christians were an innocent sect practicing pure benevolence, why did the Romans make such strenuous efforts to stamp them out?" Professor Smith asked rhetorically, and replied: "It was because the Christians engaged in magical practices, and magic was a criminal act."

Professor Smith expects lively controversy about his findings, less from documents than from people. "I'm reconciled to the attacks," he said. "Thank God I have tenure!"

The following MAGICAL RELIGIOUS RITE is only one of the many hundreds Jesus Christ had to learn and practice when he received his _education_ and _initiation_ from African teachers in North Africa's MYSTERIES SYSTEM while he lived in Egypt and Nubia.

SHADOW AND SOUL LEAVING THE TOMB [1]

... from the rubric we learn that a figure of it was to be made in gold and fastened to the neck of the deceased, and that another, drawn upon new papyrus, was to be placed under his head. If this be done "then shall abundant warmth be in him throughout, "even like that which was in him when he was upon "earth. And he shall become like a god in the under-

"world, and he shall never be turned back at any of "the gates thereof." The words of the chapter have great protective power (_i.e._, are a charm of the greatest importance) we are told, "for it was made by the cow "for her son Râ when he was setting, and when his "habitation was surrounded by a company of beings of fire."

1. See PAPYRUS OF ANI [as transl. by Sir E.A. Wallis Budge]. The scribe Ani passing through the door of his tomb; his shadow and "heart-Soul" remains outside. See page 56 for details.

xviii

Professor Smith's last sentence, with regards to his "TENURE," should not be taken lightly. From my own personal experience I know that unless he had such, he could have expected the hierarchy of those who consider themselves the sacred guardians of the magic-al allegories and mythologies, even to down-right out-and-out LIES and DISTORTIONS in Judaeo-Christian theology, would have equally destroyed him, as myself, and many other thousands in the past, and at present. He follows a very select minority which has been trying to make the average parishoners realize that there are two [2] sets of "RELIGIOUS TEACH-INGS;" one for the public that financially underwrite religious institutions and their propaganda machinery; and the other for those who make their plushed living out of the proceeds from the underwriters.

Anyone who has made any kind of concentrated research into European and European-American JUDAISM, CHRISTIANITY and ISLAM is bound to conclude that all three [3] of them are nothing more than modern plagiarized VERSIONS of the "MAGICAL RITES" of the ancient Africans of the Nile Valley [Blue and White] and Great Lakes regions of Africa, along with the ancient Asians at the West and East banks of the Tigris and Euphrates Valley of Asia. How-ever with specific concentration on the second of the three, speaking chronologically in terms of original development, any researcher can see that without SAINT PAUL there is no JESUS CHRIST and/or "CHRISTIANITY." This I have clearly pointed out in my first book – WE THE BLACK JEWS, written and published in 1937-1938, and since then in most of my other writings on history, religion and/or philosophy.

In Judaism, Christianity and Islam the Magical Writings for...

"DRIVING OUT DEVILS AND DEMONS"

are still obvious in the Hebrew Old Testament, Christian New Testament and Moslem Holy Qur'an. We find this in the Magical Incantations related to...

"THE RAISING OF THE DEAD,..AND MAKING
A BLIND MAN SEE, THE DEAF AND DUMB SPEAK."

They also made...

"VIRGINS PRODUCED OFFSPRING WITHOUT SEXUAL
INTERCOURSE OTHER THAN WITH THE GODS."

All of these MAGICAL FETES Jesus Christ allegedly performed; and all of which we noticed had taken place among the Africans of the Nile Valley and Great Lakes regions of Africa thousands of years before the "Birth Of Jesus Christ Of Nazareth" was announced to the world. They were in existence when he entered the Lodges of the Mysteries System, which had its Grand Lodge at Luxor, Egypt. RELIGIOUS MAGIC was the order of the day in Africa before, and after, Jesus Christ himself received his education from African priests and other educators in various parts of Egypt and Nubia.[1]

I have underscored Professor Smith's references to the basic sources of European and European-American [modern] Christianity..."PAUL"..., who was followed by Barnabas, Luke, John and Mark in sequential importance, just as they are listed in the Christian prophetic works of what is today called:

"CHRISTIANITY" and/or "CHRISTENDOM."

The student of "BLACK" and/or "AFRICAN STUDIES" will discover that Professor Smith's revelations about Jesus Christ's...

"ADMINISTERED NOCTURNAL, SECRET INITIATION,"

etc. were already revealed in Professor George G.M. James' STOLEN LEGACY, Sir Godfrey Higgins' ANACALYPSIS [2 vols.], Sir James Frazier's THE GOLDEN BOUGH [13 vols.], William Ashley's LIFE AND LOVE OF JESUS CHRIST [2 vols.], and countless other works over the past hundreds of years since the...

"BIRTH OF JESUS CHRIST OF NAZARETH"...

was announced by dissatisfied Jews living in Egypt, North Africa during the year ca. 4 B.C.E. Some of these works I have already quoted, particularly STOLEN LEGACY, ANACALYPSIS, LOST BOOKS OF THE BIBLE AND THE FORGOTTEN BOOKS OF EDEN, BOOK OF THE DEAD and PAPYRUS OF ANI, SIGNS AND SYMBOLS OF PRIMORDIAL MAN,...etc.

The qualification for the Black People of the world to establish their own BLACK BIBLE does not depend upon anything done by the Europeans and European-Americans who constantly thrust JUDAISM and CHRISTIANITY "a-la" European-American style on them. This equally holds true for the Asian Arabs and their Islamic Religion's JIHADS [or extermination] of African People for periods longer than the Jews and Christians against the African People and their various forms of worshiping other Gods than those of the Judaeo-Christian-Islamic MAGICAL RELIGIOUS experience. It is in fact due to its own evolution. For African [BLACK] People throughout the entire world have a heritage that gave to the rest of mankind the first concept of MAGICAL RELIGIOUS THEOLOGY and its PHILOSOPHICAL outgrowth, which predated the Hebrews' YWH, ADAM and EVE; the Christians' JESUS CHRIST, PAUL,and the POPES of Rome; and the Moslems AL'LAH and MOHAMET ibn ABDULLAH.

The following text will point out a few of these poignant facts, as they lead the student and/

---

1. See George G. M. James' STOLEN LEGACY, and Rachid's AQUARIAN GOSPEL,references to Jesus Christ's education in Egypt he received from African teachers and priests on pp. 46 – 48 of this volume.

or general reader unto other sources of conformation. For it was wisely written by "SACRED SCRIBES" of Africa these ... inspired words of the God of African People:

"MAN [African - Black People] KNOW YOURSELF."

Part of the African People knowing themselves is related to the hieroglyphic inscription below. WHY don't the African People know what is stated in the inscription? WHO killed off the priests and caused the teachings therein to be stymied? WHICH nations in Europe sent their masters of genocide to commit mass genocide of every type imaginable in order to confiscate such works as the inscription below? WAS it not people like Aristotle, Petrie, Champollion, and other pirates of their ilk, who ravaged the sacred places of the Africans and carried off their loot to Europe, Great Britain and the United States of America? Is "THOU SHALT NOT STEAL"suspended for European and European-American robbers of the graves throughout Africa, but not those who equally robbed the graves of Europe and the United States of America?

THE BLACK BIBLE IS THE ANSWER.

Hypocephalus or object placed under the head of the deceased Shai-enen to keep warmth in the body.

THE BLACK BIBLE WILL SHOW THIS ASPECT OF THE BLACK MAN'S SELF.

[THE JUSTIFICATION]   From whom does the <u>Black Man</u> secure approval for the following denial ?

"There is no need for COLOR or RACE to be emphasized within
'Negro'Clergy's presentation of Jesus Christ's mission on earth."

The statement above is commonly expressed by most "NEGRO" Christians throughout the so-called "WESTERN WORLD." What struck me with this disclaimer, however, is that the BLACK MEMBERS of the so-called Christian Clergy and up and coming BLACK Seminarians are equally regurgitating the same unrealistic propaganda, including one of the men I deal with daily - a preacher who claimed:

"I WAS CALLED BY CHRIST TO PREACH HIS WORDS TO THE ENTIRE WORLD."

But the worse of this situation was that this "NEGRO PREACHER" stated that:

"BLACK IS THE COLOR OF THE CURSE GOD PLACED UPON THE DESCEND-
ANTS OF HAM, BECAUSE OF HAM'S DISRESPECT OF HIS FATHER - NOAH.
WE ARE THE CANAANITES - HAM'S HEIRS. SLAVERY IS OUR PUNISHMENT."

Needless to say, his total contempt for the BLACK COLOR of his own SKIN is equally reflect-ed in his association of "EVERYTHING SINFUL" with being "...BLACK LIKE THE DEVIL...;" the opposite being "WHITE." But he carefully forgot that HAM was also descended from NOAH and others all the way back to "ADAM AND EVE IN THE GARDEN OF EDEN." Lastly; he could not conceive of the possibility that:

"JESUS CHRIST COULD HAVE BEEN OF ANY COLOR OTHER THAN WHITE."

For in the same context he insisted that:

"WHITE IS THE SIGN OF PURITY, WHICH IS THE SAME AS GODLINESS, ETC."

But the strangest aspect of my conversation with this man, who...

"WAS CALLED TO THE MINISTRY OF JESUS CHRIST,"

is that he cannot visualize that "COLOR" and/or "RACE" are pertinent factors in the KING JAMES [Authorized] VERSION OF THE OLD AND NEW TESTAMENT of the "<u>Holy Scriptures</u>," particularly among BLACK PROTESTANTS. Even the pointing at Michaelangelo's <u>blonde, blue eye</u> and <u>golden locks</u> "JESUS CHRIST AND THE HOLY FAMILY" he painted for Pope Julius IInd [using his own uncle for the model that became the internationally recognized European and European-American image of the Christians' God-Head] could not move my very good friend into understanding how his fellow Christians of Europe and European-America were using RACE [White-Caucasian-Semitic] and COLOR [White] to their own advantage, and BLACK [Afri-can] PEOPLE'S disadvantage, in the propagation of European and European-American [THE GREAT WHITE RACE] Judaeo-Christian anti-African and anti-Asian RELIGIOUS BIGOTRY and RACIAL PREJUDICE; all of this as seen in their condemnation of every other RELIGION and

xxii

every GOD-HEAD not of their own VERSION of Jewish and/or Christian religiosity.

Having moved from trying to make my good friend see the "WAY" in the above direction, we were able to have a much better dialogue on the matter concerning the POWER of Saint Paul over the alleged "...TEACHINGS OF JESUS CHRIST..."[2] in the Black Clergy's presentation of "CHRIST'S MESSAGE."

Certainly the Black Clergy cannot escape its responsibility to place Christianity in its correct GEO-POLITICAL and SOCIO-THEOLOGICAL perspectives in order to support its reality. And certainly Jesus Christ had, and still has, a historical background that was, and still is, denied from the time when Europeans in, and from, Rome decided to arrest his validity from the Africans of Northern, Northwestern and Northeastern Africa that introduced him over three hundred [300] years before the Nicene Conference of Bishops in ca. 322 C.E. [A.D.]. But it was at this Conference[or "Council"]the "HUMANITY OF JESUS CHRIST" was exchanged for the euphoric mythology of his equal "DIVINITY" status with his Hebrew [Jewish or Israelite] Father - "JEHOVAH" [Ywh]. This distortion of the glorious life of the "CHRIST CHILD" and "CHRIST MAN" was passed down to the Black Clergy by European and European-American slavemasters, who enslaved millions of Africans in the name of "GOD AND CHRISTIANITY." This same "GOD" was, and still is, in the context of the "GREAT WHITE FATHER" colonial paternalist that committed all forms of genocide against the African people under the banner of "CHRISTIAN MISSIONARIES" and "CIVILIZERS OF THE HEATHENS." All of this took place at a period when said BLACK CLERGY even preached to their fellow African [BLACK] People that were ruthlessly and unscrupulously uprooted from the "MOTHERLAND"[Alkebulan or Africa] by the worse infamy in human history - otherwise known as the "SLAVE TRADE." Thus it was, and still is, that the Black Clergy taught their fellow enslaved Africans, African-Americans, African-Caribbeans and African-Europeans to accept the following teaching Moses [allegedly] received from Ywh and passed down to his fellow Hebrews [Jews] for their own guide as authorized slavemasters over their own fellow Hebrews and others under the pretext of "GOD'S ORDINANCE WITH THE ISRAELITES." I extracted parts of said "ORDINANCE" from EXODUS, Chapter xx, Verses 24 - 26 and Chapter xxi, Verses 1 - 21, in which Jehovah allegedly said to the African named Moses:

...in every place where I cause my name to be remembered I will come to you and bless you. 25And if you make me an altar of stone, you shall not build it of hewn stones; for if you wield your tool upon it you profane it. 26And you shall not go up by steps to my altar, that your nakedness be not exposed on it.

21 "Now these are the ordinances which you shall set before them. 2 When you buy a Hebrew slave, he shall serve six years, and in the seventh he shall go out free, for nothing. 3 If he comes in single, he shall go out single; if he comes in married, then his wife shall go out with him. 4 If his master gives him a wife and she bears him sons or daughters, the wife and

her children shall be her master's and he shall go out alone. [5] But if the slave plainly says, 'I love my master, my wife, and my children; I will not go out free,' [6] then his master shall bring him to God, and he shall bring him to the door or the doorpost; and his master shall bore his ear through with an awl; and he shall serve him for life. [7] "When a man sells his daughter as a slave, she shall not go out as the male slaves do. [8] If she does not please her master, who has designated her for himself, then he shall let her be redeemed; he shall have no right to sell her to a foreign people, since he has dealt faithlessly with her. [9] If he designates her for his son, he shall deal with her as with a daughter. [10] If he takes another wife to himself, he shall not diminish her food, her clothing, or her marital rights. [11] And if he does not do these three things for her, she shall go out for nothing, without payment of money.

[12] "Whoever strikes a man so that he dies shall be put to death. [13] But if he did not lie in wait for him, but God let him fall into his hand, then I will appoint for you a place to which he may flee. [14] But if a man willfully attacks another to kill him treacherously, you shall take him from my altar, that he may die.

[15] "Whoever strikes his father or his mother shall be put to death.

[16] "Whoever steals a man, whether he sells him or is found in possession of him, shall be put to death.

[17] "Whoever curses his father or his mother shall be put to death.

[18] "When men quarrel and one strikes the other with a stone or with his fist and the man does not die but keeps his bed, [19] then if the man rises again and walks abroad with his staff, he that struck him shall be clear; only he shall pay for the loss of his time, and shall have him thoroughly healed.

[20] "When a man strikes his slave, male or female, with a rod and the slave dies under his hand, he shall be punished. [21] But if the slave survives a day or two, he is not to be punished; for the slave is his money.

The above citation is no less valid today than it was when the Black Clergy's co-religionist WHITE slavemasters imposed their VERSION upon their African victims of slavery and genocide. This is particularly true, because the mental depravity of the descendants of said slaves is linked directly to the historical "CARRY-OVER" from said teachings. If this is not true; WHY then the...

"WASH ME WHITER THAN SNOW, OH LORD"...

can still find the most honoured place in <u>Sunday</u> and <u>Saturday worship</u> selection of hymns to be sung before any 100 % BLACK CONGREGATION under the leadership of its "NEGRO" or "COLORED" clergyman and/or clergywoman? Because this form of MENTAL SLAVERY is no different in magnitude than the other depths of degradation Europeanized and European-Americanized WHITE-SEMITIC "Judaeo-Christian concepts" have already carried Black People. And thus, we can equally sing to the greatest pitch of our voices:

"OH LORD I HAVE CLEANSED MY SINFUL BLACK HEART; AND I'M READY FOR THE GREAT WHITE WAY!"

We should be able to observe from the above that "RACE, COLOR" and "SEX" are as much a part of the Judaeo-Christian-Islamic religious syndromes as they are a component part of the basic socio-political fabric that is the United States of America and all of the other European and European-American governments of the world. For it is the people that comprises any government - capitalist, communist, socialist, feudalist, or whatever else there may be socio-politically.

These concepts were not accidentally contrived by the Africans upon their arrival in the "THIRTEEN BRITISH COLONIES" that became in 1776 C.E. "THE UNITED STATES OF AMERICA," following one group of Europeans enslavement of another group that ended in the

xxiv

freedom of the European-Americans [WHITE, CAUCASIAN-INDO-EUROPEAN-ARYAN-SEMITIC, etc.] alone; none of the other ethnic or racial groups that equally fought against Great Britain having gained one iota of freedom therefrom. In this experience the African [BLACK] People envolved were not allowed to develop their own African Heritage from this point, no more so than they were permitted by the British colonialists; neither were they allowed to bring forward their African RELIGIONS that they had to hide to practice; nor were they allowed to practice any other of their African culture they had developed before becoming CHATTLE SLAVES for Reverend [later Bishop] Bartolome de LasCasas and Pope Julius IInd of the Roman Catholic Church in the early half of the Sixteenth Century C.E., and ever since, all of which began when the Church of Christendom sent four thousand [4000] Africans called "MOORS" from Spain to the Island of Hispañiola [today's Santo Domingo and Haiti] following their lost of power over the Iberian Peninsula in 1485 C.E. These concepts were forced upon the African People while they served as SLAVES in the Caribbeans, the South American Continent, Central America, and finally on the North American Continent; all of this along with their de-Africanization, and their final brainwashing that took place as they were Europeanized and European-Americanized by their slavemasters, even to the point of losing their common identity - their AFRICAN NAMES, and even forced to accept their slavemasters names - otherwise distorted into what is today called "CHRISTIAN NAMES."

The fact that one person can reduce another to the point where the reduced personality accepts him or her self as INFERIOR to the other is sufficient JUSTIFICATION for any form of rebellion and/or insurrection, even physically, against such an enslaver or enslavers. But the period of AWAKENING for each is not the same for all. However, some of the slaves were never asleep. For their minds were totally FREE as they had been in their native "Motherland - Alkebu-lan" [Africa; see map on page 108 of this volume].

When the dormant and non-dormant slaves found out that they were equally enslaved by the slavemasters of Europe and European-America [both of the so-called Judaeo-Christian philosophy taught in Judaism and Christianity], they noticed that the same people who controlled the institutions of SLAVERY also created and developed COLONIALISM, IMPERIALISM, CHRISTIAN MISSIONS and the MAKING OF THE HOLY SCRIPTURES. Knowing this: what should they have done that any other group of normal people would have done? Certainly their first step had to be the removal of the MENTAL SHACKLE that detoriated their minds. But what is the "MENTAL SHACKLES" most powerful drug? It was in the past, as it is now, "ESOTORICAL RELIGION".. particularly as promulgated by Judaism, Christianity and Islam -

a - la - European, European-American and Arabian-Asian styles. And; what basic lesson there is behind all of this? The answer:

THE MERE RELATIONSHIP BETWEEN SLAVE AND MASTER MAKES FOR
THE MOST UNNATURAL MARRIAGE BETWEEN BOTH.

Is it not RELIGION, particularly the three most commonly practised in the so-called "Western World" - Judaism, Christianity and Islam, that is still perpetuating said relationship with its teaching of...

"TURN THE OTHER CHEEK"...

to the descendants of the former chattle slaves, and present mental slaves? All of these theologians have carefully forgotten that the basic foundation of all three have stemned from an AFRICAN ORIGIN. And, is it not the leaders of said institutions that mostly dominate African [BLACK] People's MORAL and SECULAR value judgment? Since these facts exist, then African People must have any RELIGION and any GOD-HEAD African People the world over are envolved with, even if they must be converted to suit African People's specific needs in the "Western Hemisphere," the United States of America being no exception. Their GOD-HEAD must reflect the aspirations of the struggle for freedom as all other ex-SLAVES GOD-HEAD has had to do in aiding his "CHOSEN PEOPLE" to rid themselves of their imposed "INFERIOR MENTALITY" their self-appointed slavemasters from Europe, and those of the United States of America, imposed upon them through the European and European-American VERSIONS of the Christian and Hebrew [Jewish] NEW and OLD TESTAMENT; all of which the slavemasters have defined as "AUTHORITY" and "TRUTH" for themselves, as well as for their SLAVES. But the First Step to this obnoxious relationship is that the slaves' "GOD" and "GOD-DESS" must be like the slaves, of the slaves, and for the slaves against the slaves self-appointed masters and others that threaten the "GOD INSPIRED" love between said HOLY and DIVINELY MADE UNION. For said slaves [African or Black People] forebearers are the "CHOSEN PEOPLE" of their own "GOD" or "GODDESS;" just as the slavemasters are the "CHOSEN PEOPLE" of their own "GOD" or "GODDESS" that assists them in their enslavemen of people all over the world in colonialism and imperialism supported by missionary activities.

The major question behind all of this logical relationship, rhetorical or otherwise, is: which one of the available RELIGIONS known to the African People is correct as it stands today? The answer, as I see it! NOT ONE. No! NOT ONE. Why? Because all three of the so-called "MAJOR WESTERN RELIGIONS" - Judaism, Christianity and Islam, as written in the Europen and European-Americanized VERSIONS of the Five Books Of Moses [Pentateuch, Holy

Torah or Old Testament], Christian Holy Bible [New Testament] and the Moslem Holy Qur'an have been revised and re-revised with distortions inserted in every dimension possible to perpetuate the mythological concept that all of the African People were, and still are, created by some "GOD-HEAD" or another to be. . .

"HEWERS OF WOOD AND DRAWERS OF WATER". . .

for all of the other races of the world, particularly for the Europeans and European-Americans of what is left of the "Jewish" and "Christian" RELIGIONS. Each of these Caucasianized and Semiticized "HOLY SCRIPTURES" failed to account for the fact that the GENESIS and FOUNDATION of their being were with the teachings by the Africans along the Nile River [BLUE and WHITE] Valley and Great Lakes regions of Central Africa.

What does all of this suggest? That the African People MUST equally revise all of the...

FIVE BOOKS OF MOSES, the HOLY BIBLE, and the HOLY QUR'AN

to make their God's teachings responsive to their own needs and aspirations; just as the European People shown on pages xvii and xxx of this volume. For a people's GOD-HEAD must serve them equally as all other peoples' GOD-HEAD serve them. Thus, they MUST have their own "HOLY SCRIPTURES" that recite what they want their GOD-HEAD to have said in the past, and to say today, and will say in the future; all of which MUST be revised periodically as their condition changes. The Europeans and European-Americans [WHITE PEOPLE] did this with their -

VULGATE, DUOAY-RHAMES, GUTTENBERG, KING JAMES [Authorized]
OLD AND NEW TESTAMENT, AMERICAN STANDARD, JEHOVAH WITNESS,
LATTER DAY SAINTS OF THE MORMONS, CHRISTIAN SCIENCE, HOLY
ROLLERS, COMMON PEOPLES,

etc., etc., etc., almost endlessly,"VERSION" of the "God inspired Holy Scriptures;" all of which reflect their own RACIAL and/or ETHNIC, COLOR and CULTURAL, enviroment and aspirations. The Africans and African-Americans are equally entitled to do the same, and anything else they so desire with said teachings that were distorted from the original worship of their own God-Head - "TEM, RA" or "AMEN - RA," etc. Or must the African People continue to depend upon "The Penintental Tyrant" or the "Slave Trader Reformed" image exhibited in the psychology of the docile human being, according to the following picture by Thomas Branagan as their only hope, while they equally await a RELIGIOUS MIRACLE to free them for "Christ's Second Coming" and/or "Moses' Intercession With Jehovah?" They wait; because they cannot FREE themselves from their presently enslaved mentality which esotorical Judaeo-Christian MAGIC led them into. This, of course, is no worse than the enslavement their fellow Africans suffered under Islam hundreds of years before the Europeans superceded Arab slavery in all of North, Northwest, East, Northeast, and Central Africa. The picture below[1] represents the LOWEST EBB, next only to the MENTAL and PHYSICAL DEATH to which any human being can sink; a slave down on his knees praying to his slavemaster's GOD-HEAD.

Even the European and European-American slavemasters' "GOD" must have detested this form of mental masturbation and spiritual ejaculation; a slave believing that his master's "GOD" would go against his master's interest - his property, which is the SLAVE himself.

The solution to all of the esoterical RELIGIOUS sexualities definitely stands within our minds as a common bond of African People. But we must draw upon the strength we inherited from our ancient indigenous African ancestors along the Nile River Valley and Great Lakes regions of Central Africa, equally from all of the other parts of the more than eleven million [11,000,000] square miles of our own "Motherland - Alkebu-lan" [which the Greeks renamed "AFRICA" or "AFRIKA" in the 6th Century B.C.E.].Using all of these theosophical vibrations of our ancient MAGICAL RELIGIOUS RITES and TEACHINGS that began in the Grand Lodge of Luxor [Thebes] by our fellow Africans who came down to Egypt from Central Africa and founded their MYSTERIES SYSTEM that created the FIRST [or original] BIBLE in ca. 4100 B.C.E. -

THE BOOK OF THE COMING FORTH BY DAY AND BY NIGHT,

which produced the alleged African...

"PAGAN PAST, PRIMITIVE BACKGROUND, CANNIBALISTIC APPETITE, INFERI-
OR RACIAL STOCK, INCONGRUOUS FACIAL CHARACTERISTICS, BLACK SIN...;

and equally our African...

"MAGICAL RITES AND SPIRITUAL ENCANTATIONS IN THE PYRAMID AND
COFFIN TEXT, NEGATIVE CONFESSIONS, AND OTHER INSCRIPTIONS..;"

all of which produced the basic foundation for Judaism, Christianity and Islam, from the beginning of their own GENESIS, must be reactivated. In so doing, we must re-establish...

'OUR OWN AUTHORITY, OUR OWN MORALITY, AND OUR OWN GOD-HEAD.'

1. See T. Branagan's THE PENITENTAL TYRANT, or SLAVE TRADER REFORMED. A copy can be had at Princeton University's Library, Princeton, New Jersey; Y. ben-Jochannan's CULTURAL GENOCIDE IN THE BLACK AND AFRICAN STUDIES CURRICULUM, pp. 141 -143.

In this major undertaking we are bound to take <u>First Things First</u>. Thus, the <u>First Step</u> must be...

THE PRODUCTION OF OUR OWN BLACK BIBLE.

With the African [BLACK] People's "<u>philosophical, theosophical</u>" and "<u>juridical</u>" values of esoterical "LAW AND ORDER" comes OUR own "<u>Morality</u>." With OUR own "Morality," a new renaissance of OUR own <u>Reality</u>. With OUR own "<u>Reality</u>," a new dimension for the ultimate "<u>Liberation</u>" from OUR own -

MENTAL MASTURBATION and PHYSICAL EJACULATION -

constantly exhibited as a direct result of OUR [African People] accepted <u>Europeanized</u> and <u>European-Americanized</u> VERSIONS of the Judaeo-Christian-Islamic RELIGIONS that have inprisoned African People's minds from the beginning of the SLAVE TRADE in ca. 640 C.E. to this very day. For although these are but a mere few of the MENTAL SHACKLES that enslaved African People to date, they must be removed as a "<u>First Step</u>." Then we will simultaneously have the "FIRST SHACKLE" of Black People's mental enslavement abated, and as such, remembering that:

A SLAVE AND HIS MASTER CANNOT RULE THE SAME PLANTATION IN THE
MUTUAL BENEFIT
OF BOTH.

Since it is the "WORD" that is "GOD," why not the Black Man's "WORD?" Or shall We [African People] have to ask once again:

"ARE WE NOT HUMAN BEINGS TOO?"

If we must ask such an academic question again this late into the 20th Century C.E., more than <u>one hundred and eight</u> [108] <u>years</u> following the so-called "EMANCIPATION PROCLAMA- TION:" what has OUR <u>Black Clergy</u> done other than lead us like "JUDAS GOATS" at the head of <u>sheep for the slaughter</u>?

Our revered ancestors painted their GODS and GODDESSES as they were: why do we use other GODS and GODDESSES unlike our selves? And if it is in fact true that

"GOD MADE MAN IN HIS OWN IMAGE:"

what are we? Certainly an <u>African</u> [BLACK] <u>Interpretation</u> of GENESIS to REVELATION is desperately overdue in these areas of the BLACK [God] IMAGE. This we can readily note in the following article on pages xxx - xxxi of this volume.

Just as our forerunners, we too will have to control our GOD'S "HOLY WORDS" to say whatever we want them to have said in the past, presently, and in the future. For this we have seen all the time by European and European-American theologians. But what is it about us

that a 'PANEL OF AFRICAN SCHOLARS TRANSLATING THE BIBLE' cannot do for ourselves as the PANEL below for themselves? NOTHING WHATSOEVER! As we read what
the PANEL below did to EZEKIEL 36 : 4, we should have been able to see all of the plagiarization that took place from the time of the Council Of Jamnia to the Council Of Bishops
Of The Nicene Conference. But: does this not further validate –

THE NEED FOR A BLACK BIBLE?

Panel of Jewish Scholars Translating the Bible

Dr. Harry M. Orlinsky   Rabbi Solomon Grayzel   Rabbi Max Arzt

Rabbi Bernard J. Bamberger   Dr. H. L. Ginsberg

---

1. See THE NEW YORK TIMES, Monday, May 21, 1973; and p. 35 for the story about the
activities of the PANEL and its performance to date.

xxx

By EDWARD B. FISKE

The Bible was written by individuals—familiar figures like David and anonymous authors or editors known only by such cold scholarly names as "J" or "Deutero-Isaiah."

Translations, though, are made by committees, which may be the result of Parkinson's Law encroaching on the process of divine revelation, but which is justified as a matter of scholarly necessity.

"To do a good translation you have to know not only the languages, but also something about archeology, folklore, poetry, ritual law and many other fields," said Dr. Harry M. Orlinsky, professor of Bible at the Hebrew Union College-Jewish Institute of Religion in Manhattan. "No one person can know enough by himself."

Together 20 Years

Dr. Orlinsky speaks from experience. He is a member of a committee that for nearly two decades has been working on a new English translation of the Bible sponsored by the Jewish Publication Society of America. The finished work, which is due in two years, will replace the version published by the society in 1917.

Out of loyalty to their collective product, most translation teams are about as eager to divulge their internal deliberations and differences of opinion as David was to publicize his conversations with Bathsheba. Recently, however, the team of Jewish scholars agreed to let a visitor sit in on a weekly working session.

The scholars sat around a long folding table at one end of Dr. Orlinsky's cluttered office at the seminary. On the table was a mass of reference books and perhaps a dozen English translations, from the King James Version to the New English Bible.

In addition to Dr. Orlinsky the scholars were Rabbi Bernard J. Bamberger, rabbi emeritus of Temple Sharray Tefila in Manhattan; Rabbi Solomon Grayzel, professor of history at Dropsie University in Philadelphia; Rabbi Max Arzt, vice chancellor of the Jewish Theological Seminary in Manhattan, and Dr. H. L. Ginsberg, professor of Bible at the same seminary.

Encountering Ezekiel

The passage for the day was Ezekiel 36 to 38. which includes the prophetic vision of the valley of the "dry bones" and their coming to life. The basis for discussion was a draft translation prepared by Rabbi Harry Freedman, an Orthodox member of the team, who lives in Australia. Other rabbis in the group represent the Conservative and Reform branches of contemporary Judaism.

The scholars have been working as a group since 1955, so they approached their work in a friendly, relaxed and confident manner with frequent touches of humor.

The first problem to arise was a reference in verse 36:4 to Israel becoming "a prey and derision" to surrounding nations. For some time they wondered out loud whether the idea of "exploitation" ought to be injected in the translation and whether "laughingstock" would be better than "derision."

Other Versions

In the middle of the debate Dr. Orlinsky stood up and began sifting through the stack of other translations to see how the New English Bible rendered it.

"We've been robbed, fellows," he announced. "Where's the New English Bible?" He found it and turned the pages. "It says 'all plundered and despised.' Boy, that's not even close!"

Shortly afterward everyone agreed on "a prey and a laughingstock," but no one knew how to spell the latter. Dr. Orlinsky went for a dictionary on a nearby shelf and settled the matter. "One word," he said.

The next big problem came in verse 33, with the phrase wehoshabti et-he-arim, which Rabbi Freedman translated "I will repopulate your cities." Rabbi Artz frowned and said that he was "allergic" to this idiom and suggested "rebuild." Dr. Orlinsky proposed "people your cities again." Rabbi Artz responded that this "sounds like a population explosion." But he saw that the consensus was against him and accepted "people."

During the deliberations, Rabbi Grayzel, as secretary of the team, sat at the end of the table with a stub of a pencil taking down the revisions as they came along. "When I get home I have to transcribe all this," he explained. "I tell you, the life of a secretary is no cinch."

The team of scholars decided years ago that they would try to capture the meaning of Hebrew idioms rather than follow literal word-by-word translations. Thus in Genesis 4:26, where the King James reads "he called his name Enos," the new Jewish version says simply "he named him Enosh."

Such a problem arose in verse 36:9, which in the King James is translated as, "For behold, I am for you, and I will turn unto you, and ye shall be tilled and sown." Rabbi Freedman suggested that the first part be translated "For I have plans for you."

Everyone agreed that the King James was too literal and Rabbi Freedman's draft too free. "It sounds pretty sexy—I have plans for you," said Dr. Orlinsky. After several proposals and counterproposals they settled on "For I will care for you."

An Institute Dilemma

Any group of translators faces certain inevitable stylistic decisions—such as whether it is permissible to occasionally, in the interests of more natural phrasing, split an infinitive. This came up in verse 36:27, where the draft proposed the phrase "faithfully to observe my rules."

Dr. Orlinsky suggested changing it to read "to faithfully," but Rabbi Grayzel, whose instincts reflect his years as an editor at the Jewish publication Society, objected. "I was brought up to never do it," he said.

Dr. Orlinsky defended the new permissiveness. "Most great Americans split infinitives," he declared. "You can split the atom, but not the infintive." Rabbi Bamberger rose to the host's defense. "It's stilted," he said. Rabbi Grayzel mumbled dryly, "I see no stilts here."

Finally, Rabbi Arzt intervened and asked Rabbi Grayzel: "You feel strongly on that, Sol?"

"It grates on me," confessed Rabbi Grayzel, throwing up his hands. The unstated ground rules are that when someone feels strongly about such a matter he gets his way. The infinitive remained in its virginal state.

The scholars noted in interviews that while they were interested only in translation, they sometimes found themselves dragged into theological debates.

Deuteronomy 25:5, for instance, has traditionally been understood as declaring that when a man dies without leaving a child, his brother must take the widow as his wife in order to perpetuate the name of the deceased.

Another tradition, however, asserts that, the Hebrew word ben should, in this instance, be interpreted as "son" rather than "child." This would mean that the brother would not be obliged to enter into this so-called "Levirate" marriage with the widow if she had a daughter.

In contrast to the 1917 Jewish version, the new team went with "son." "That's what we think it means," Dr. Orlinsky said. "A daughter doesn't perpetuate the name."

Products of Their Time

Beginning with the Torah (the first five books of the Old Testament) in 1962, the translations have been published in piecemeal fashion as completed books were ready. The most recent was Isaiah, and Psalms, one of the books produced by another committee that was formed in 1967 to help out, is scheduled to be released later this year.

The scholars pointed out in interviews that Bible translations are inevitably products of their times and often have social and even political overtones.

St. Jerome produced the Vulgate, or Latin translation of the Christian Bible, shortly after Christianity became the official religion of the Roman Empire. Luther's German translation and the King James Version were weapons in the Protestant Reformation, a struggle that had implications for the emerging nationalism and the efforts by commerical interests to displace feudalism.

During the 19th century, the principal English translation of the Jewish Bible was one made by Rabbi Isaac

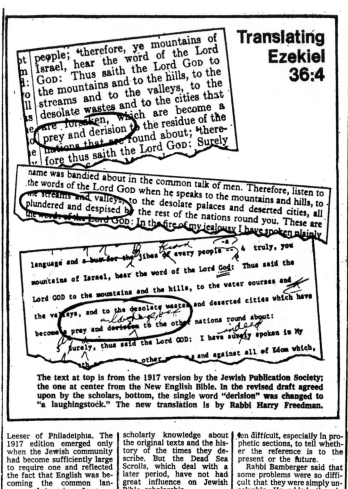

Translating Ezekiel 36:4

people; therefore, ye mountains of Israel, hear the word of the Lord GOD: Thus saith the Lord GOD to the mountains and to the hills, to the streams and to the valleys, to the desolate wastes and to the cities that are forsaken, which are become a prey and derision to the residue of the nations that are found about; therefore thus saith the Lord GOD: Surely

name was bandied about in the common talk of men. Therefore, listen to the words of the Lord GOD when he speaks to the mountains and hills, to the streams and valleys, to the desolate palaces and deserted cities, all plundered and despised by the rest of the nations round you. These are the words of the Lord GOD: In the fire of my jealousy I have spoken plainly

language and a butt for the jibes of every people — 4 truly, you mountains of Israel, hear the word of the Lord God: Thus said the Lord GOD to the mountains and the hills, to the water courses and the valleys, and to the desolate wastes and deserted cities which have become a prey and derision to the other nations round about: 5 Surely, thus said the Lord GOD: I have surely spoken in My ... other ... and against all of Edom which,

The text at top is from the 1917 version by the Jewish Publication Society; the one at center from the New English Bible. In the revised draft agreed upon by the scholars, bottom, the single word "derision" was changed to "a laughingstock." The new translation is by Rabbi Harry Freedman.

Leeser of Philadelphia. The 1917 edition emerged only when the Jewish community had become sufficiently large to require one and reflected the fact that English was becoming the common language of American Jews.

New Scholarship

The current Jewish translation was undertaken to incorporate not only changes in the American language since 1917 but also new scholarly knowledge about the original texts and the history of the times they describe. But the Dead Sea Scrolls, which deal with a later period, have not had great influence on Jewish Bible scholarship.

The scholars said that translating Hebrew poses special problems because the texts frequently change the grammatical person without notice. In addition, Hebrew tenses are such that it is often difficult, especially in prophetic sections, to tell whether the reference is to the present or the future.

Rabbi Bamberger said that some problems were so difficult that they were simply unsolvable. He added, though, that this doesn't discourage anyone. "In such cases," he said, "we just put in a footnote saying, 'Don't worry, fellows, we don't know what it means either'."

Although there is no need to depend upon the above "JEWISH SCHOLARS" decision to change their own forerunners religious teachings, while at the same instance noting that amongst them there is not a single BLACK RABBI or DOCTOR of like "scholarship"on their PANEL; does this not support...

THE NEED FOR A BLACK BIBLE?

As my associate and fellow AFRICAN STUDIES professor, George E. Simmonds, reminded me of the history related to the MAGICAL RELIGIOUS TEXTS on the stalae below as he was checking and proofreading this manuscript; that I should teach my students to read and write various hieroglyphic scripts; I realized that too many of my students had to take practically everyone of the so-called "EGYPTOLOGISTS" words for whatever they told them are the facts in the history and culture of the Africans of ancient Egypt and other Nile Valley and Great Lakes High-Cultures. But even beyond this, each one should have at least a reading knowledge of Hebrew, Greek, Latin and Arabic , at least enough for an understanding of the allegorical facts presented to you in the various VERSIONS of the so-called Old Testament, New Testament and Holy Qur'an. I was further convinced that the distortions cannot change. For you will find that much of the INTERPRETATIONS and TRANSLATIONS of this document from one European language to another is loaded with all sorts of distortions and down-right out and out lies which can be only classified as willful WHITE RACISM and SEMITIC RELIGIOUS BIGOTRY of the type that is never excelled anywhere.

[The "CIPPUS OF HORUS" from Golenischeff's Metternichstele] [1]

---

1. Each student should try to decipher the above inscription and compare results.

In the Black Bible "FILTH" of the mind, and of the body, will be equally considered "an abomination unto [BLACK PEOPLE] me," as it did in ancient times by our ancestors along the Nile and Great Lakes High-Cultures, and equally among those of the South, Central and West African continent. The type of mental "FILTH" I refer to is quite dominant in all of the plagiarizations in the so-called HOLY BIBLES [New and Old Testament] from the Council of Jamnia to the Council of Nicene. The ancient indigenous African ancestors said the following about mental and physical "FILTH:"

> " That which is an abomination unto me, that
> " which is an abomination unto me let me not eat.
> " That which is an abomination unto me, that which is
> " an abomination unto me is filth; let me not eat of it
> " instead of the cakes [which are offered unto] the
> " Doubles (*kau*). Let it not light upon my body; let
> " me not be obliged to take it into my hands; and let

[The scribe Ani and his wife standing in a stream drinking water.]

" me not be obliged to walk thereon in my sandals."[1]

"WATER," that which our ancient African ancestors used in their stories about the "CREATION OF THE WORLD" and in the worship of the SUN, MOON, STARS, ANIMALS, PROCREATION, etc. in the person of...

"THE ONE AND ONLY I AM – TEM, RA, AMEN-RA, ATEN, GOD, THE WORD," etc. This also holds true for Goddesses, who equally were involved in the making of mankind. They also "made man God" like the pharaohs from the FIRST through the SIXTH to EIGHT Dynasty. Here is where a major departure from the ORIGINAL BIBLE... The Book Of The Coming Forth By Day And By Night... was taken by the first translators who changed the Africans' "SACRED WORDS OF GOD" written by his "Holy inspired scribes" for his "CHOSEN [Black] PEOPLE."

Just how much of the above will the "PANEL OF JEWISH SCHOLARS TRANSLATING THE BIBLE" return according to the original the African named "Moses" handed down?

---

1. See Sir E.A. Wallis Budge's PAPYRUS OF ANI, plate 16.

[PRELUDE]   The contrived, manufactured and believed GOSPEL according to ruthless rumors about...

"Elijah Mohammad and Malcolm X's leadership; and the threat of physical violence by the "Black Muslims"[1] trying to dominate Black and White Ameri-America with the intent of taking both over...," etc., etc., etc., etc., etc.,

almost endlessly, which caused pandemonium and acute paranoia throughout the "White Communities" of the United States of America, along with the "Middle-Class me-too-ers of the Negro Communities," just a few short years ago, seem to be somewhat true today with respect to the Reverend-Teacher Albert Cleage and his "BLACK CHRISTIAN NATIONALIST MOVEMENT."[2] This type of propaganda causes many questions to arise daily. The most significant of them is: why does not a similar type of threat of physical violence ever evolve from the so-called "typical Negro [Colored] Christian, Israelite [Jewish, etc.] or Orthodox Moslem parishoners " who follow the conventional teachings in the standardized "FORMS" and "VERSIONS" of the Hebrew Old Testament, Christian New Testament, and/or Moslem Qur'an? The answer is to be found in the interpretations of each of these "HOLY BOOKS," from either a European, European-American or African and African-American perspective. In the case of the Honourable Prophet Elijah Mohammad and the Honourable Mwalimu [or Teacher] Albert Cleage, they have been able to recognize that the so-called "HOLY BOOKS," as they are presently written, have been made to perpetuate the "LIFE-STYLE" and "ETHNO-CENTRICITY" of the people who plagiarized the "ORIGINALS" and adopted the "END RESULTS" to represent their own concept of their GOD-HEAD...who, of course, looks like them, represent them in their every endeavour, and even fight their battles against all others outside of their own ETHNIC CLAN - members of the so-called "GREAT WHITE [Caucasian, Indo-European Aryan, Semitic] RACE." BLACK BROTHERS - Mohammad and Cleage - unlike most of the "NEGRO" or "COLORED" politically oriented "preachers of the Black Clergy" in the so-called "Western World," recognizing the above facts and the mental condition of Black People in RELIGION, are doing what they found to be necessary to change the moral condition required in each of their own - "ALL BLACK PHILOSOPHY;" all praises be to them. Never the less, both have failed to make the major "FINAL [first] STEP" in producing the one thing that is a 'MUST' for the rebirth of their fellow African [BLACK] People's mental state of being; that is:

'THE PRODUCTION OF OUR OWN VERSION OF THE HOLY BOOKS;" WHICH WAS INSPIRED BY OUR OWN HOLY SCRIBES;" FROM OUR OWN "ONE AND ONLY TRUE GOD" [Ywh, Oledumare, Jesus Christ, Al'lah, Ngai, Damballah Ouedo,etc]; AS OUR OUR GOD'S ONE AND ONLY "CHOSEN PEOPLE."

1

Yet, the answer may still be not in a Black People's VERSION, but in a -

COMPLETELY NEW BLACK BIBLE.

The end result of the apparent decision of Mohammad and Cleage to continue using the standardized and/or orthodox "VERSIONS" of a European [Caucasian-Semitic-Aryan] "HOLY BIBLE" or an Asian [Arab, Hamitic, Adomic, etc.] "HOLY QUR'AN" would indicate that they are preaching what they appearently found no time to document. And,that they have not yet established their own final "WRITTEN AUTHORITY" of just who, or what, is "GOD" [Ra, Ywh, Jesus Christ, Al'lah, Oledumare, Ngai, etc.]. Also, that they too rely somewhat upon their oppositions' [DEVIL'S] "versions" of the color of...

"TRUTH, UNTRUTH, GODLINESS, UN-GODLINESS, RELIGIOUS-MAGIC;"
and for the...

"INTERPRETATION OF THE WORD."

The first question this latter fact causes to arise is:

ARE THERE NO COMPETENT HOLY [Black] SCRIBES AMONG THESE TWO
LEADERS THOUSANDS OF FAITHFUL FOLLOWERS WHO ARE CAPABLE
OF THE NECESSARY SCHOLARSHIP REQUIRED FOR RECORDING THE
VARIANCES BEING PREACHED BY THEIR OWN SPIRITUAL PROPHETS -

Mohammad and Cleage; just as the scribes shown on pages xvii and xxx of this volume? At this juncture the question must them be:

WHO MAKES A HOLY SCRIBE LIKE ANY OF THOSE ON PAGES xvii AND xxx
OTHER THAN THE PEOPLE HE IS TO WRITE HIS "HOLY WORDS" ABOUT?

Certainly the literature each of these two groups [Black Muslims[1] and Black Christian Nationalists[2]] produces validate the fact that they do have such competence around and about them. And most certainly both of their teachings are as "GODLY" as the teachings of any of the other leaders like those who told, and are now telling, stories about YWH, JESUS CHRIST and AL'LAH. They were in the past, and still remain today, as they will ever be in the future; merely HUMAN BEINGS like anyone of us.

The second question, a result of the first, is:

WHY HAVE THEY [Mohammad and Cleage] NOT CALLED A "SCHOLARLY"
GATHERING OF THEIR OWN SCRIBES TO BEGIN THE NECESSARY GROUND-
WORK AND RESEARCH TOWARDS THIS MONUMENTAL GOAL; A MUST...?

The answer to this question is conjectural; as the main principals seem to be mute on this area of their "LEADERSHIP."

---

1. A name given "The Nation Of Islam" by Prof. Eric Lincoln in his book about them of like name. The Holy Lamb Prophet Elijah Mohammad is their leader.
2. Headed by the Hon. Reverend-Teacher [Walimu] Albert Cleage.

As one who teaches within the area of the "HISTORY" and "HERITAGE" of the African People, equally in the field of "COMPARATIVE RELIGIONS, " I am aghast at the lateness of both of these leaders in this venture! WHY? Because I see the basically overriding need for BLACK RELIGIOUS WORKS on the part of African People who can no longer tolerate the CAUCASIAN-SEMITIC-JUDAEO-CHRISTIAN IMAGERY OF AN AFRICAN-LESS [black] AND ASIAN-LESS [brown] MAGICAL-RELIGIOUS JUDAISM, CHRISTIANITY AND ISLAM; all of which had their GENESIS in Africa and Asia; and moreso, to be able to detail much more effectively with those who still find African People to be like the following from page 1 of Professor C. P. Groves' THE PLANTING OF CHRISTIANITY IN AFRICA, Volume I. Professor Groves wrote:

> "...it is the paradox of this vast continent" [Africa] "that
> while sharing in the earliest history of the human race, it
> was yet not opened up until the late nineteenth century."

Professor Groves' assertion that Africa"...was yet not opened up...," etc., is typically the same position held by Professor M.D.W. Jeffreys and most of the current "liberal" and "orthodox AUTHORITIES on Africa and African People. This equally holds true for those who called themselves "academicians, especially those who prefer to be associated with the "Christian Missionaries" and "Jewish Theologians" that corrupted African people's religious teachings in the past, at present, and are preparing to continue said distortion and plagiarization way into the future. But the TRUTH is that there has never in history been a period in man's behaviour throughout the continent when Africa "...was yet not opened up..." to all. It seems that any place where European and/or European-American [WHITE] Judaeo-Christians have never been is always labeled by them...

"UNDISCOVERED, CLOSED, SECRETIVE, DANGEROUS, PRIMITIVE, AND
WAS YET NOT YET OPENED UP."

However, the first appearance of any of them who gain control of any place inhabited by people other than their own ETHNIC or RELIGIOUS group suddenly becomes...

"SAFE, DISCOVERED, AND 'YET WAS OPENED UP,' WORTHY OF GOD'S GRACE,"
etc. But this is providing their own GOD-HEAD [Ywh, Jesus Christ, etc.] becomes the...

"THE ONE AND ONLY TRUE GOD" ABOVE THE EXISTING GOD THEY MEET.
Other religious historians and theologians like Professor C. P. Groves, who suffered from an extreme case of "NEGROPHOBIA" in their works, must be equally examined and cited. For example: Dr. Lothrop S. Stoddard in his book, THE RISING TIDE OF COLOUR, page 68, added his support for the African People's submission by military force to his fellow European

and European-American Judaeo-Christian missionaries and colonialists. He wrote:

> Of course Christianity has made distinct progress in the Dark
> continent. The natives of the South African Union are predominantly
> Christianized. In east-central Africa Christianity has also gained
> many converts, particularly in Uganda, while on the West African
> Guinea coast Christian missions have long been established and have
> generally succeeded in keeping Islam away from the Seaboard.

It should be needless to say that Dr. Stoddard continued in the normal Judaeo-Christian manner on page 90 of the same book. He wrote:

> From the First glance we see that, in the Negro, we are in
> the presence of a being differing profoundly not merely from the
> white man but also from those human types which we discovered
> in our surveys of the brown and yellow worlds. The black man is,
> indeed, sharply differentiated from the other branches of mankind.
> His outstanding qualities is super-abundant animal vitality. In this
> he easily surpasses other races. To it he owes his intense emo-
> tionalism. To it, again, is due his extreme fecundity, the Negro
> being the quickest of the breeders. This abounding vitality shows
> in many other ways, such as the Negro's ability to survive harsh
> conditions of slavery under which other races have succumb. Last-
> ly, in the ethnic crossings, the Negro strikingly displays his pre-
> potency, for black blood, once entering a human stock, seems never
> really bred out again.

Still not satisfied with his obvious overdose of "ACUTE NEGROPHOBIA," the good doctor
reached his climax in his religious and racist mental masturbation when he wrote the following on pages 96 and 97:

> ... Certainly, all white men, whether professing Christians or not,
> should welcome the success of missionary efforts in Africa. The de-
> grading fetishism and demonology which sum up the native pagan cults
> cannot stand, and all Negroes will some day be either Christian or
> Moslems. In so far as he is Christianized, the Negro's savage in-
> stincts will be restrained and he will be disposed to acquiece in white
> tutelage. In so far as he is Islamized, the Negro warlike propensi-
> ties will be inflamed, and he will be used as the tool of Arab Pan-
> Islamism seeking to drive the white man from Africa and make the
> continent his very own.

There are those who, under any circumstance whatsoever, and irrespective of the above,
would not understand that the use of "COLOR, RACE" and "ETHNIC ORIGIN" make their
European and European-American "VERSION" of the "HOLY BOOK" whatever it is to each
parishoner. For example: They cannot comprehend that the areas of the "WORLD" mentioned in the "BOOK OF GENESIS" could not have included the United States of America or any
other part of the so-called "Western Hemisphere;" as the authors of said FIRST BOOK OF
MOSES [Genesis] failed to mention that there were millions upon millions of people, and
millions of square miles of landmasses in Africa and Asia, before anyone knew that a MOSES
existed. Even around the Nile Valley and the Tigris and Euphrates Valley they were not con-

4

cious of the existence of people who lived on the planet Earth; all of whom had "WORLDS" of their own. Moreover, they were not conscious of any nation west of the eastern limits of Greece in Europe; southwest of the First Cataract of Egypt and Nubia, also south of Kenya, in Africa; south of the City of Mecca at the eastern coast of the Red Sea, east of the Persian Kingdom, and north of the northern limits of the Tigris and Euphrates River in Asia. Thus the "WORLD OF GENESIS," which began with the "WORLD" of Adam, Eve and Noah, then of Abraham, Isaac, Jacob, Joseph, and others that are too extensive in numbers to list here, was similar to the HYPOTHETICAL MAP shown below... ,which was drawn according to the "Holy Scriptures" by "God-inspired Scribes" in the BOOK OF GENESIS.

We must reexamine the entire text of the BOOK OF GENESIS [or First Book Of Moses] with specific emphasis on the geography, palaeontology, cultural anthropology, archaeology and demography of its African and Asian Peoples and their homelands. Of course our FIRST STEP is with the theory of "THE CREATION OF THE" [chosen Hebrews, Christians, Moslems] WORLD;" pinpointing the "LOCATION OF THE GARDEN OF EDEN;" finding "THE LAND OF NOD;" and marking off the limits of "THE AREA OF THE GREAT DELUGE" [flood].

Which of the earlier of the contemporary works, other than those written by the so-called "HEBREW SCRIBES" of the Council of Jamnia that ended as late as ca. 500 B.C.E., validates

5

these claims? NONE. Not a single line was written about any "...CREATION OF THE WORLD BY..." a Hebrew"...GOD..." named "...YWH" [Jehovah, Jesus Christ or Al'lah] before an indigenous African called "MOSES" [Drawn Out Of Water] allegedly passed down his "FIVE BOOKS" of plagiarized African works dealing with the <u>Magical-Religious Rites and Incantations</u> from the Nile Valley <u>Mysteries System</u> that European and European-American Jews and Christians have since called the PENTATEUCH and/or OLD TESTAMENT, also HOLY TORAH. All of this is inspite of the fact that most European and European-American "<u>Talmudic Jews</u>" have stated that:

> "The chronological beginning of the "WORLD" completes
> 5734 years old as of the month of September [1974 C.E.]."

But if this is in fact the "TRUTH;" then we must subtract the present year 1974 C.E. [A.D.] from 5,734 years to secure the "YEAR ONE" [1] when the Jewish, Christian and Moslem "GOD [Ywh, Jesus Christ, Al'lah] CREATED THE [Hebrew] WORLD," which would have been sometime around ca. 3,760 <u>Before the Christian Era</u> [B.C.E.]. Yet using anyone of the chronological dynastic dates shown on pages seven [7] and eight [8] following, we will discover that the...

"YEAR OF THE CREATION OF THE [Judaeo-Christian-Islamic] WORLD"... was equivalent to the same "YEAR" when the indigenous Africans of the Nile Valley and Great Lakes High-Cultures had already reached somewhere between the end of their very FIRST DYNASTY - ca. 5867 to 3892 B.C.E. and the SECOND DYNASTY - ca. 5615 to 3639 B.C.E. The High-Cultures [civilizations] along the Blue and White Nile River and the Great Lakes regions were Punt, Itiopi, Meröe, Ta-Nehisi [Nubia] and Ta-Merry [Egypt]; each no later than ca. 3,892 B.C.E. The "FIRST DYNASTY" was initiated in Ta-Merry [Egypt, according to Moses and his Hebrew HOLY TORAH] by an African from Ta-Nehisi [Zeti, Nubia or El Sud - - Sudan] named AHA or NARMER [whom Herodotus, the "first European historian," called "MENES" in his history book he named EUTERPE in ca. 457 - 450 B.C.E.]. May all of the students and general readers, at this juncture in the text, remember that <u>not a single European nation was in existence during the FIRST</u> [ca. 3892 B.C.E.] <u>through the TWENTIETH Dynasty</u> [ca. 1091 B.C.E], <u>including the first one - Greece.</u> So far the peoples involved are only Africans and Asians. Yet all of the African High-Cultures along the WHITE and BLUE Nile Valley, Atbara River Valley and the Great Lakes regions were already reaching their FIRST ZENITH in their very long history. But the Hebrew's "WORLD OF GENESIS" was not only preceded by all of the kingdoms of the preDYNASTIC periods of the

Nile Valley history, particularly Egypt, Meröe, Nubia, Itiopi and Punt. Yet,the First Dynasty in ca. 3892 B.C.E. was the point of equation before each and everyone of the so-called FIVE BOOKS OF MOSES [Pentateuch, Old Testament or Holy Torah], beginning with the FIRST BOOK or "GENESIS" which even followed many more thousands of years before the FIRST DYNASTY of Pharaonic Reign.The African worshipers of TEM and/or RA's "WORLD," thousands of years before the Hebrew's "WORLD," went back beyond the SEBELLIAN SILT PYRAMIDS period - ca. 250,000 - ca. 6000 B.C.E.

DATES OF EGYPTIAN DYNASTIES BY EUROPEAN "AUTHORITIES IN [1] EGYPTOLOGY" COMPARED TO MANETHO'S ORIGINAL WORKS

Period or DYNASTY	Manetho (280 B.C) DATE	Champollion- Figeac (?A D) DATE	Lepsius (1858AD) DATE	Brugsh (1877AD) DATE	Mariette (?AD) DATE
	First Book				
1	9K, 253Y	5,867*	3,892*	4,400*	5,004*
II	9K, 302Y	5,615	3,639	4,133	4,751
III	9K, 214Y	5,318	3,338	3,966	4,449
IV	8K,.284Y	5,121	3,124	3,733	4,235
V	9K,˙248Y	4,673	2,840	3,566	3,951
VI	6K, 203Y	4,225	2,744	3,300	3,703
VII	70K, 0Y, 70D	4,222	2,592	3,100	3,500
VIII	27K, 146Y	4,147	2,522	?	3,500
IX	19K, 409Y	4,047	2,674**	?	3,358
X	10K, 185Y	3,947	2,565**	?	3,249
XI	192K,2300Y, 70D	3,762	?,423	?	3,064
XII	7K, 160Y	3,703	2,380	?	2,851
XIII	?	3,417	2,136	2,235	?
XIV	76K, 184Y	3,004	2,167	?	2,398
XV	?	2,520	2,101	?	2,214
XVI	32K, 518Y	2,270	1,842	?	?
XVII	86K, 151Y	2,082	1,684	?	?
VIII	16K, 263Y	1,822	1,581	1,700	1,703
	Second Book				
XIX	7K, 209Y	1,473	1,443	1,400	1,462
XX	12K, 135Y	1,279	1,269	1,200	1,288
XXI	7K, 130Y	1,101	1,091	1,100	1,110
XXII	9K, 126Y	971	961	966	980
XXIII	4K, 28Y	851	787	766	810
XXIV	1K , 6Y	762	729	733	721
XXV	3K, 40Y	718	716	700	715
XXVI	9K, 150Y, 6M	674	685	666	665
XXVII	8K, 124Y, 4M	524	525	527	527
XXVIII	1K , 6Y	404	525	?	406
XXIX	4K, 20Y, 4M	398	399	399	399
XXX	3K, 38Y	377	378	378	378
	Third Book				
XXXI***	????????	399	340	340	340

---

1. See BLACK MAN OF THE NILE AND HIS FAMILY, p. 131. You will observe that the comparative Hebrew Calendar dates shown on the following page - 8 - are based upon the First Dnasty date of ca. 3892 B.C.E., which I have used throughout this volume for comparisions.

Because of the extent to which the dates of the preceding Calendar far exceeds the following of the Hebrews' WORLD OF GENESIS in terms of time and authenticity, it will not
be necessary to introduce other material information of a <u>Histo-Religious</u> nature detailing
the earlier indigenous African High-Cultures that even go back chronologically over <u>one</u>
<u>million</u> [1,000,000] <u>years</u> into mankind's pre-antiquity at the Great Lakes regions of Central
Alkebu-lan [Afrika, Africa, etc.]. They are already detailed in BLACK MAN OF THE NILE
AND HIS FAMILY, Chapter II : Prehistoric African Homosapiens, pages 73 - 98, equally as it
is shown in CULTURAL GENOCIDE IN THE BLACK AND AFRICAN STUDIES CURRICULUM,
Chapter 13: Anthropology - The Weapon Of Black Cultural Genocide, pages 104 - 120. All of
the historical periods above preceded the <u>Comparative Chronological Chart</u> below:

THE MANETHONIAN NILE LISTS [1]

The Dynastic Sections	The measures of the ex-pired and calculated nations in the several book-sections	The measures of the as-sociated calculations in the third book-section	Duration of the Cata-clysmic Sections	Durations of the Exp-rene Sections	The Patriarchs and the years of time in it's waging between their birth only.	The Samaritan numbers	The Septuagint numbers	The Hebrew numbers
	Metric noctas.	Metric noctas	Nilo years.	Nilo years.		Sacred years.	Lunar years.	Nilo years.
XIX.	 209	....	204	....	Terah	70	170	70
XVIII.	} 263	....	262	....	Nahor	79	179	29
	Amos 25 B	26 B	....	....	Serug	130	130	30
XVII.	.... 151 B	2×151 B	....	151 B	Reu	132	132	32
XVI.	.... 518 B	2×518 B	....	518 B	Peleg......	130	130	30
XV.	 284	....	284	....	Eber	134	134	34
XIV.	.... 184 B	184 B	....	184 B	Salah......	130	130	30
XIII.	.... 453 B	453 B	....	453 B	(Cainan II.)	160	130	160
XII.	 160	....	160	....	Arphaxad...	135	135	35
XI.	.. 2× 16	....	16	....	Shem......	100	100	100
	{.... 43 B	43 B	43 B	(43 B)				
					Sums ...	1140	1370	490
X.	.... 185 B	185 B	....	185 B	Noah......	500	500	500
IX.	.... 409 B	409 B	....	409 B	Lamech....	53	188	182
VIII.	.... 146 B	146 B	....	146 B	Methuselah..	67	187	187
VII.	.... 0·2 B	0·2 B	....	....	Enoch	65	165	65
VI.	 203	....	197	....	Jared.. ...	162	262	162
V.	 248	....	248	....	Mahalaleel.	65	165	65
IV.	 284	....	284	....	Cainan I...	70	170	70
III.	 214	....	214	....	Enos	90	190	90
II.	 302	....	302	....	Seth	105	205	105
I.	 263	....	263	....	Adam	130	230	130
	2)4523·2	2)2740·2 B			Sums ..	1307	2262	1556
	2261·6	1370·1 B						
					Post-Noachid section ..	1140	1370	490
					Ante-Noachid section ..	1307	2262	1556
			2417	2016	Sums total..	2447	3632	2016

It is suggested that all of the students specializing in AFRICAN and/or BLACK STUDIES
familiarize themselves with similar information in the following introductory works: Y. ben-
Jochannan and George E. Simmonds' THE BLACK MAN'S NORTH AND EAST AFRICA; Y.
ben-Jochannan's AFRICAN ORIGINS OF THE MAJOR WESTERN RELIGIONS;[2] THE BLACK

---

1. See BLACK MAN OF THE NILE AND HIS FAMILY, p. 213. You will notice that the differences between the Nile Lists and the Dynastic Dates are many; depending upon each author.
2. This is VOLUME I in the series of THE BLACK MAN'S RELIGION, publ. date 1973.

MAN'S RELIGION: THE MYTH OF GENESIS AND EXODUS, AND THE EXCLUSION OF THEIR AFRICAN ORIGIN. The last three books, along with the other two mentioned above the Nile Lists chart, are already listed on your required reading assignment. The following supportive historical works should be added and used in conjunction with those already mentioned: George G.M. James' STOLEN LEGACY; Eva B. Sandford's THE MEDITERRANEAN WORLD; J.C. deGraft-Johnson's AFRICAN GLORY; Sir James Frazier's THE GOLDEN BOUGH [13 vols.]; Sir Godfrey Higgins' ANACALYPSIS [2 vols.]; Gerald Massey's EGYPT THE LIGHT OF THE WORLD; James H. Breasted's THE DAWN OF CIVILIZATION; Gaston Maspero's THE DAWN OF CIVILIZATION; Joel A. Rogers' WORLD'S GREAT MEN OF COLOR [2 vols.]; Sir Ernest A. Wallis Budge's BOOK OF THE DEAD and PAPYRUS OF ANI; Dr. Albert Churchward's ORIGIN AND EVOLUTION OF THE HUMAN RACE; Churchward's SIGNS AND SYMBOLS OF PRIMORDIAL MAN; Herodotus' THE HISTORIES; Count C.F. Volney's RUINS OF EMPIRE; and many more, some of which shall be included as you continue throughout the text of this volume, also in the Added Bibliography at the end.

[IDENTIFICATION OF THE "GARDEN OF EDEN"] It is the biblical figure named "Abraham,"[1] allegedly "...the first of the line of the Hebrews...,"[2] who is also said to have been "...the first to introduce the God Ywh[3] to the Hebrew people..." that was equally passed on by Moses in GENESIS..., which Moses later detailed with other stories he learned at the Lodges of the Mysteries System of the Nile Valley to produce the Hebrews, Christians and Moslems' -

"...CREATION OF THE WORLD...."

This story included the geographic location of the so-called...

"GARDEN OF EDEN"

around the birthplace of the "First Hebrew Patriarch - Abraham." Thus, one is expected to assume that said "HEBREW WORLD OF GENESIS" was centered around the vicinity of the area presently called...

"THE FERTILE CRESCENT,"

as outlined on the map on the following page, also as shown on page 5 of this volume.

The development of these facts, so far stated, should be sufficient for the necessary evidence to prove that mankind's oldest FOSSIL-ANCESTORS must have been buried somewhere within the earth's layers along the perimeter of the "Fertile Crescent."

---

1. Also called "ABRM, AVRAM, ABRAM, AVRAM, ABRAHAH," etc.
2. Also called "JEHOVAH, ADONI, GOD, I AM, REDEEMER," etc.

The Fertile Crescent & Garden Of Eden

ca. 3760 - 3500 B.C.E. [B.C.]

Inspite of the map above and the facts connected to the story related thereto, to date it is still around the Great Lakes regions of Central Africa, particularly at the OLDUVAI GORGE, and also at the most southerly tip of Monomotapa, and equally at the most northerly tip of the Sahara, that mankind's most ancient FOSSIL-ANCESTORS are being unearthed, which is demonstrated graphically on the map shown below.

NAME OF AREA
+ 1 Broken Hill
+ 2 Diredawa
+ 3 Singna
+ 4 Springbak or Tulnplaats
+ 5 Boskop
+ 6 Hopefield
+ 7 Tulnplaats
+ 8 Vaal River region
+ 9 Asselar
+10 Mechta-el-Arbi
+ 11 Rabat
+ 12 Hau Fteah
+ 13 Ngorongoro Crater Tanzania

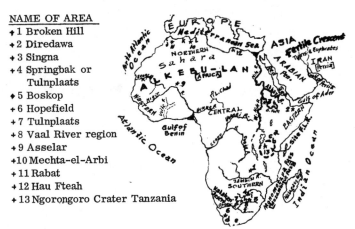

MAIN SITE
a. Gamble's Cave
b. Olduvai and Eyasi
c. Kanam and Kanjera
d. Cape Flats and Fish Hoek
e. Matjes River and Tzitzikama
f. Florisbad
g. Taung
h. Sterkfrontein
i. Makapansgat
j. Sidi Abderrahman
k. Ternifine
l. Afalou-bou Rhummel

FOSSIL-FIELD MAP OF AFRICA
ca. 1966 C.E. [A.D.]

Examples of the Caucasian-Semitic-Indo-European Aryan RACISM that were necessary to make the indigenous African FOSSIL-MEN appear to have been European, or WHITE, are shown on pages 22, 24 and 25 of THE BLACK MAN'S RELIGION, Volume II.[1] Within this same context to date we can only produce a FOSSIL-FIND called NEANDERTHAL MAN of no more than four hundred thousand [400,000] years old throughout all of Europe. And "JAVA MAN" of the Malayan Peninsula is only five hundred thousand [500,000] years, the oldest throughout all of Asia. But all of the FOSSIL-FINDS throughout the "FOSSIL-FIELD MAP" above predated all of Europe and Asia; two of them even beyond the astonishing figure of two million seven hundred and fifty thousand [2,750,000] years old. One known as "ZINJANTHROPUS boise" is one million seven hundred and fifty thousand [1,750,000] years old; the other is not yet named.[2] Obviously then, it is only rational to assume that the true "GARDEN OF EDEN" of the Black Bible is Central Africa- around the OLDUVAI GORGE of Tanzania. This is the area circled with the very heavy broken lines on the FOSSIL-FIELD MAP on page 10. However, it is a MUST that each student reexamines the details of the Hebrew "...God's [Ywh's] Creation of man and woman in the Garden of Eden..." sometime around ca. 3760 B.C.E., less than six thousand [6000] years ago,[3] according to the following extract from GENESIS, Chapter ii, Verses 1 - 9:

2 Thus the heavens and the earth were finished, and all the host of them. 2And on the seventh day God finished his work which he had done, and he rested on the seventh day from all his work which he had done. 3 So God blessed the seventh day and hallowed it, because on it God rested from all his work which he had done in creation.
4 These are the generations of the heavens and the earth when they were created.
In the day that the LORD God made the earth and the heavens, 5 when no plant of the field was yet in the earth and no herb of the field had yet sprung up—for the LORD God had not caused it to rain upon the earth, and there was no man to till the ground; 6 but a mist went up from the earth and watered the whole face of the ground— 7 then the LORD God formed man of dust from the ground, and breathed into his nostrils the breath of life; and man became a living being. 8And the LORD God planted a garden in Eden, in the east; and there he put the man whom he had formed. 9And out of the ground the LORD God made to grow every tree that is pleasant to the sight and good for food, the tree of life also in the midst of the garden, and the tree of the knowledge of good and evil.

Should the Black ["Holy Scripture"] Bible recite the same type of Jewish or White "Semitic" CREATION STORY inspite of the facts already revealed with respect to the FOSSIL-FINDS throughout all of 'Africa''and other places in Asia? Or, should it not reflect the fact that the true "GARDEN OF EDEN" was more than likely around''Central Africa's''OLDUVAI GORGE? This is not according to the "INSPIRED WORDS OF [the Jewish] GOD;" but instead, the fact in which no amount of esoterical belief and hypothetical conjecture within Judaism, Christian-

1. See Y. ben-Jochannan's CULTURAL GENOCIDE IN THE BLACK AND AFRICAN STUDIES CURRICULUM, pp. 104 - 135.
2. Ibid.
3. According to the Hebrew [Jewish] Calendar this is the year 5733 since God created the world.

ity and Islam is necessary. The same equally holds true for the "FIRST MAN" and "FIRST WOMAN," neither of whom was named "ADAM" or "EVE," but more than likely something near the African name given to "ZINJANTHROPUS boise" - already mentioned in this volume.

[THE MAKING OF PEOPLE] As to the construction of the so-called "TWO FIRST PEOPLE," one out of "CLAY" and the other from the "RIB" of the first; what should the Black Bible say? Should it not take into account God's EVOLUTIONARY PROCESSES being equally as valid as God's KNEADING MAN INTO BEING FROM CLAY? And at this juncture: Will the Black Bible have any "FORBIDDEN FRUIT TREE" by which God will be shown playing a childish game of HIDE AND SEEK, or CATCH, with both of His first creations - ADAM AND EVE? Obviously the God of the Black Bible will not object to NORMAL SEXUAL INTERCOURSE between His first two people he provided with matching GENITAL ORGANS - a male penis and female vagina. This, of course, is not in keeping with the Judaeo-Christian-Islamic "ORIGINAL SIN" syndrome you have found in the White Bible according to GENESIS, Chapter ii - iv, of which the following extract from Chapter ii, Verses 13 - 24 is quoted:

> 13 The name of the second river is Gi'hon; it is the one which flows around the whole land of Cush. 14And the name of the third river is Ti'gris, which flows east of Assyria. And the fourth river is the Eu·phra'tes.
> 15 The LORD God took the man and put him in the garden of Eden to till it and keep it. 16And the LORD God commanded the man, saying, "You may freely eat of every tree of the garden; 17 but of the tree of the knowledge of good and evil you shall not eat, for in the day that you eat of it you shall die."
> 18 Then the LORD God said, "It is not good that the man should be alone; I will make him a helper fit for him." 19 So out of the ground the LORD God formed every beast of the field and every bird of the air, and brought them to the man to see what he would call them; and whatever the man called every living creature, that was its name. 20 The man gave names to all cattle, and to the birds of the air, and to every beast of the field; but for the man there was not found a helper fit for him. 21 So the LORD God caused a deep sleep to fall upon the man, and while he slept took one of his ribs and closed up its place with flesh;' 22 and the rib which the LORD God had taken from the man he made into a woman and brought her to the man. 23 Then the man said,
> "This at last is bone of my bones
>   and flesh of my flesh;
> she shall be called Woman,d
>   because she was taken out of Man."e
> 24 Therefore a man leaves his father and his mother and cleaves to his wife, and they become one flesh.

Since there is no record of any MARRIAGE CONTRACT ever issued to either "Adam" or "Eve" in the Bible, and no MARRIAGE between them is mentioned in the Hebrew, Christian and/or Islamic context; why did God allow SEXUAL INTERCOURSE between Adam and Eve before, and after, they produced three offsprings - namely "CAIN, ABEL" and "SET?" It is obvious that the Black Bible would have to conclude that this biological process was indeed ordained by "...THE GOD OF EV[E]OLUTION..." [nature]. And, that this biological function is in fact "RIGHTEOUS" and "GODLY," instead of "UNRIGHTEOUS" and "UNGODLY." This would be much more in keeping with the African [BLACK] People's premise of the "EXTENDED FAMILY" concept; that which does not include such anti-Godliness as the perpetuation of CHILD-

BIRTH with the stigma of...

"ILLEGITAMACY , OUT OF WEDLOCK SEXUAL LOVE CHILD, BASTARD," ETC.,
and other such inhuman terms related to the so-called "ORIGINAL SIN" syndrome and penalty;
all of which is attributed to Moses' story about "ADAM AND EVE IN THE GARDEN OF EDEN"
and their very first SEXUAL INTERCOURSE and PREGNANCY. This aspect of a perverted religious theory must give away to the natural EVOLUTION of child-birth - the only logical understanding reality of the BIOLOGICAL PROCESSES OF NATURAL REPRODUCTION relative to the
PROCREATION OF MANKIND, without which there will be no more HUMAN BEINGS - Adam
and Eve not withstanding. For one has to remember that the Hebrew, Christian and/or Moslem's
"GOD" [Ywh, Jesus Christ and/or Al'lah] called upon His own WOMAN [or Goddess] when He
hollered at the tip of His voice:

"LET US MAKE MAN IN OUR OWN LIKENESS."
This we find in GENESIS [the First Book Of Moses], Chapter i, Verse 26. Certainly it was to
His WOMAN God was speaking. And this is what the BLACK BIBLE will have to say about such
a glorious couple of SPIRIT-BEINGS or GOD-HUMAN-BEINGS; of whom Black People must say:

'ALL PRAISES BE TO THE GOD AND GODDESS OF PROCREATION.'
[CRIME and PUNISHMENT] Since the "Original Sin" syndrome came by way of the penalty
placed on human beings for SEXUAL INTERCOURSE committed with the SEX ORGANS provided by God; this will be omitted from the Black Bible. At least, this is what is logical to believe
inspite of the current biblical teaching. Then there would be no reason to have BLACK WOMEN
condemned forever to all sorts of horrible experiences in CHILD-BEARING and/or CHILD-
BIRTH as a retribution for "EVE'S ORIGINAL SIN"...having INTERCOURSE with her man -
"ADAM" - whom God allegedly "MADE HER FOR." For there will be no "SIN" connected in
the Black Bible with respect to making...

"MAN" [female and male] "IN OUR OWN LIKENESS."
However, using the present White Bible; would the...

"LET US MAKE MAN IN OUR OWN LIKENESS," ETC.,
not suggests that GOD [a male] was talking to his GODDESS [a female]? Noting the biological
reality and necessity in making MAN [male and female]; would it not have been logically possible
for any GOD [Ywh, Jesus Christ and Al'lah included] to have been addressing another GOD [a
male] or GODS in the process of making another like...

"THEIR KIND, AND EACH ACCORDING TO ITS KIND, AND GOD WAS SATISFIED,"
according to GENESIS [the Hebrew or Jewish First Book Of Moses] Chapter i, Verse 20?

Since we have noticed that there was in use along the Nile Valley High-Cultures Planned

Parenthood and "FERTILITY CONTROL METHOD" before ca. 1555 B.C.E., a PRESCRIPTION of said period is shown below under the heading of "EBERS PAPYRUS." We should, however, understand that any RELIGIOUS PROHIBITION in this direction in the 20th Century C.E. will be that much more "PRIMITIVE" in reality than the efforts in the same type of antiquity we have already deemed "UNCIVILIZED" and "PRIMITIVE;" for it cannot enter the pages of the BLACK BIBLE anytime. Thus there will be no "TET BUCKLE" [as shown on page 61 of this volume] to prevent the "SERPENT" from crawling down any "FORBIDDEN FRUIT TREE" for the sole purpose of tempting "THE FIRST WOMAN - EVE" while "THE FIRST MAN - ADAM," the latter whom God provided with a NATURAL MATING COUPLER, stand by idly not knowing what to do biologically with his own NATURAL MATE until a common "REPTILE" has to enlighten him to the function of the MALE PENIS and the FEMALE VAGINA. Stranger yet, there was no CONTRACEPTIVE DEVICE like the following the indigenous African [BLACK] People developed along the Nile Valley High-Cultures for Eve to have used to avoid herself getting pregnant for her man - Adam - whom she was made for by "God":

EBERS PAPYRUS[1]
ca. 1555 BC
<u>PRESCRIPTION FOR FERTILITY CONTROL</u>
Plan Parenthood of the Nile

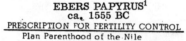

1. A compendium of medical inscriptions left by Africans along the Nile Valley, particularly in Ta-Merry, Ta-Nehisi, Itiopi, Meröe and Puanit. A prescription for a medical tampon designed to prevent pregnancy, requiring the following: "A mixture of the tips of the shrub of accacia and honey, made into a tampon and inserted into the vagina in the form of an elongatedly thin sup-

In no way whatsoever the previous remarks ignore the fact that the earliest HOLY BOOKS of the Africans along the High-Cultures of the Nile River Valley and the major Great Lakes regions have shown stories about...

"VIRGIN BIRTHS, RESURRECTIONS, REINCARNATIONS, ANGELS, GHOSTS," and a host of other mythological [fundamental]figures and allegorical stories about them in the same context as those passed on down to Judaism, Christianity and Islam. However, said ancient Africans had every reason to believe as they did; for although they were extremely wiser than most of their neighbouring peoples of their era, they supposedly did not have much of the information on the PRODUCTION and REPRODUCTION of human beings we know today. Of course this is providing one desires to overlook the Ebers Papyrus on Planned Parenthood done before ca. 1555 B.C.E. But we noticed that the ancient indigenous Africans did not provide us with any evidence that shows they were knowledgeable of any practical first-hand information about OUTER SPACE other than with the observatory instruments they had in compiling the necessary data they used in preparing their Stellar and Solar calendars in about 10,000 to 4100 B.C.E. At the same instance, they did not leave us information on any of their deceased brethren who had returned from the "NETHER" [or "Other"] "WORLD" after having met with the Great I Am - God: PTAH, TEM, RA, etc. Ywh, Jesus or Al'lah was not.

We have to remember that as ancient as their RELIGIOUS TEXTS[2] were, they had already gone through countless REVISIONS during various periods before the First Dynasty [ca. 5867, 5004, 4400 or ca. 3892 B.C.E.] , depending upon whose chronological listing one is using]; each time, because the unexpected results showed that:

NOT ONE OF THEM RETURNED FROM THE DEAD
AND LIVED AMONG THOSE HE [she] KNEW BEFORE
DEATH AND RESURRECTION INTO THE BEYOND.[3]

We do not need any more proof of this than the following from "The Doctrine Of Eternal Life" found in the PYRAMID TEXT, which preceded the OLD TESTAMENT by thousands of years.

1. Rise up thou   Teta   this.   Stand up thou mighty one

---

pository." The chemical reaction is that accacia fermentation breaks down into lactic acid, one of the active spermicidal agents used in CONTRACEPTIVE JELLIES today. See BLACK MAN OF THE NILE AND HIS FAMILY, p. 283 for further details.
2. PYRAMID TEXT, COFFIN TEXT, OSIRIAN DRAMA, PAPYRUS OF ANI, etc.
3. See PYRAMID TEXT, Recueil de Travaux, t. v, p. 36

being strong.   Sit thou   with   the gods,   do thou   that which

did   Osiris in   the great house   in   Ånu.   Thou hast received

thy *såh*,   not   shall be fettered   thy foot   in   heaven, not

shalt thou be turned back   upon   earth.

2.   Hail   to thee,   Tetá   on   this thy day   [when]   thou art

standing before Rā [as] he cometh from   the east, [when]   thou art

endued with   this thy *såh*   among   the souls.

3.   [His] duration of life   is   eternity,   his limit of life   is   everlastingness

in   his *såh*.

4.   I am   a *såh*   with his soul.

In the same context, African People in the United States of America and elsewhere have been
calling upon Michaelangelo and Pope Julius IInd European and European-American's VERSION
of the <u>African-Asian Jesus Christ</u>[1] to save them from European and European-American persecutors, persecution and genocide that began in ca. 1506 C.E. with Reverend [later on made
Bishop] Bartolome de LasCasas and Pope Julius IInd of the Roman Catholic Church.[2] The latter
two initiated the infamous SLAVE TRADE of Africans called "MOORS" [Moros] from Spain;
<u>a period of infamy that lasted at least four hundred and sixty-seven [467] years.</u> And; not a
single "GOD," Jesus Christ included, has ever removed said bondage. Thus, it is obvious
that such a "GOD" needs to be changed. If not; at least <u>the current approach recommended</u>

---

1. See BLACK MAN OF THE NILE AND HIS FAMILY, pp. 379 - 381.
2. See AFRICAN ORIGINS OF THE MAJOR "WESTERN RELIGIONS," pp. 73 - 137.

to appeal to said "GOD" needs to be by some other mean than current European and European-American theology. The Black Bible MUST state what it SHALL be.

[GOD: HE or SHE]   Since Judaism, Christianity and Islam made it possible to reduce the FEMALE IMAGE from one of SLAVERY to a mere object of "DISGRACE, SCORN, CONTEMPT" and/or "SIN," God was a natural in either of these three religons to be presented as a 'CELEBATE UNI-SEXUAL' [or perverted] PURE WHITE POWER SOURCE OF GLORY. In the same context, since the "ADAM AND EVE'S SIN" syndrome had to be maintained at all cost by the "MORAL PURISTS"that condemned all who were born as a result of SEXUAL INTERCOURSE, God's ORIGIN had to be equally UNI-SEXUAL as the FIRST MAN - Adam - He allegedly "CREATED OUT OF DIRT." Thus the corruption of the "HUMAN SOUL" attributed to SEXUAL INTERCOURSE, whether the couple is married or unmarried; and the one and only ingredient necessary for the NATURAL production and reproduction of the human's daily GENESIS must be equally condemned and defamed. The Black Bible would correct this demeaning aspect of Man's MOTHER, DAUGHTER, SISTER, and other female relationships. For it is only through the female's canal of REINCARNATION [1] and/or "RESURRECTION,"[2] otherwise from up and down - VIE - the falopian tube and womb that is connected to the vagina, that "CREATION" really takes place; and out of it "DEATH" immediately begins simultaneously with "LIFE" still in progress. This is the major area of "CREATION" that Europeanized and European-Americanized Judaeo-Christian-Islamic teachings have totally distorted in their own VERSION of the original "FERTILITY CONCEPTS" and METHODS from whence the principle of

" CREATION THROUGH VIRGIN BIRTH"[3]

arose in the Book Of The Coming Forth By Day And By Night of the Africans' Mysteries System.

Certainly the concept of the reproduction of mankind through SEXUAL INTERCOURSE was nothing new to the inhabitants of the ancient Nile Valley and Great Lakes regions of Africa. Methods for the control of "FERTILITY" resulting from SEXUAL INTERCOURSE were widely demonstrated throughout many of the ancient papyri and books of the Mysteries System teachings, rituals, paintings and hieroglyphic texts. Even the "GODS" were shown to have produced each others through the process of SEXUAL INTERCOURSE between themselves and their GODDESSES. On the following page we even see a dramatic representation of the Goddess ISIS hold-

---

1. See BLACK MAN OF THE NILE AND HIS FAMILY, pp. 375 - 377.
2. See PAPYRUS OF ANI, Chapter CLVII.
3. See references to the TET BUCKLE on p. 60 of this volume; also BLACK MAN OF THE NILE AND HIS FAMILY, pp. 375 - 377; and ISIS AND OSIRIS, pp. 106 - 108.

ing her infant child...<u>God</u> - HORUS

BLACK MADONNA AND CHILD[1]

Note that the picture on the following page was drawn before the showing of <u>Mary's</u> BREAST became "UNGODLY" and "OBSCENE." You will also note that she is feeding <u>Jesus Christ</u> on her breast in the same manner and position as ISIS fed her own VIRGIN offspring - the <u>God</u> "HORUS." This 16th Century C.E. [A.D.] painting is presently tabooed among the <u>puritan</u> [orthodox] <u>Christians</u>, all of whom even believe that:

"JESUS CHRIST DID NOT NURSE ON HIS MOTHER'S [the Virgin] BREASTS" like any of the other normal baby boys of his era in Asia - where he was born, and Africa where he was raised and schooled. These were the normal aspects of Jesus before he was proclaimed

"RESURRECTED FROM THE DEAD AND ASCENDED INTO HEAVEN."

1. A Middle Kingdom statue: Bronze, height 5 inches. Courtesy of Berlin-Charlottenburg, Staatliche Museen der Stiftung PreuBischer Kulturbesitz, Egyptian Department; and Y. ben-Jochannan and G.E. Simmonds' THE BLACK MAN'S NORTH AND EAST Africa, p. 85; BLACK MAN OF THE NILE AND HIS FAMILY, pp. 375 - 377.

Mary Nursing The "Christ-Child"[1]

The 'PURE AND LILY-WHITE PURITANIC IDEALISM' that crept into Judaism, Christianity and Islam has no ancient tradition at the source of these RELIGIONS in Africa and Asia.
It is strictly the result of a European cultural carryover that even experienced the development of a contraption for SEALING OFF A WOMAN'S VAGINA as a safeguard against her in-
fidelity. It was called a "CHASTITY BELT." This type of low life Paulite anti-sexual perversion never entered the African and Asian High-Cultures until the idea was transfered to these
two continents by European and European-American colonialists, imperialists, and their so-
called "Christian Missionaries" that aided and abetted the infamous slave trade, imperialism,
colonialism and neo-colonialism in the African and Asian homelands to the present day. Paulite anti-sexual perversion was also imposed upon the African and Asian peoples within and outside of their continents. Such conduct was especially reprehensible. Yet FERTILITY RIGHTS

1.See Dr. Albert Churchward's SIGNS AND SYMBOLS OF PRIMORDIAL MAN, p. 126. Dr.
Churchward called this Christian "Virgin and Child" figure the "EARTH MOTHER." It was
the most common name for all of the "FERTILITY [Mother] SYMBOLS" of the ancient world.
It was painted by Michaelangelo on the Cisteen Chapel's ceiling for Pope Julius IInd in ca. 1512.

It is a Symbol of Superhuman type of Motherhood depicted
in primitive art by the Aborigines, who had no other way to
express their ideas, and a stone or tree was a symbol of the mother
—the primitive birthplace.

have been related to the <u>Magical Religious Culture</u> and its <u>Physical Glorification Of Creation Rites</u> among the African and Asian Peoples. In maintaining said SPIRITUALITY, along with the necessary "RITUALS" attached to its theosophical teachings and practices, the Africans and Asians included this <u>extra Magical Religious source of origin</u> to compliment the incantations developed for the worship of the FEMALE REPRODUCTIVE TRACT in the highest of esteem; its virtue being symbolized as the "GODDESS OF FERTILITY" in everyone of HER religious experiences. Thus FERTILITY became the...

"GODLINESS OF MAN, AND THE SACREDNESS OF WOMAN'S FUNCTION."
And behold her stature as "GODDESS" besides her GOD. But GOD'S MOTHER of yesteryear became the demoted "GODMOTHER" of the Judaeo-Christian-Islamic theologians of today.

??? WHY ???

One should note that the BLACK BIBLE <u>can not,</u> therefore, <u>see any of the offsprings of said</u> "HOME OF CREATION" [woman's reproductive organs], "HEAVEN" no less, ... <u>producing anything other than</u> "PURITY." For "PURITY" <u>is the byproduct of</u> FERTILITY..., <u>which is in fact</u> GOD IN CREATION. Thus, in said esotorical value there can be no such <u>holier-than-thou</u> labels like...

"BASTARDS, OUT OF WEDLOCK LOVE CHILD, MONGRELS, MISFITS,"...
and other such <u>unwanteds</u> we are conditioned to despise in our Judaeo-Christian-Islamic <u>perverted anti-sexual intercourse</u> puritanical ethics. Then BLACK LIFE will be truly GODLY. And "GOD" shall have truly ...

"CREATED EVERYONE EQUALLY."
Here is one point where the <u>Black Bible</u> must correct this horrible type of abuse against all BLACK WOMEN and not follow the celebate anti-SEXUAL INTERCOURSE directives of [St.] Paul,[1] who was later outdone by [St.] Augustine;[2] both of whom are most responsible for much of Christendom's anti-SEXUAL stand on Jesus Christ of Nazareth. Of course there can be no doubt that they too were equally corrupted in their own vicious attacks upon WOMEN generally, and on SEXUAL INTERCOURSE specifically, all of which they copied from the teachings of the Hebrew writers who charged Moses with passing down the story about the condemnation of the 'FIRST SEXUAL INTERCOURSE' between humans..."ADAM AND EVE IN THE GARDEN OF EDEN." This was recognized by the ancient Hebrew rabbis as they dealt with their own

---

1. See Paul's EPISTLE TO THE ROMANS, Chapter i : 1 - 27; vii : 1 - 7
2. See Augustine's CONFESSION, Book X , Chapter XXX; THE CITY OF GOD, Book XIII, Chapter 1 - 6 ; and ON CHRISTIAN DOCTRINE, Book I, Chapter 17, 24 and 27.

<u>mental masturbation</u> and <u>sexual perversion</u> in addition to the <u>distortion</u> about...

EVE'S SUBMISSION TO ADAM IN THE GARDEN OF EDEN ...,ETC. -
all of which is stated in GENESIS, Chapter iii, Verses 16 - 17 and Chapter iv. Verses 1 - 2,
according to the following extract:

AND Ad'-am knew Eve his wife; and | 2 And she again bare his brother A'-bĕl.
she conceived, and bare Cain, and | And A'-bĕl was a keeper of sheep, but
said, I have gotten a man from the LORD. | Cain was a tiller of the ground.

[LOVE: HEART or MIND]   The <u>Black Bible</u> will have to clarify a grave semantical error that
is commonly the cause of many dissolutions of peaceful cohabitation and marriage, next only
to money and a few other material things...; that is:

'LOVING WITH ONE'S HEART.'
This greatest of all of the moderate myths in the <u>various bibles</u> was developed out of the
Greeks distortion of the indigenous Africans of the Nile Valley symbolism of the...

"WEIGHING OF ANI'S HEART AGAINST THE FEATHER OF TRUTH"

[Ani before Osiris]   [Gods in the Chamber of the Gods]

[Ani led by Anubis to   [Anubis weighing Ani's "Heart"   [Osiris leads Ani
 his "Heart" weighed]   in the "Scale Of Justice Truth"]   to "Judgment Hall]

etc.[1] found in the BOOK OF THE DEAD and PAPYRUS OF ANI, Chapter XXXB, etc., etc., etc.

---

1. The hieroglyphic inscription tells of the deceased scribe named Ani getting his "Heart"
weighed preparatory to entering the "NETHER WORLD" [Heaven]. See English traslation by
Sir Ernest A. Wallis Budge's BOOK OF THE DEAD and PAPYRUS OF ANI, Chapter XXXB;
also y. ben-Jochannan's BLACK MAN OF THE NILE AND HIS FAMILY, p. 122.

This distortion of African religiosity has caused people to actually believe that their think -
ing process is centered in their 'HEART VALVE'rather than within the confines of their BRAIN.
It is an obsession that is particularly dominant among the "Fire and damnation heavenly bound
Save Soul sisters and brothers;" all of whom believe that:

"CHRIST SPEAK'S TO US [them] THROUGH OUR HEART."
But the sole purpose of the "HEART" is biological; to pump blood throughout the network of
blood vessels and nerve centers of the body; and absolutely nothing else. This fact equally
seems not to matter with the Black Clergy. But the gravest aspect of this tradegy lies in their
most obnoxious disregard for the obvious human functions. And this type of stupidity is at its
zenith when one who is scientifically knowledgeable equally adopts the same emotionally ir-
rational stand of "THINKING" and/or "LOVING" with one's "HEART." The classic example
of this is shown in the following from one of the "Commandments" in EXODUS, Chapter xx,
Verses 1 - 17:

"THOU SHALL LOVE THE LORD THY GOD WITH ALL THINE HEART, "
etc. Each student should by now be more than familiar with the source and continuation of the
above quotation; but a refresher look at page 21 should assist at this juncture. The "HEART"
story was originally for the "HEREAFTER JUDGMENT SCENE." This will give you a very
good understanding of the plagiarism that took place in the distortions of the indigenous Africans' Mysteries System teachings the Hebrews used to produce their so-called FIVE BOOKS
OF MOSES, which were further plagiarized and distorted by both the Christians and the Moslems to produce their New Testament and Holy Qur'an.

It is impossible for an intelligent person to accept that the maintenance and perpetuation
of "IGNORANCE" is necessary for one to "...BE IN HARMONY WITH GOD." Neither can
anyone comprehend the need to continue such a myth because it may have been condoned by
our grand ancestors for thousands of years. Nor can anyone fail to notice the damage it has
already done, and is still doing, along with the other equally distorted RELIGIOUS teachings
it produces, and not struggle to get rid of it. For "IGNORANCE" of any kind whatsoever should
only exist in the absense of "KNOWLEDGE." Such teaching in RELIGION is no exception to this
rule. For there is no place in the teachings of any African God or Goddess where said ultimate
manifestation of CREATION was ever proposed, condoned or sponsored in "IGNORANCE" of
any kind. Such has never existed, not even through careless and wanton errors that became
knowledgeable to those who were, or are, in control of African RELIGIOUS institutions. And
surely RELIGIOUS BIGOTRY, caused by the direct result of "IGNORANCE;' has no place whatsoever in the BLACK BIBLE.

22

One must place Professor James H. Cone's attempt at BLACKENING Jesus Christ of Nazareth through his alleged ENSLAVEMENT mysticism in the following extract from his BLACK THEOLOGY and BLACK POWER[1] in a similar category as the "ignorance" displayed with respect to "Loving With One's Heart." For example, Professor Cone wrote that:

> Jesus' work is essentially one of liberation. Becoming a slave himself, he opens realities of human existence formerly closed to man. Through an encounter with Jesus, man now knows the full meaning of God's action in history and man's place within it.
>
> The Gospel of Mark describes the nature of Jesus' ministry in this manner: "The time is fulfilled, the Kingdom of God is at hand; repent and believe the Gospel" (1:14-15). On the face of it, this message appears not to be too radical to our twentieth-century ears, but this impression stems from our failure existentially to bridge the gap between modern man and biblical man. Indeed, the message of the Kingdom strikes at the very center of man's desire to define his own existence in the light of his own interest at the price of his brother's enslavement. It means the irruption of a new age, an age which has to do with God's action in history on behalf of man's salvation. It is an age of liberation, in which "the blind receive their sight, the lame walk, the lepers are cleansed, the deaf hear, the dead are raised up, the poor have the good news preached to them" (Luke 7:22). This is not pious talk, and one does not need a seminary degree to interpret the message. It is a message about the ghetto, and all other injustices done in the name of democracy and religion to further the social, political, and economic interests of the oppressor. In Christ, God enters human affairs and takes sides with the oppressed. Their suffering becomes his; their despair, divine despair. Through Christ the poor man is offered freedom now to rebel against that which makes him other than human.
>
> It is ironical that America with its history of injustice to the poor (especially the black man and the Indian) prides itself as being a Christian nation. (Is there really such an animal?) It is even more ironic that officials within the body of the Church have passively and actively participated in these injustices. With Jesus, however, the poor were at the heart of his mission: "The last shall be first and the first last" (Matt. 20:16).

What else is there in Professor Cone's language that does not fall within the same light as the usage of the "HEART" in biblical parlance? Quite a lot. He did not find it equally impossible to BLACKEN Tillich,[1] Reinhold Niebuhr,[2] Karl Barth,[3] Friedrich Nietzche,[4] and count-

. See James H. Cone's BLACK THEOLOGY and BLACK POWER, pp. 7, 54, 84 - 85
. Ibid., p. 13
. Ibid., pp. 31, 34, 37 - 38, 45 - 46, 49, 60, 70, 70 - 71n, 84n, 87 - 88, 148 - 149.
. Ibid., pp. 101, 127 - 129

less other WHITE theologians' theories and theses he adopted, all of whom taught of a God that allowed BLACK VICTIMS like Professor Cone himself to suffer under European and European-American Judaeo-Christian RELIGIOUS torture. For they too were the sponsors that manufacture other theologians who continue perpetuating the same type of RACIST SLAVE SYSTEM inserted into the various European and European-American VERSIONS of the Jewish Old Testament and Christian New Testament. Professor Cone, like so many of the other "Negro" [not Black] professors in the field of European-American style Judaeo-Christian The-ology, presented a total "COP-OUT" when he alluded to Jesus as a BLACK MAN because of his common suffering like Black People. For if Jesus was in fact BLACK; it was because...

THE PIGMENT OF HIS SKIN WAS BLACK LIKE ANY BLACK MAN OR WOMAN
OF THE HARLEMS AND TIMBUCTOOS OF THE ENTIRE WORLD TODAY.

Not because of any historical evidence, whatsoever, showing that Jesus - the Christ - was

"...A SLAVE HIMSELF...."

[GOD'S COLOR?] Professor Cone's 'Black God,' which he must have vizualized when he first decided to write about a "BLACK THEOLOGY"... etc.,failed miserably to be valid in terms of the NEED FOR A BLACK BIBLE to be placed among the African People of the world. For he too vasillated over the ETHNIC, RACIAL, COLOR and NATIONAL ORIGIN of his God - Jesus Christ of Nazareth, which is the opposite of his teachers PURE WHITE BLONDE Jesus Christ, holy family [Joseph and Mary] and heaven shown in all of the picture-bibles printed in the United States of America, Great Britain and Europe. The BLACK BIBLE cannot vasillate on either of these points. However, the precedence of a "BLACK [God] MESSIAH" like those of the Africans of Egypt and other High-Cultures of the Nile River [blue and white] Valley and Great Lakes regions of Alkebu-lan [Africa] was established before the following from [St.] MATTHEW, Chapter ii, Verses 13 - 15:

> 13 Now when they had departed, behold, an angel of the Lord appeared to Joseph in a dream and said, "Rise, take the child and his mother, and flee to Egypt, and remain there till I tell you; for Her'od is about to search for the child, to destroy him." 14And he rose and took the child and his mother by night, and departed to Egypt, 15 and remained there until the death of Her'od. This was to fulfil what the Lord had spoken by the prophet, "Out of Egypt have I called my son."

The first...

"PRINCE OF PEACE, MESSIAH, SAVIOUR, REDEEMER, OSAGYEFO," ETC...
on record was an African pharaoh of Ta-Merry [Egypt],of whom thousands upon thousands of volumes have been written. This African was no other than Pharaoh Amenhotep IV, other-wise known as "AKHENATEN." He was not Professor Cone's Jesus Christ, irrespective of how many European and/or European-American WHITE theologians and authorities he quoted

24

for his authority on <u>Jesus Christ's</u> COLOR because of his alleged <u>enslavement</u>. This BLACK MESSIAH or "CHRIST" [anointed one] reigned over all of the Upper and Lower Nile Valley High-Culture, from the Kimit [Mediterranean] Sea up to the Sixth Cataract, during ca. 1370 - 1352 B.C.E. For a comparative analysis of his facial characteristics and those of another BLACK PHARAOH - his predecessor <u>Pharaoh Djoser</u>[1] of the IIIrd Dynasty, ca. 2780 - 2680 B.C.E. - the following pictures of their statues are shown; others appear on page 27.

Nefer-xeperu-Rā- ·on of the Amen-hotep netei hetj
uā-en-Rā,.   Sun,   L'ast (Amenophis IV.).   Aū-en-Āten.

Left: Pharaoh Akhenaton or Amen-hotep IV, the "FIRST CHRIST"[2] whom many have also called "THE FATHER OF THE TRINITARIAN CONCEPT." Note the so-called "NEGROID CHARACTERISTICS" of this African that were, and still are common in most Africans today.

Right: Pharaoh Djoser's ("Cheops") statue; a tribute to the so-called "NEGROID CHARACTERISTICS" of the Nile Valley Africans. The pharaoh, who commissioned the renowned African architect, Imhotep, to design and build the "WORLD'S FIRST BUILDING OF STONE" - the Step Pyramid at Sakhara (Saqqara).

Ser.

Akhenaten was called "THE PRINCE OF PEACE" more than <u>one thousand three hundred and fifty-two</u> [1,352] <u>years</u> before the "<u>birth of Jesus Christ</u>[3] of Nazareth" - the Christians' GOD - in approximately 30 to 4 B.C.E. [or B.C.] - depending upon whose chronological chart or calendar one uses; for even <u>Christians</u> cannot agree on the date of Jesus' "<u>birth</u>" or "<u>death</u>."

1. See BLACK MAN OF THE NILE AND HIS FAMILY, Chapter I: Who Were/Are The Africans?, pp. 1 - 14 for further details and criticisms about Pharaoh Akhenaten [Amenhotep IV].
2. Jesus Christ [or Krystos] is the Greek translation of the Hebrew "JOSHUA THE ANOINTED." The Greeks were the first to record his story while they were with the Africans in Ta-Merry [which biblical history records as "Egypt"].

We have to remember that Matthew's declaration, which we read on page 24, was not supported by the Hebrew Prophet Isaiah that preceded him [in the Old Testament]by a few hundred years. This we can observe in the following extract from ISAIAH, Chapter lxvi, Verses 15 - 16:

> 5 "For behold, the LORD will come in fire, and his chariots like the storm-wind, to render his anger in fury, and his rebuke with flames of fire. 6 For by fire will the LORD execute judgment, and by his sword, upon all flesh; and those slain by the LORD shall be many.

One can clearly see that the type of entrance for "THE LORD TO COME IN FIRE...", according to Isaiah, was not the same manner in which Jesus Christ entered this world. However, irrespective of MATTHEW, Chapter ii, Verses 13 - 15, which showed Jesus Christ was typically the same as his African cousins he met in Egypt, where he had been taken for protection against King Herod; it should be equally noted that Osiris and Akhenaten superceded him as the first BLACK MESSIAH . Matthew allegedly wrote the following:

> 13 Now when they had departed, behold, an angel of the Lord appeared to Joseph in a dream and said, "Rise, take the child and his mother, and flee to Egypt, and remain there till I tell you; for Her'ôd is about to search for the child. to destroy him." 14And he rose and took the child and his mother by night, and departed to Egypt, 15 and remained there until the death of Her'ôd. This was to fulfil what the Lord had spoken by the prophet, "Out of Egypt have I called my son."

Flanders Petrie [the first of the European and European-American archaeologists, and one of the first to have illegally removed the Africans' artifacts from many pyramids and other sacred places of Egypt, Nubia and Meröe he looted] had in his collection of stolen treasures a sketch drawn by one or more ancient Africans of Egypt or Nubia depicting a head of a typical member of "Royal Egyptian" origin - typical to any of the other Africans who ruled over Egypt up to the XIVth Dynasty [ca. 1675 B.C.E.], and once again from the XXIVth to the XXVIth Dynasty [ca. 718 - 527 B.C.E.], which is shown on the following page   along with a picture of the "God Of Medicine" - Imhotep and another Pharaoh - Amonemhat III rd.

The pictures on the following page should assist each student and general reader to understand that Egypt, at least until the XVth Dynasty - ca. 1675 B.C.E. , was an "ALL BLACK NATION" of indigenous African [BLACK] People.

Of course Professor James H. Cone might not have known anything about the facts so far stated. And he must have forgotten that until Michaelangelo painted his own version of the so-called "HOLY FAMILY" - Joseph, Mary and Jesus Christ [all of which originated with Africa's "BLACK MADONNA AND CHILD"...otherwise called "ISIS AND HORUS"] for Pope Julius IInd during the XVIth Century C.E., the standard image of all three was in fact "BLACK" like

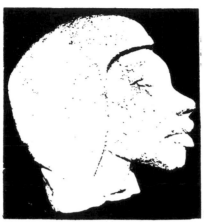

Maat-en-Rā, son of the Sun,

Amen-em-ḥāt (III.)

Bronze Statue of IMH(..
(Paris Museum Col.)

..t... of the Head of A Royal Egyptian
(T.W. Petrie Coll.)

Pharaoh AMONEMHAT III
XIIth Dynasty
(Cairo Museum)

their Egyptian model. ; not WHITE, as he converted them to suit European WHITE RACISM...
as shown on page 19 of this volume. Professor Cone should have had no problem whatsoever
over Mary, who was originally called the "BLACK MADONNA" by the earliest Christians of
North and East Africa; this is providing he had done his home work on the history of the Christian Religion and its origin in Africa, and not so much on PURE WHITE THEOLOGY, WHITE
THEOLOGIANS and their WHITE BIBLES...The King James Authorized Version Of The Old
And New Testament not excluded. This title - "BLACK MADONNA" - was adopted as the
symbol of Mary's ability to produce an off-spring, her son Jesus Christ. For Isis, the forerunner of the "VIRGIN MARY, " was also known as "THE GODDESS OF FERTILITY." Sir
Godfrey Higgins made this point very clear in his major work, ANACALYPSIS, Volume I,
when he wrote the following about Isis and her son HORUS [Hor, Horis, Orus, Osiris, Siris]:

> The Bull was the body into which Osiris transmigrated after his death; and, lastly, the
> Hebrew name for bull is שׁוּר *sur*. Orpheus has a hymn to the Lord Bull. Iswara of India or
> Osiris, is the husband of Isi or of Isis; and Surya is Buddha. Can all these coincidences be the
> effect of accident?
> " Osiris, or Isiris, as Sanchoniathon calls him, is also the same name with Mizraim, when the
> " servile letter M is left out." The reason of the monogram M being prefixed to this, and to
> many other words, will be shewn by and by.
> I have some suspicion that *O-siris* is a Greek corruption; that the name ought, as already men-
> tioned, to be what it is called by Hellanicus, *Ysiris* or *Isiris*, and that it is derived from, or rather

1. For further details see BLACK MAN OF THE NILE AND HIS FAMILY, Chapter I, p. 199.

27

I should say is the same as, *Iswara* of India. Iswara and Isi are the same as Osiris and Isis—the male and female procreative powers of nature.

"Iswara, in Sanscrit, signifies Lord, and in that sense is applied by the Bramans to each of "their three principal deities, or rather to each of the forms in which they teach the people to "adore Brahm, or the GREAT ONE . . . . Brahma, Vishnu, and Mahadeva, say the *Puranics*, "were brothers: and the Egyptian triad, or Osiris, Horus, and Typhon, were brought forth by "the same parent."

Syria was called Suria. Eusebius says the Egyptians called Osiris, Surius, and that, in Persia, *Surē* was the old name of the sun.

In the sol-lunar legends of the Hindoos, the Sun is, as we have seen, sometimes male and sometimes female. The Moon is also of both sexes, and is called *Isa* and *Isi*. Deus Lunus was common to several nations of the ancient world.

The peculiar mode in which the Hindoos identify their three great Gods with the solar orb, is a curious specimen of the physical refinements of ancient mythology. *At night and in the West, the Sun is Vishnu: he is Brama in the East and in the morning:* and from noon to evening, he is Siva.

The adoration of a black stone is a very singular superstition. Like many other superstitions this also came from India. Buddha was adored as a square black stone; so was Mercury; so was the Roman Terminus. The famous Pessinuntian stone, brought to Rome, was square and black. The sacred black stone at Mecca many of my readers are acquainted with, and George the Fourth did very wisely to be crowned on the square stone, nearer black than any other colour, of Scotia and Ireland.

Dr. Shuckford has the following curious passage: "We have several representations in the "draughts of the same learned antiquary *(Montfaucon)*, which are said to be Isis, holding or "giving suck to the boy Orus; but it should be remarked, that Orus was not represented by the "figure of a new-born child: for Plutarch expressly tells us, that a new-born child was the "Egyptian picture of the sun's rising." Plutarch and Montfaucon were both right. Orus was the sun, and the infant child was the picture of the sun, in his infancy or birth, immediately after the winter solstice—when he began to increase. Orus, I repeat, is nothing but the Hebrew word אור *aur*, lux, light — the very light so often spoken of by St. John, in the first chapter of his gospel. Plutarch says, that Osiris means a benevolent and beneficent power, as does likewise his other name OMPHIS. In a former book I have taken much pains to discover the meaning of Omphi. After all, is it any thing but the OM, with the Coptic emphatic article *Pi?*

There is no more reason for calling Isis the moon, than the earth. She was called by all the following names: Minerva, Venus, Juno, Proserpina, Ceres, Diana, Rhea seu Tellus, Pessinuncia, Rhamnusia, Bellona, Hecate, Luna, PolymorphusDæmon. But most of these have been shewn to be in fact all one—the Sun. Isis, therefore, can be nothing but the sun, or the being whose residence was the sun. This being we have seen was both masculine and feminine: I therefore conclude that Isis was no other than the first cause in its feminine character, as Osiris was the first cause in the masculine. The inscriptions cited above, upon the temples of Isis, completely negative the idea of her being the moon. From Pausanias we learn that the most ancient statue of Ceres amongst the Phigalenses was black; and in chap. vi., that at a place called Melangea, in Arcadia, was a Venus who was black, the reason for which, as given by him, evidently shews that it was unknown. At Athens, Minerva Aglaurus, daughter of Cecrops, was *black*, according to Ovid, in his Metamorphoses. Jerom observed, that "Juno has her priestesses devoted to one "husband, Vesta her perpetual virgins, and other idols their priests, also under the vows of "chastity." The Latin *Diana* is the contract of *Diva Jana*. Gale says they styled the moon "Urania, Juno, Jana, Diana, Venus, &c.; and as the sun was called Jupiter, from יה *(ie,) ja,*

28

' πατηρ, and Janus from יה *(ie) Jah, the proper name of God;* so Juno is referred to the moon, " and comes from יה *(ie) Jah,* the proper name of God, as *Jacchus* from יה *(ie) ja*-chus. Amongst " the ancient Romans Jana and Juno were the same." That the moon was the emblem of the passive generative power cannot be denied, but this was merely astrological, not religious. She was not considered the passive power itself, as the sun was himself considered the active power,— but merely as the planets were considered: for though the planet was called Jupiter, as I have before observed, that *planet* was not considered Lord of heaven, the Great Creator.

Higgins and Shuckford were further supported by the original source from whence came the concept of a "BLACK MADONNA" [Goddess Of Fertility], as shown on page 18 and below.

ISIS and the Infant HORUS,
BLACK MADONNA & CHILD
(F.W. Petrie Coll.)

29

One has to note that Isis was always shown BREAST-FEEDING her "VIRGIN SON" -
God...HORUS. The latter was the "VIRGIN SON" whom Jesus Christ succeeded as:

"THE ONE AND ONLY GOD OF THE WORLD."

This is another of the thousands of artifacts illegally removed from Egypt and Nubia by
Flanders Petrie, as noted by the label on the picture on page 29. This picture of the Statue
Of The Black Madonna and Child is for the student's further evaluation of the characteristics
common to the Africans of Egypt prior to the arrival of the Asians and Europeans as conquer
It was sculptured thousands of years prior to the birth of Pharaoh Akhenaten who reigned
over all of Egypt during the XXVIth Dynasty; reputedly "The First Prince Of Peace" and only
"Anointed One."

The following from Sir Ernest A. Wallis Budge's BOOK OF THE DEAD, pages 178 - 179
should equally help to clarify ISIS originality that preceded the Virgin Mary's "IMMACULAT
CONCEPTION" by at least four to five thousand years...ca. 5867 B.C.E. - ca. 30 or 4 B.C.
[the possible date of Jesus - the Christ's - birth], which we can also see on page 32 of this
volume. Note that Isis was also called "AST" and "SET." According to Budge, Chabas wrote
the following about her from an inscription in the "HYMN OF OSIRIS:"[1]

Àst or Set ⌂, the seventh member of the company
of the gods of Ànu, was the wife of Osiris and the mother
of Horus ; her woes have been described both by Egyptian
and Greek writers.[2] Her commonest names are " the great
" goddess, the divine mother, the mistress of words of power
" or enchantments"; in later times she is called the "mother
of the gods," and the "living one." She is usually depicted
in the form of a woman, with a headdress in the shape of a
seat ⌂, the value of the hieroglyph for which forms her
name. The animal in which she sometimes became
incarnate was the cow, hence she sometimes wears upon
her head the horns of that animal accompanied by plumes
and feathers. In one aspect she is identified with the
goddess Selk or Serq, and she then has upon her head a
scorpion, the emblem of that goddess ; in another aspect
she is united to the star Sothis, and then a star ✶ is added
to her crown. She is, however, most commonly represented
as the mother suckling her child Horus, and figures of her
in this aspect, in bronze and *faïence*, exist in thousands.
As a nature-goddess she is seen standing in the Boat of the
Sun, and she was probably the deity of the dawn.

---

1. For further detail and artifacts related to Osiris and Isis the following should be consulte
[2] Chabas, *Un Hymne a Osiris* (in *Revue Archeologique*, t. XIV, pp. 65 ff.);
Horrack, *Les Lamentations d'Isis et de Nephthys*, Paris, 1866 ; *The Festival
Songs of Isis and Nephthys* (in *Archaeologia*, Vol. LII, London, 1891);
Golénischeff, *Die Metternichstele*, Leipzig, 1877 ; Plutarch, *De Iside et
Osiride*. etc.

Below, and on the following page, the student will see some of the many GODS and GOD-DESSES of the ancient Africans of Egypt and other Nile Valley and Great Lakes High-Cultures, including HORUS [or Osiris] and his VIRGIN MOTHER - <u>Isis</u>:

GODS and GODDESSES of THE BOOK OF THE COMING FORTH BY DAY of Ta-Merry[1]

Amuletic figures of Egyptian gods and goddesses.

HORUS I.—THE DIFFERENT NAMES OR ATTRIBUTES OF HORUS AND AMSU, THE RISEN HORUS OR HORUS IN SPIRIT

Horus—The first Man-God
Horus—I. U. or I. A. U. = Jesus.
Horus—The Light of the World.
Horus—God of Life.
Horus—God of the Four Quarters, N. E. S. W.
Horus—God of the Pole Star.
Horus—God of Light.
Horus—Creator of Himself and Heir of Eternity.
Horus—Child of Isis.
Horus—King of the North and South.
Horus—Guide of the Northern Horizon.
Horus—In Spirit (Amsu).
Horus—Guardian of Sut.
Horus—Lord of Dawn and Evening Twilight.

Horus—The Mighty One of the Teshert Crown.
Horus—In the Resurrection.
Horus—The Child-suckling.
Horus—The Great Spirit.
Horus—The Seven Powers of
Horus—Of the Two Horizons.
Horus—As Hawk or Vulture or Eagle Hawk.
Horus—As Young Ear of Corn.
Horus—As Her-Shef or Khnemu—He who is on his lake.
Horus—The Anointed Son of the Father.
Horus—The Red Calf (Type of Horus the Child).
Horus—In the Tree.
Horus—On the Cross.

Horus—Lord of the Northern and Southern Horizon.
Horus—Fettering Sut (or binding or chaining Satan).
Horus—Prince of the Emerald Stone.
Horus of the Triangle.
Horus—The Great One — The Mighty One.
Horus—The Great Chief of the Hammer or Axe.
Horus—Lord of Tattu.
Horus—The Blind.
Horus—The Tears of.
Horus—The Followers of.
Horus—The Feet of.
Horus—The Divine Healer.
Horus—The Master.
Horus—In the Tank of Flame (Baptiser with Fire).
Horus—The Good Shepherd with the Crook upon His Shoulder.
Horus—With Four Followers on the Mount.
Horus—With the Seven Great Spirits on the Mount.
Horus—As the Fisher.
Horus—As the Lamb.
Horus—As the Lion.
Horus—Of Twelve Years.
Horus—With the Tat (Cross).
Horus—Made a man at 30 years in his Baptism.
Horus—The Healer in the Mountain.
Horus—The Exorciser of Evil Spirits, as the Word.
Horus—Who gives the Waters of Life.
Horus—In the Bush of Thorns (as Unbu).
Horus—The Just and True.
Horus—The Bridegroom with the Bride in Sothis.

Horus—As " I am the Resurrection and the Life."
Horus—Prince of Peace.
Horus—Who descends into Hades.
Horus—Lord of the Two Eyes or Double Vision
Horus—The Manifesting Son of God.
Horus—As Child of the Virgin.
Horus—The Sower of Good Seed (and Sut the Destroyer).
Horus—Carried off by Sut to the Summit of the Mount Hetep.
Horus—Contending with Sut on the Mount.
Horus—One of Five Brethren.
Horus—The Brother of Sut, the betrayer.
Horus—Baptised with water by Anup.
Horus—Who exalted His Father in every Sacred Place.
Horus—The Weeper.
Horus—The Lifted Serpent.
Horus—In the Bosom of Ra (his Father).
Horus—The Avenger.
Horus—He who comes with Peace.
Horus—The Afflicted One.
Horus—The Lord of Resurrection from the House of Death.
Horus—As the type of Eternal Life.
Horus—The Child Teacher in the Temple (as Iu-em-Hetep).
Horus—As Ma-Kheru (the Witness unto Truth).
Horus—As the Lily.
Horus—Who came to fulfil the Law.
Horus—Walking the Water.
Horus—The Raiser of the Dead.
Horus—One with his Father.
Horus—Entering the Mount at Sunset to hold Converse with his Father.
Horus—Transfigured on the Mount.

Horus had two mothers : Isis, the Virgin, who conceived him, and Nephthys, who nursed him.
He was brought forth singly and as one of five brothers.
Jesus had two mothers : Mary the Virgin, who conceived him, and Mary, the wife of Cleophas, who brought him forth as one of her children.
He was brought forth singly and as one of five brethren.
Horus was the Son of Seb, his father on earth.
Jesus was the son of Joseph, the father on earth.
Horus was with his mother, the Virgin, until 12 years old, when he was transformed into the beloved son of God, as the only begotten of the Father in heaven.
Jesus remained with his mother, the Virgin, up to the age of 12 years, when he left her " to be about his Father's business."
From 12 to 30 years of age there is no record in the life of Horus.

From 12 to 30 years of age there is no record in the life of Jesus:
Horus at 30 years of age became adult in his baptism by Anup.
Jesus at 30 years of age was made a man of in his baptism by John the Baptist:
Horus, in his baptism, made his transformation into the beloved son and only begotten of the Father—the holy spirit, represented by a bird.
Jesus, in his baptism, is hailed from heaven as the beloved son and only begotten of the Father, God—the holy spirit that is represented by a dove.

After you have carefully examined these presentations, ask yourself: Is it not because of RACIAL considerations that the BLACK MADONNA from Africa was converted to the WHITE MADONNA in Europe? Or: Is it instead coincidental? This instructor, or teacher, which ever

1. See Dr. Albert Churchward's SIGNS AND SYMBOLS OF PRIMORDIAL MAN, pp. 421, 422 and 423. One should not forget to examine the Judaeo-Christian-Islamic "HOLY WORKS" for another look at the origin of the above as stated by Judaism, Christianity and Islam. For we have seen that "AMEN" is still carried in them without the proper designation as one of the GODS of Judaism, Christianity and/or Islam. Yet each of these three offsprings from the Mysteries System maintained that "AMEN", the first name of "RA," means "SO BE IT."

you prefer, cannot deny that it is the former, bearing in mind that only one picture in any of the colored graphical presentations in all of the European and European-American OLD and NEW TESTAMENT show a Black person...the so-called "WISE MAN FROM ETHIOPIA;" one of the "THREE" that allegedly visited little Jesus Christ immediately after his birth. Of course this totally ignored the fact that Jesus Christ's mother - MARY - sent him over to Africa to hide amongst his African [or "Negro"] relatives according to MATTHEW, Chapter ii, Verses 1 - 15. This extract is already shown [Verses 13 - 15]on page 26;and it should be reviewed at this time.

Returning back to the color of the GODS Abraham, Moses, Jesus Christ and/or Mohamet ibn Abdullah, along with hundreds more, worshiped, Sir Godfrey said the following about them:

In Montfaucon, a black Isis and Orus are described in the printing, but not in the plate. I suspect many of Montfaucon's figures ought to be black, which are not so described.

Pausanias states the Thespians to have had a temple and statue to Jupiter the Saviour, and a statue to Love, consisting only of a rude stone ; and a temple to Venus Melainis, or *the black*.

Ammon was founded by Black doves, Ατρε-Ιωνες. One of them flew from Ammon to Dodona and founded it.

At Corinth there was a black Venus.

In my search into the origin of ancient Druids, I continually found, at last, that my labours terminated with something *black*. Thus the oracles at Dodona, and of Apollo at Delphi, were founded by BLACK doves. Doves are not often, I believe never really, black.

Osiris and his Bull were black ; all the Gods and Goddesses of Greece were black : at least this was the case with Jupiter, Bacchus, Hercules, Apollo, Ammon.

The Goddesses Venus, Isis, Hecati, Diana, Juno, Metis, Ceres, Cybile, are black. The Multimammia is black in the Campidoglio at Rome, and in Montfaucon, Antiquity explained.

The Linghams in India, anointed with oil, are black: a black stone was adored in numbers of places in India.

It has already been observed that, in the galleries, we constantly see busts and statues of the Roman Emperors, made of two kinds of stone ; the human part of the statue of *black* stone, the drapery *white* or *coloured*. When they are thus described, I suppose they are meant to be represented as priests of the sun ; this was probably confined to the celebration of the Isiac or Egyptian ceremonies.

9. On the colour of the Gods of the ancients, and of the identity of them all with the God Sol, and with the Cristna of India, nothing more need be said. The reader has already seen the striking marks of similarity in the history of Cristna and the stories related of Jesus in the Romish and heretical books. He probably will not think that their effect is destroyed, as Mr. Maurice flatters himself, by the word Cristna in the Indian language signifying black, and the God being of that colour, when he is informed, of what Mr. Maurice was probably ignorant, that in all the Romish countries of Europe, in France, Italy, Germany, &c., the God Christ, as well as his mother, are described in their old pictures and statues to be black. The infant God in the arms of his black mother, his eyes and drapery white, is himself perfectly black. If the reader doubt my word, he may go to the cathedral at Moulins—to the famous chapel of the Virgin at Loretto—to the church of the Annunciata—the church of St. Lazaro, or the church of St. Stephen at Genoa—to St. Francisco at Pisa—to the church at Brixen, in the Tyrol, and to that at Padua—to the church of St. Theo-

33

dore, at Munich, in the two last of which the whiteness of the eyes and teeth, and the studied redness of the lips, are very observable ;—to a church and to the cathedral at Augsburg, where are a black virgin and child as large as life:—to Rome, to the Borghese chapel Maria Maggiore—to the Pantheon—to a small chapel of St. Peter's, on the right-hand side on entering, near the door ; and, in fact, to almost innumerable other churches, in countries professing the Romish religion.

There is scarcely an old church in Italy where some remains of the worship of the BLACK VIRGIN and BLACK CHILD are not to be met with. Very often the black figures have given way to white ones, and in these cases the black ones, as being held sacred, were put into retired places in the churches, but were not destroyed, but are yet to be found there. In many cases the images are painted all over and look like bronze, often with coloured aprons or napkins round the loins or other parts ; but pictures in great numbers are to be seen, where the white of the eyes and of the teeth, and the lips a little tinged with red, like the black figures in the Museum of the India Company, shew that there is no imitation of bronze. In many instances these images and pictures are shaded, not all one colour, of very dark brown, so dark as to look like black. They are generally esteemed by the rabble with the most profound veneration. The toes are often white, the brown or black paint being kissed away by the devotees, and the white wood left. No doubt in many places, when the priests have new-painted the images, they have coloured the eyes, teeth, &c., in order that they might not shock the feelings of devotees by a too sudden change from black to white, and in order, at the same time, that they might furnish a decent pretence for their blackness, viz. that they are an imitation of bronze : but the number that are left with white teeth, &c., let out the secret.

Isis and Horus, along with all of the hundreds of other BLACK GODS and GODDESSES along the Nile Valley and Great Lakes regions of Central Alkebu-lan, were the first DIVINI-TIES the Hebrew Patriarch - ABRAHAM - called upon as he moved himself into the MAGICAL RELIGION his Chaldean parents learnt from the Ethiopians that conquered his homeland - Chaldea - before and following his birth; all of which is further detailed on the following pages of this volume. It was the beginning of the advance MAGICAL RELIGIOUS training he too received when he went to Alkebu-lan to seek food, clothing, shelter and education; very similar to all that Moses and others later equally received in Ta-Merry and Ta-Nehisi. Thus we read the following extract from Volume I, pages 62 and 63, of Sir Godfrey Higgins' ANACALYPSIS - an analysis of some of the many GOD-HEADS Abraham worshiped and called upon for assistence before, and after, he went to Alkebu-lan [Africa]. These GODS included a few of the so-called SIXTEEN CRUCIFIED SAVIOURS before Jesus - the Christ; all of them BLACK and from Alkebu-lan, or BROWN from Asia; not a single WHITE one, even the two [2] from Europe; He wrote:

4. The fact that Abraham worshiped several Gods, who were, in reality, the same as those of the Persians, namely, the creator, preserver, and the destroyer, has been long asserted, and the assertion has been very unpalatable both to Jews and many Christians ; and to obviate or disguise what they could not account for, they have had recourse, in numerous instances, to the mistranslation of the original, as will presently be shewn.

The following texts will clearly prove this assertion. The Rev. Dr. Shuckford pointed out the fact long ago ; so that this is nothing new.

In the second book of Genesis the creation is described not to have been made by Aleim, or the Aleim, but by a God of a double name—יהוה אלהים *Ieue Aleim ;* which the priests have translated LORD God. By using the word LORD, their object evidently is to conceal from their readers several difficulties which arise afterward respecting the names of God and this word, and which shew clearly that the books of the Pentateuch are the writings of different persons.

Dr. Shuckford has observed, that in Genesis xii. 7, 8, Abraham did not call upon the name of the LORD as we improperly translate it ; but invoked God in the name of the Lord (i. e. Ieue) whom he worshiped, and who appeared to him ; and that this was the same God to whom Jacob prayed when he vowed that the Lord should be his God. Again, in Gen. xxviii. 21, 22, והיה יהוה לי לאלהים erit Dominus mihi in Deum ; and he called the place בית אלהים *(Bit aleim),* Domus Dei. Again, Shuckford says, that in Gen. xxvi. 25, Isaac invoked God as Abraham did in the name of this Lord, יהוה Ieue or Jehovah. On this he observes, " It is very evident that Abraham " and his descendants worshiped not only the true and living God, but they invoked him in the " name of the Lord, and they worshiped the Lord in whose name they invoked, so that two per- " sons were the object of their worship, God and this Lord : and the Scripture has distinguished " these two persons from one another by this circumstance, that *God no man hath seen at any* " *time nor can see,* but the Lord whom Abraham and his descendants worshiped was the person " who appeared to them."

In the above I need not remind my reader that he must insert the name of *Ieue* or *Jehovah* for the name of Lord.

Chapter xxi. verse 33, is wrong translated : when properly rendered it represents Abraham to have invoked *(in the name of Jehovah)* the everlasting God. That is, to have invoked the ever-lasting God, or to have prayed to him in the name of Jehovah—precisely as the Christians do at this day, who invoke God in the name of Jesus—who invoke the first person of the Trinity in the name of the second.

The words of this text are, ויקרא-שם בשם יהוה אל עולם et *invocavit ibi in nomine* IEUE *Deum æternum.*

The foregoing observations of Dr. Shuckford's are confirmed by the following texts :

Gen. xxxi. 42, " Except the God of my father, the God of Abraham, and the fear of Isaac," &c.

Gen. xxxi. 53, " The Gods of Abraham, and the Gods of Nahor, the Gods of their father, judge betwixt us, אלהי אביהם. Dii patris eorum, that is, the Gods of Terah, the great-grandfather of both Jacob and Laban. It appears that they went back to the time when there could be no dispute about their Gods. They sought for Gods that should be received by them both, and these were the Gods of Terah. Laban was an idolater, (or at least of a different sect or religion—Rachel stole his Gods,) Jacob was not ; and in consequence of the difference in their religion, there was a difficulty in finding an oath that should be binding on both.

In Gen. xxxv. 1, it is said, *And (*אלהים *Aleim) God said unto Jacob, Arise, go up to Bethel, and dwell there ; and make there an altar unto God (*לאל *LAL) that appeared unto thee, when thou fleddest from the face of Esau thy brother.* If two Gods at least, or a plurality in the Godhead, had not been acknowledged by the author of Genesis, the words would have been, *and make there an altar unto me, that,* &c. ; or, *unto me, because I appeared,* &c.

Genesis xlix. 25, מאל אביך ויעזרך ואת שדי ויברכך, a Deo tui patris et adjuvabit te ; et omnipo-tente benedicet tibi. By the God (Al) of thy father *also* he will help thee, and the Saddai (Sdi) *also* shall bless thee with blessings, &c.

It is worthy of observation, that there is a marked distinction between the *Al* of his father who will help him, and the *Suddi* who will bless him. Here are two evidently clear and distinct Gods, and neither of them the destroyer or the evil principle.

*Even by the God (*אל *Al) of thy father, who shall help thee : and by the Almighty,* שדי *omnipo-*

tente, who shall bless thee with blessings of heaven above, blessings of the deep that lieth under, blessings of the breasts and of the womb. The *Sdi* or *Saddi* are here very remarkable ; they seem to have been peculiarly Gods of the blessings of this world.

Deut. vi. 4, יהוה אלהינו יהוה אחד. This, Mr. Hales has correctly observed, ought to be rendered Jehovah our Gods is one Jehovah.

The doctrine of a plurality, shewn above in the Pentateuch, is confirmed in the later books of the **Jews.**

Isaiah xlviii. 16, ועתה אדני יהוה שלחני ורוחו. Et nunc Adonai Ieue misit me et spiritus ejus : And now the Lord (Adonai) Jehovah, hath sent me and his spirit.

Not only did the <u>Black People of Africa</u> presented the world with their multiplicity of GODS; they included the science of MAGICAL-RELIGION. And they also presented the SYM-BOLISMS connected to all of the so-called "MODERN RELIGIONS" - Abraham's <u>Judaism</u>, Jesus Christ's <u>Christianity</u> and Mohamet's <u>Islam</u>. Dr. Albert Churchward, on page 23 of his outstanding book - SIGNS AND SYMBOLS OF PRIMORDIAL MAN, showed the following depiction and comments about one of the thousands of the Africans' MAGICAL-RELIGIOUS symbols:

"THE TUAT AND THE TWELVE HOURS OF THE NIGHT."

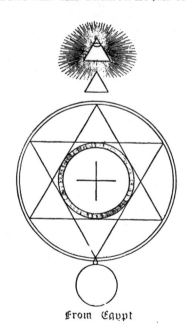

From Egypt

Dr. Churchward was certain that:

' This the Egyptians depicted most graphically, and the records are still

36

extant in the book of "THAT WHICH IS THE UNDERWORLD,"which they have divided into twelve divisions: "The Tuat and the Twelve Hours of the Night," which is hewn in stone in the Great Pyramid of Gizeh. In the Christian doctrine the twelve gates of heaven were taken from this.[1]

On pages 303 and 304 of ANACALYPSIS, Volume I, Sir Godfrey Higgins wrote the following clarification of the BLACK identity of the entire "VIRGIN MARY and the CHRIST-CHILD" concept, which he carefully related to an African and/or Asian BLACK origin of the GODS and GODDESSES of the Hebrews, Christians and Moslems:

CHAPTER II

Adoration of the Virgin and Child —Carmelites attached to the Virgin—Virgin of the Sphere-- Festival of the Virgin—German and Italian Virgin—Mansions of the Moon— Montfaucon—Multimammia— Isis and the Moon—Celestial Virgin of Dupuis—Kircher—Jesus Ben Panther —Lunar Mansions

1. In the two following chapters I shall repeat, with some important additions, or shall collect into one view, what has been said in a variety of places in the foregoing work, respecting the Queen of Heaven, the Virgin Mary, and her son Iaw; to which I shall also add some observations respecting the famous God Bacchus.

In very ancient as well as modern times, the worship of a female, supposed to be a virgin, with an infant in her arms, has prevailed. This worship has not been confined to one particular place or country, but has spread to nearly every part of the habitable world. In all Romish countries to this day, the Virgin, with the infant Jesus Christ in her arms, is the favourite object of adoration ; and it is, as it has been observed before, a decisive proof that the Christ, the good shepherd, the Saviour of the Romish church of Italy, is the same as the person of the same name in India; that he is, like him, described to be black, to be an Ethiopian. It seems that if a person wanted a fact to complete the proof of the identity of the person of Cristna and the Romish Jesus, he could not have invented any thing more striking than this, when all the other circumstances are considered. But though they were both black, I think they had both the name of Crish, or Christ, or Χρησος, from a word in a very ancient language, (the parent both of the Greek and the Sanscrit,) having the meaning of *Benignus*, of which I shall say more hereafter. We will now try to find out who the celebrated virgin, the mother of this person, was.

The Virgin Mary, in most countries where the Roman faith prevails, is called the Queen of Heaven: this is the very epithet given by the ancients to the mother of Bacchus, who was said to be a virgin. The Rev. Dr. Stukeley writes, " Diodorus says Bacchus was born of Jupiter (mean-
" ing the Supreme) and Ceres, or as others think, Proserpine."—" Both Ceres and Proserpine
" were called Κορη, which is analogous to the Hebrew עלמה virgo, παρθενος, LXX., Isaiah vii. 14:
" Behold a virgin shall conceive. It signifies eminently *the* virgin. Αθηναιοι Διονυσον τ Διος
" και Κορης σεβεσιν. Arrian, Alex. II. The Egyptians called this same person Bacchus, or the
" sun-deity, by the name of *Orus*, which is the same as the Greek word Κορος aspirated. The
" heathen fables as oft confound Bacchus's mother and wife."

" Ovid, Fasti iii., makes Libera, the name of Ariadne, Bacchus's pretended wife, whom Cicero,
" de Nat. Deor., makes to be Proserpina, Bacchus's mother. The story of this woman being
" deserted by a man, and espoused by a God, has somewhat so exceedingly like that passage,
" Matt. i. 19, 20, of the blessed virgin's history, that we should wonder at it, did we not see the
" parallelism infinite between the sacred and the profane history before us.

" — Ariadne was translated into heaven, as is said of the Virgin, and her nuptial garland was
" turned into an heavenly crown : she was made queen of heaven."

Testis sidereæ torta corona Deæ.   Propert..iii. 17.

" — There are many similitudes between the Virgin and the mother of Bacchus in all the old
" fables ; as for instance, Hyginus (Fab. 164) makes Adoneus or Adonis the son of Myrrha.
" Adonis is Bacchus beyond controversy."

Ogygia me Bacchum vocat
Osirin Egyptus putat
Arabica gens Adoneum.   Auson.

" Adonis is the Hebrew אדני (Adni) Adonai, which the Heathens learned from the Arabians—
" one of the sacred names of the Deity.   Mary or Miriam, St. Jerome interprets Myrrha Maris :
" Mariamne is the same appellation of which Ariadne seems a corruption.   Orpheus calls the mo-
" ther[1] of Bacchus, Leucothea, a sea Goddess.
" — Nonnus in Dyonys. calls Sirius star Mœra, Μαιρης.   Hesychius says, Μαιρα κυον το
" αςρον.   Our Sanford hence infers this star to mean Miriam, Moses's sister.   Vossius de Idolat.
" approves of it.   Μαίρα by metathesis is Μαρια."[2]

Thus we see that the Rev. and learned Gentleman, Dr. Stukeley, has clearly made out, that the
story of Mary, the queen of heaven, the mother of אדני (Adni) Adonis, or the Lord, as our book
always renders this word, with her translation to heaven, &c., was an old story long before Jesus
of Nazareth was born.   After this, Stukeley observes, that Ariadne, the queen of heaven, has upon
her head a crown of twelve stars.   This is the case of the queen of heaven in almost every church
on the continent.

2. In the service or liturgy of the Carmelites, which I bought in Dublin at the Carmelite monastery, the Virgin is called Stella Maris ; that is, in fact, the star of the sea—" Leucothea"—
Venus rising from the sea.

All monks were Carmelites till the fifth century.[3]   After that time, from different religious mo-
tives, new orders branched off from the old one, and became attached to new superstitions : but
the Carmelites always remained, and yet remain, attached in a peculiar manner to the Virgin Mary,
the Regina Stellarum.[4]

---

[1] Nurse.   [2] Stukeley, Pal. Sac. No. I. p. 34.   [3] Priestley, Hist. Cor. Vol. II. p. 403.

[4] I am of opinion that a certain class of persons, initiated into the higher mysteries of the ancients, were what are
called Carmelites Therapeutæ and Esseniens, or that they constituted a part of, or were formed out of, these sects, and
were what we now call Freemasons.   They were also called Chaldæi and Mathematici.   I think that the rite of circumcision was originally instituted for the characteristic mark of the fraternity or society.   I doubt its being a religious
community solely.   Abraham brought circumcision from Urr of the Chaldees.   When the Jewish tribe was declared a
priestly tribe it was circumcised, part of the secret rites were thrown open to all, probably the tribe refused any longer
to be excluded from them, and the rite no longer continued the secret symbol.   We read of three hundred and eighteen
servants trained in Abraham's own house.   On these persons, the Apostle, St. Barnabas, the companion of St. Paul, has
the following passage :
" For the Scripture says, that Abraham circumcised three hundred and eighteen men of his house.   But what, there-
" fore, was the mystery that was made known to him ?   Mark the eighteen and next the three hundred.   For the
" numeral letters of ten and eight are I H, and these denote Jesus ; and because the cross was that by which we were
" to find grace, therefore he adds, Three hundred : the note of which is T (the figure of his cross).   Wherefore by two
" letters he signified Jesus, and by the third his cross.   He who has put the engrafted gift of his doctrine within us
" knows that I never taught to any one a more certain truth : but I trust ye are worthy of it."—Epist. Barnabas, Sect.
ix. ed. Wake.
This epistle of St. Barnabas was formerly read in the Romish churches ; but the Protestants do not allow it to be
genuine.   One reason why Jones contends that it is spurious is, because it says that Abraham circumcised 318 men of
his family, which is not now in the text.   But the Hebrew word which Jones renders circumcised חניכיו Anikiu, in one
sense means initiated, and this justifies Barnabas.   In fact, this word hnikiu is our initiate.   (Jones on Canon, Pt. III.
ch. xli. p. 449.)   If what I suspect be true, viz. that circumcision was the mark or test of initiation, Barnabas the Apostle
might not understand the full import of the Greek ; but he cannot be supposed to have been ignorant of the Hebrew ..

From all of the evidence at our command it is obvious that Jesus Christ could not have been any different in "COLOR" and/or "RACE" than the other members of his family in Israel, Egypt, Meröe, Nubia, Ethiopia and Punt. And, as an "ISRAELITE" or "PALESTINIAN" of "The Line Of David"..., he must have been a descendant of the same "CANAANITE" [Black or "Negro"] ORIGIN" from "The Line Of Noah." This is providing the story about...

"NOAH AND THE GREAT DELUGE" [flood]

in the BOOK OF GENESIS [First Book Of Moses] is not fiction. From the geneaology of Jesus Christ according to the Hebrews, Christians and Moslems' HOLY SCRIPTURES, we can use the following from EXODUS, Chapter i, Verses 1 - 7 for mankind generally:

1 These are the names of the sons of Israel who came to Egypt with Jacob, each with his household: 2 Reuben, Simeon, Levi, and Judah, 3 Is'sa-chär, Zeb'û-lûn, and Benjamin, 4 Dan and Naph'ta-li, Gad and Ash'er. 5 All the offspring of Jacob were seventy persons; Joseph was already in Egypt. 6 Then Joseph died, and all his brothers, and all that generation. 7 But the descendants of Israel were fruitful and increased greatly; they multiplied and grew exceedingly strong; so that the land was filled with them.

For Jesus Christ's genealogy, particularly, it is the following from MATTHEW, Chapter i, Verses 1 - 17 we must read:

1 The book of the genealogy of Jesus Christ, the son of David, the son of Abraham.
2 Abraham was the father of Isaac, and Isaac the father of Jacob, and Jacob the father of Judah and his brothers, 3 and Judah the father of Per'ez and Zē'rah by Tä'mar, and Perez the father of Hez'ron, and Hezron the father of Räm, 4 and Räm the father of Am-min'à-dab, and Amminadab the father of Näh'shon, and Nahshon the father of Sal'mon, 5 and Sal'mon the father of Bō'az by Rä'hab, and Boaz the father of O'bed by Ruth, and Obed the father of Jesse, 6 and Jesse the father of David the king.
And David was the father of Solomon by the wife of U-rī'ah, 7 and Solomon the father of Rē-hô-bō'àm, and Rehoboam the father of A-bi'jàh, and Abijah the father of Asa,b 8 and Asab the father of Je-hosh'à-phat, and Jehoshaphat the father of Jō'ràm, and Joram the father of Uz-zi'àh, 9 and Uz-zī'àh the father of Jō'thàm, and Jotham the father of Ā'haz, and Ahaz the father of Hez-ê-ki'àh, 10 and Hez-ê-ki'àh the father of Mà-nas'sèh, and

Manasseh the father of Amos,c and Amosc the father of Jō-si'àh, 11 and Jō-si'àh the father of Jech-ô-ni'àh and his brothers, at the time of the deportation to Babylon.
12 And after the deportation to Babylon: Jech-ô-ni'àh was the father of She-al'ti-el,d and She-alti-eld the father of Ze-rub'bà-bel, 13 and Ze-rub'-bà-bel the father of A-bi'ûd, and Abiud the father of E-li'à-kim, and Eliakim the father of Ā'zôr, 14 and Ā'zôr the father of Zā'dok, and Zadok the father of Ā'chim, and Achim the father of E-li'ûd, 15 and E-li'ûd the father of El-ê-ā'zàr, and Eleazar the father of Mat'thàn, and Matthan the father of Jacob, 16 and Jacob the father of Joseph the husband of Mary, of whom Jesus was born, who is called Christ.
17 So all the generations from Abraham to David were fourteen generations, and from David to the deportation to Babylon fourteen generations, and from the deportation to Babylon to the Christ fourteen generations.

Someone seemed to have overlooked the fact that Jesus Christ's relatives go back to the "Canaanites" [the so-called "Cursed Black" Hebrews],"Noah,"and even to "Adam and Eve."

Herodotus, Eusebius, Josephus and Polybius gave us added information about the genealogy of the people of Africa with whom Jesus Christ lived and studied. Herodotus even extended his comments to cover what is today called "THE MIDDLE EAST" - a geographic area formed by the "U - SHAPE" contour from the western limits of Turkey in Europe, bounded by the limits of the eastern end of the Mediterranean Sea, and ending with the western limits of Egypt, as shown on the map on page 10 of this volume. For it was sometime around ca. 457 - 450 B.C.E. that Herodotus wrote the following in his book on history [the first in Europe], which he called THE HISTORIES, Book II:[1]

"THE COLCHIANS, EGYPTIANS AND ETHIOPIANS HAVE THICK LIPS,
BROAD NOSE, WOOLLY HAIR, AND THEY ARE BURNT OF SKIN,"

etc. Thus, to say that "Jesus Christ was BLACK" solely on the basis that"...he was persecuted and mistreated like Black People today...;" or because "...he became a slave...;" which so many of the "Negro" and/or "Colored" cop-out clergy have been insinuating in their cowardly teachings on a "BLACK CHRIST," is only due to fear of repercussion from racist WHITE-CAUCASIAN-SEMITIC Judaeo-Christian theologians whom they have always quoted as ...

"THE SOLE AUTHORITY ON CHRISTIANITY;"

which, of course, included their being...

"THE SOLE AUTHORITY ON JESUS."

The height of this irony is that there seems not to be a single Black Man or Black Woman considered an "AUTHORITY" on anything within Christendom, Judaism and/or Islam today who is quoted "AUTHORITATIVELY" in any Black Seminary or Black Church of a solitary Black Community throughout the United States of America. This is more than hypocritical inferiority; it is CRIMINAL. And it shows the deep sense of MORAL and RACIAL BANKRUPTCY within the membership of the Black Clergy as a unit. The cause is basically 'academic jingoism' directed against those it confuses and corrupts in making them believe that academic degrees in RELIGION and THEOLOGY are in themselves "TRUTH" and "AUTHORITY;" and with one such academic kosher certificate automatically comes knowledge about the "BEGINNING" and "ENDING" of the world. But if Jesus Christ was in fact "BLACK;" it had to be that the pigment of his SKIN was "BLACK." Equally, to speak of "BLACK SIN" and "WHITE RIGHTEOUSNESS" is only in keeping with the WHITE [Caucasian-Indo-European-Aryan-Semitic] racist mythology that crept into the THEOLOGY of Judaism, Christianity and Islam. For such a mythological concept was necessary when the European and European-American imperialist colonizers, slave traders and owners, along with their Christian Missionaries, found it necessary to validate their own conscience for their acts of slavery and genocide perpetuated against the African People, and those of Asia. Thus it was, and still is, that they have related their theological WHITE RACISM from the following Jewish myth about "NOAH'S CURSE" he allegedly placed upon "HAM'S [Noah's youngest son] DESCENDANTS...THE CANAANITES." The alleged "CURSE" reads, according to GENESIS, Chapter ix, Verses 25 - 27 of the Sixth [6th] Century C.E. BABYLONIAN TALMUD written by racist and bigoted ghettorized European rabbis and

40

Talmudist fanatics:[2]

> Now I cannot beget the fourth son whose children
> I would have ordered to serve you and your bro-
> thers! Therefore it must be Canaan, your first
> born, whom they enslave. And since you have dis-
> abled me...doing ugly things in blackness of
> night, Canaan's children shall be born ugly and
> black! Moreover, because you twisted your head
> around to see my nakedness, your grandchildren's
> hair shall be twisted into kinks, and their eyes
> red; again because your lips jested at my mis-
> fortune, theirs shall swell; and because you ne-
> glected my nakedness, they shall go naked, and
> their male members shall be shamefully elongated!
> Men of this race are called Negroes, their fore-
> father Canaan commanded them to love theft and
> fornication, to be banded together in hatred of
> their masters and never to tell the truth.i

[SLAVERY and GOD] "Slaves Obey Your Master." This is one of the commands the Jewish,
Christian and Moslem's GOD issued in favour of SLAVEMASTERS, according to the so-called
"Holy Scriptures" written by GOD'S HOLY INSPIRED SCRIBES. Obviously Jesus Christ, or
should one say 'PAUL'S STATEMENT ABOUT JESUS CHRIST' on the subject of "SLAVERY, "
failed to empathize with the infamous conditions of the "SLAVES" of his era. But today the
Black Clergy finds itself in the same position Jesus and Paul were on SLAVERY. And they
have equally failed to tell their fellow African People, particularly their Black Parishoners
who keep them in luxurious living, that the CURSED SLAVE syndrome mentality is as racist
today in the so-called "MODERN VERSIONS" of the New Testament as it was in the Old Testament. Another example of this is shown in the following extract from the CONFRATERNITY
VERSION OF THE OLD TESTAMENT OF THE HOLY BIBLE.[1] It deals with the same "Noah's
Curse" on page 40; with God's approval no less. Thus, in this "VERSION" Noah told his youngest son Ham - the father of the "CURSED" child [Noah's grandson] - "CANAAN":[2]

> Cursed be Canaan,
> A servant of servants shall he be unto
> his brethren.
> And he said,
> Blessed be Jehovah, the God of Shem;
> And let Canaan be his servant.
> God enlarge Japhet,
> And let him dwell in the tent of Shem;
> And let Canaan be his servant.

---

1. See English translation in M. Markan's HERODOTUS' HISTORIES; Wilson Armistead's
A TRIBUTE TO THE NEGRO, pp. 121 - 130; Basil Davidson's THE AFRICAN PAST, pp.
46 - 48; and Aubrey Selincourt's HERODOTUS' THE HISTORIES.
2. See Robert Graves and Robert Patai's HEBREW MYTHS, pp. 121 - 122; and Yosef ben-
Jochannan's BLACK MAN OF THE NILE AND HIS FAMILY, pp. 11 - 44; also CULTURAL
GENOCIDE IN THE BLACK AND AFRICAN STUDIES CURRICULUM, pp. 22 - 35.

Is it not strange that the Hebrew God – JEHOVAH – was not equally... The God Of Ham...,
and of Ham's Offsprings [Noah's grandchildren], as he was of Shem's and Japhet's? The alleged
fact that Jesus Christ, or was it Paul, approved the enslavement of the African People - the
so-called "Canaanites" ["CURSED Negroes] is best dramatized in the following extract from
COLOSSIANS, Chapter iii, Verses 18 - 25:

18 Wives, be subject to your hus-bands, as is fitting in the Lord. 19 Hus-bands, love your wives, and do not be harsh with them. 20 Children, obey your parents in everything, for this pleases the Lord. 21 Fathers, do not provoke your children, lest they be-come discouraged. 22 Slaves, obey in everything those who are your earthly masters, not with eyeservice, as men-pleasers, but in singleness of heart, fearing the Lord. 23 Whatever your task, work heartily, as serving the Lord and not men, 24 knowing that from the Lord you will receive the in-heritance as your reward; you are serving the Lord Christ. 25 For the wrongdoer will be paid back for the wrong he has done, and there is no partiality.

The SLAVE PACT between Jesus Christ and the SLAVEMASTERS of his era is further supported by EPHESIANS vi : 5 - 9, PETER ii : 18, and TIMOTHY i : 2 - 9. But, not one of these
so-called "SLAVE PACTS" by the Hebrew and Christian GODS is acceptable for the Black Bibl
This will include "the greatest of the Christian Church Fathers" - an African named Augustine
[later made "Saint] from Numidia, North Alkebu-lan - failure to display any of the same under
standing and compassion for his fellow Africans that were SLAVES of the Roman conquerors
from Europe. For he was to severely obsessed with the problem of having Mary's [Jesus Christ
mother] "PHYSICAL VIRGIN STATE" accepted by the whole world, even though she had other
children, such as James the Lesser - who was"older than Jesus,"and also "Jesus' cousin." WH
Because Augustine, himself, like most of the members of the Black Clergy today, was a SYS-
TEM'S man. Thus he too responded in an obsessive manner against his fellow BLACKS who
were in MENTAL and PHYSICAL SLAVERY. His "Middle Class Status" personality, like that
of the "Negro" [Black?] Clergy today, overcame his "CHRISTIAN MORALITY." All of this we
can observe in the following extract from [St.] Augustine's THE CITY OF GOD:[3]

free, by serving not in crafty fear, but in faith-ful love, until all unrighteousness pass away, and all principality and every human power be brought to nothing, and God be all in all.

CHAP. 16. Of equitable rule

And therefore, although our righteous fa-thers had slaves, and administered their domes-tic affairs so as to distinguish between the con-dition of slaves and the heirship of sons in re-gard to the blessings of this life, yet in regard to the worship of God, in whom we hope for eternal blessings, they took an equally loving oversight of all the members of their household. And this is so much in accordance with the nat-ural order, that the head of the household was called paterfamilias; and this name has been so generally accepted, that even those whose rule

---

1. GENESIS, Chapter ix, Verses 20 - 29. The footnote comments in the CONFRATERNITY
VERSION OF THE OLD TESTAMENT by the Reverend Joseph Grispino, S.M.L. deals directl
against the Sixth Century rabbis racist VERSION of this aspect of GENESIS.
2. Ham was Canaan's father. Noah's alleged "CURSE" was directed against his unborn grandson and all of his descendants following.
3. THE CITY OF GOD, Book XIX, Chapter 15 - 16 [translation by Marcus Dods in: Great Bool
of the Western World, Vol. 18, 1952].

is unrighteous are glad to apply it to themselves. But those who are true fathers of their households desire and endeavour that all the members of their household, equally with their own children, should worship and win God, and should come to that heavenly home in which the duty of ruling men is no longer necessary, because the duty of caring for their everlasting happiness has also ceased; but, until they reach that home, masters ought to feel their position of authority a greater burden than servants their service. And if any member of the family interrupts the domestic peace by disobedience, he is corrected either by word or blow, or some kind of just and legitimate punishment, such as society permits, that he may himself be the better for it, and be readjusted to the family harmony from which he had dislocated himself. Witness that man of God, Daniel, who, when he was in captivity, confessed to God his own sins and the sins of his people, and declares with pious grief that these were the cause of the captivity. The prime cause, then, of slavery is sin, which brings man under the dominion of his fellow—that which does not happen save by the judgment of God, with Whom is no unrighteousness, and Who knows how to award fit punishments to every variety of offence. But our Master in heaven says, "Every one who doeth sin is the servant of sin." And thus there are many wicked masters who have religious men as their slaves, and who are yet themselves in bondage; "for of whom a man is overcome, of the same is he brought in bondage." And beyond question it is a happier thing to be the slave of a man than of a lust; for even this very lust of ruling, to mention no others, lays waste men's hearts with the most ruthless dominion. Moreover, when men are subjected to one another in a peaceful order, the lowly position does as much good to the servant as the proud position does harm to the master. But by nature, as God first created us, no one is the slave either of man or of sin. This servitude is, however, penal, and is appointed by that law which enjoins the preservation of the natural order and forbids its disturbance; for if nothing had been done in violation of that law, there would have been nothing to restrain by penal servitude. And therefore the apostle admonishes slaves to be subject to their masters, and to serve them heartily and with good-will, so that, if they cannot be freed by their masters, they may themselves make their slavery in some sort

Certainly the precedence Augustine used for his "AUTHORITY" in the Vulgate Version appears in the following extract from EXODUS, Chapter xxi, Verses 1 - 7. It purports to be GOD'S instruction to Moses and his fellow Hebrew SLAVEMASTERS with respect to their treatment of their own fellow Hebrew SLAVES, and other non-Hebrew SLAVES. This aspect of Judaism is carefully played down by its omission from all of the SERMONS by the Black Clergy on SLAVERY, equally in the Theological Teachings by "Negro Theologians." It states:

21 "Now these are the ordinances which you shall set before them. 2 When you buy a Hebrew slave, he shall serve six years, and in the seventh he shall go out free, for nothing. 3 If he comes in single, he shall go out single; if he comes in married, then his wife shall go out with him. 4 If his master gives him a wife and she bears him sons or daughters, the wife and her children shall be her master's and he shall go out alone. 5 But if the slave plainly says, 'I love my master, my wife, and my children; I will not go out free,' 6 then his master shall bring him to God, and he shall bring him to the door or the doorpost; and his master shall bore his ear through with an awl; and he shall serve him for life. 7 "When a man sells his daughter as a slave, she shall not go out as the male slaves do.

[PAUL or CHRIST?] Augustine, a disreputable young man that was himself reformed into a valiant and most revered "son of Africa," exhibited the same type of unconscious hatred Paul had for women and sexual intercourse; which is understandable. This is especially true, particularly when one reads about his sordid youth in Carthage, North Africa he detailed in his CONFESSION. He wrote it during ca. 400 - 402 C.E. while serving as Bishop Of Hippo Magnus. But Augustine's ANTI-SEXUAL and ANTI-SOCIAL intolerance was already established in another precedence within the teachings of one of his most favorite "FOLLOWERS OF CHRIST... SAUL OF TARSUS," the man who was one of the PERSECUTORS and PROSECUTORS of his fellow Hebrews for the Roman imperialist conquerors of Palestine [Israel]; who also changed his name to "PAUL," and was later made a "SAINT" by the Roman Catholic Church when it changed Christendom's structure. For it is Paul that most of the members of the Black Christian Clergy always quote; not JESUS CHRIST, whom Paul never saw. It is equally Paul, according to his various "LETTERS" to people and places, that the Black Clergy idolizes...

"IN THE NAME OF JESUS CHRIST."

Thus it is that the Black Christians are reduced to "PAULITES," in reality. Again, it was Paul and Barnabas who taught the following according to ACTS, Chapter xv, Verses 12 - 21:

12 And all the assembly kept silence; and they listened to Bär'na·bàs and Paul as they related what signs and wonders God had done through them among the Gentiles. 13After they finished speaking, James replied "Brethren, listen to me. 14 Sym'ē·ŏr has related how God first visited the Gentiles, to take out of them a people for his name. 15And with this the words of the prophets agree, as it is written, 16 'After this I will return, and I will rebuild the dwelling of David, which has fallen; I will rebuild its ruins, and I will set it up.

17 that the rest of men may seek the Lord, and all the Gentiles who are called by my name, 18 says the Lord, who has made these things known from of old.' 19 Therefore my judgment is that we should not trouble those of the Gentiles who turn to God, 20 but should write to them to abstain from the pollutions of idols and from unchastity and from what is strangled and from blood. 21 For from early generations Moses has had in every city those who preach him, for he is read every sabbath in the synagogues."

Paul also taught the following about his own obsession over the female reproductive organs, which Augustine found necessary to cite in the following manner:

47. An example of the *temperate* style is the celebrated encomium on virginity from Cyprian: "Now our discourse addresses itself to the virgins, who, as they are the objects of higher honour, are also the objects of greater care. These are the flowers on the tree of the Church, the glory and ornament of spiritual grace, the joy of honour and praise, a work unbroken and unblemished, the image of God answering to the holiness of the Lord, the brighter portion of the flock of Christ. The glorious fruitfulness of their mother the Church rejoices in them, and in them flourishes more abundantly; and in proportion as bright virginity adds to her numbers, in the same proportion does the mother's joy increase. And at another place in the end of the epistle, 'As we have borne,' he says, 'the image of the earthly, we shall also bear the image of the heavenly.'[1] Virginity bears this image, integrity bears it, holiness and truth bear it; they

bear it who are mindful of the chastening of the Lord, who observe justice and piety, who are strong in faith, humble in fear, steadfast in the endurance of suffering, meek in the endurance of injury, ready to pity, of one mind and of one heart in brotherly peace. And every one of these things ought ye, holy virgins, to observe, to cherish, and fulfil, who having hearts at leisure for God and for Christ, and having chosen the greater and better part, lead and point the way to the Lord, to whom you have pledged your vows. Ye who are advanced in age, exercise control over the younger. Ye who are younger, wait upon the elders, and encourage your equals; stir up one another by mutual exhortations; provoke one another to glory by emulous examples of virtue; endure bravely, advance in spirituality, finish your course with joy; only be mindful of us when your virginity shall begin to reap its reward of honour."

It was the same Paul who made Jesus Christ's MANHOOD appeared to have been free

---

1. See the VULGATE VERSION OF THE OLD AND NEW TESTAMENT, along with other VERSIONS on pp. 82 - 86 of this volume. A few changed "SLAVES" to "SERVANTS;" but not when the ISRAELITES [Hebrews, Jews, etc.] are shown as the "SLAVES" to non-Hebrews. Today the SLAVES to the Hebrews are shown as "SERVANTS" in every bible since the 20th Century.

of any FEMALE relationship whatsoever;[1] free from SEXUAL desires; free from the NEED FOR LOVE; and even free from any HUMAN EMOTION for his own mother's tender loving care. Paul's "JESUS CHRIST" did not try to laugh; not even to show NORMAL ANGER when he LASHED THE MONEY CHANGERS in the Temple. This man also demanded of Timothy that he...

"LET THE WOMAN LEARN IN SILENCE WITH ALL SUBJECTION."[1]

Yet millions follow Paul's VIRGINITY" syndrome in the BOOK OF THE BIRTH OF MARY, one of the most vital doctrine of Christendom in the so-called LOST BOOKS OF THE BIBLE extracted from the original KOINE BIBLE [NewTestament]; all of which was suppressed on the order of Pope Sylvester upon the advice of his underlings at the Nicene Conference Of Bishops - which met upon an Edict[2] by the Roman Emperor Constantine "the great" during the tenth year [ca. 312-322 C.E.] of his reign. Paul's obsession over SEX even made Mary herself"...BORN OF A VIRGIN BIRTH...," etc., according to the following:

The GOSPEL of the BIRTH OF MARY.[3]

[In the primitive ages there was a Gospel extant bearing this name, attributed to St. Matthew, and received as genuine and authentic by several of the ancient Christian sects. It is to be found in the works of Jerome, a Father of the Church, who flourished in the fourth century, from whence the present translation is made. His contemporaries, Epiphanius, Bishop of Salamis, and Austin, also mention a Gospel under this title. The ancient copies differed from Jerome's, for from one of them the learned Faustus, a native of Britain, who became Bishop of Riez, in Provence, endeavoured to prove that Christ was not the Son of God till after his baptism; and that he was not of the house of David and tribe of Judah, because, according to the Gospel he cited, the Virgin herself was not of this tribe, but of the tribe of Levi; her father being a priest of the name of Joachim. It was likewise from this Gospel that the sect of the Collyridians, established the worship and offering of manchet bread and cracknels, or fine wafers, as sacrifices to Mary, whom they imagined to have been born of a Virgin, as Christ is related in the Canonical Gospel to have been born of her. Epiphanius likewise cites a passage concerning the death of Zacharias, which is not in Jerome's copy, viz. "That it was the occasion of the death of Zacharias in the temple, that when he had seen a vision, he, through surprise, was willing to disclose it, and his mouth was stopped. That which he saw was at the time of his offering incense, and it was a man standing in the form of an ass. When he was gone out, and had a mind to speak thus to the people, Woe unto you, whom do ye worship! he who had appeared to him in the temple took away the use of his speech. Afterwards when he recovered it, and was able to speak, he declared this to the Jews, and they slew him. They add (viz. the Gnostics in this book), that on this very account the high-priest was appointed by their lawgiver (by God to Moses), to carry little bells, that whensoever he went into the temple to sacrifice, he, whom they worshipped, hearing the noise of the bells, might have time enough to hide himself, and not be caught in that ugly shape and figure."—The principal part of this Gospel is contained in the Protevangelion of James, which follows next in order.]

It is obvious that the non-SEXUAL activities of Mary, her mother, and grandmother, according to the above extract, were impossible to sell to anyone. Equally, the absence of any male attached to Mary, her mother and grandmother's lives made their claims of becoming MOTHERS through "VIRGIN CONCEPTION" and "BIRTH" more than ludicrous. Thus one of the

---

1. See 1 TIMOTHY, 2 : 1 - 15 for further details about Paul's charge to Timothy.
2. See THE LOST BOOKS OF THE BIBLE, etc., "Introduction;" A. Finch's HISTORY OF THE ROMAN EMPIRE; and James Hasting's ENCYCLOPEDIA OF RELIGION AND ETHICS [13 vols]. Pope Sylvester reigned from ca. 314 to 336 C.E. [or A.D.].
3. See THE LOST BOOKS OF THE BIBLE AND THE FORGOTTEN BOOKS OF EDEN, p. 17.

reasons for the extraction of the BOOK OF THE BIRTH OF MARY, along with many others, from the original BOOKS OF THE NEW TESTAMENT ["God's Holy Srcipture," no less].

If the NEW TESTAMENT, otherwise known as the KOĨNE BIBLE when it was written in ca. 52 - 100 C.E. with everyone of the original BOOKS therein - including the so-called "Lost Books Of The Bible"- was...

"GOD'S INSPIRED WORDS TO HIS HOLY SCRIBES"...

before the Nicene Conference [Council] Of Bishops in ca. 322 - 325 C.E.; When did the same "GOD" passed down His new "SACRED COMMAND" to remove any of His "SACRED BOOKS" that was purposely suppressed from His "CHOSEN PEOPLE" - the Christians? Or are we to assume that the 219 Bishops assigned to the Nicene Conference, all of whom fought verbally and physically against each others to secure their own VERSION of Jesus Christ's "BIRTH, LIFE, DEATH, RESURRECTION" and "DIVINITY,"[1] were given some kind of a 'SECRET MESSAGE BY GOD," of which no one else was aware? Obviously; there was no such 'MESSAGE.' Yet these same men, human beings like anyone of us today and of the past, decided which "BOOKS OF THE BIBLE ARE THE INSPIRED WORKS OF GOD" and which ones "ARE NOT." They also decided that:

"MARY WAS A PHYSICAL VIRGIN BEFORE, AND AFTER, JESUS' BIRTH" approximately 1974 to 1978 years ago.[2] It was equally they who also decided that:

"JESUS CHRIST IS THE ONLY TRUE GOD OF THE TRINITY - THE FATHER, THE SON, AND THE HOLY GHOST" [today's "Spirit"].

20th Century C.E. Christian Theoiogians of every color have even made the "HOLY GHOST" in the original New Testament a "HOLY SPIRIT." This is to conform with their much more modern semantics. "GHOST," they said:

"SOUNDS TO MUCH LIKE THE HEATHEN'S DEITY OF THE PAST AND PRESENT." These precedences the Black Clergy wholeheartedly endorsed without question to please their WHITE diviners - their "AUTHORITIES."

Certainly the proclamation of the...

"BIRTH, LIFE, DEATH, RESURRECTION" and "DIVINITY OF JESUS CHRIST"...

has been a point of controversy for millions upon millions of "Christians" and "non-Christians" all over the entire world![3] All of the points of conflict related to said controversy can be best at-

---

1. See BOOK OF THE BIRTH OF MARY, Chapter i, Verse 1 [in: LOST BOOKS OF THE BIBLE and THE FORGOTTEN BOOKS OF EDEN, p. 17].
2. Ibid., and all of the Chapters. There is a question of his "date of birth" - 4 B.C. or 0 B.C.
3. See also Y. ben-Jochannan's CULTURAL GENOCIDE IN THE BLACK AND AFRICAN STUDIES CURRICULUM, p. 38; and BLACK MAN OF THE NILE AND HIS FAMILY, pp 340-393.

tributed mainly to the MYTHS and ALLEGORIES around the "LIFE" and "DIVINITY" concepts of Christ's actual "HUMANITY." This problem becomes excessively obscure as time brings on much more abundant expansions of the details told about him by each person to the other; each adding his or her own VERSION to each detail. But it is Rachid's AQUARIAN GOSPEL that attempts to detail the missing aspects cited in Jesus Christ's "LIFE" from the age of "TWELVE" [12] to "THIRTY - THREE" [33]. Professor George G.M. James, however, who was deeply influenced by Christ's HUMANITY wrote the following about his education in Africa on page 178 of STOLEN LEGACY:

> (6) *All the great religious leaders from Moses to Christ were Initiates of the Egyptian Mysteries*
> This is an inference from the nature of the Egyptian Mysteries and prevailing custom.
> (a) The Egyptian Mystery System was the One Holy Catholic Religion of the remotest antiquity.
> (b) It was the one and only Masonic Order of Antiquity, and as such.
> (c) It built the Grand Lodge of Luxor in Egypt and encompassed the ancient world with its branch lodges.
> (d) It was the first University of history and it made knowledge a secret, so that all who desired to become Priests and Teachers had to obtain their training from the Mystery System, either locally at a branch lodge or by travelling to Egypt.
> We know that Moses became an Egyptian Priest, a Hierogrammat, and that Christ after attending the lodge at Mt. Carmel went to Egypt for Final Initiation, which took place in the Great Pyramid of Cheops. Other religious leaders obtained their preparation from lodges most convenient to them.
> (e) This explains why all religions, seemingly different, have a common nucleus of similarity; belief in a God; belief in immortality and a code of ethics. Read Ancient Mysteries by C. H. Vail, p. 61; Mystical Life of Jesus by H. Spencer Lewis; Esoteric Christianity by Annie Besant, p. 107, 128-129; Philo; also read note (2) Chapter III for branch lodges of the ancient world.

Of course the following from SECTION XI, Chapter 47 and 48 of the AQUARIAN GOSPEL OF JESUS THE CHRIST[1] is much more definitive on Christ's education in Africa than Professor James.' It states:

Life and Works of Jesus in Egypt

CHAPTER 47

Jesus with Elihu and Salome in Egypt. Tells the story of his journeys. Elihu and Salome praise God. Jesus goes to the temple in Heliopolis and is received as a pupil.

AND Jesus came to Egypt land and all was well. He tarried not upon the coast; he went at once to Zoan, home of Elihu and Salome, who five and twenty years before had taught his mother in their sacred school.

2 And there was joy when met these three. When last the son of Mary saw these sacred groves he was a babe;

---

1. See Rachid's AQUARIAN GOSPEL OF JESUS THE CHRIST, pp. 87 - 89.

47

3 And now a man grown strong by buffetings of every kind; a teacher who had stirred the multitudes in many lands.

4 And Jesus told the aged teachers all about his life; about his journeyings in foreign lands; about the meetings with the masters and about his kind receptions by the multitudes.

5 Elihu and Salome heard his story with delight; they lifted up their eyes to heaven and said,

6 Our Father-God, let now thy servants go in peace, for we have seen the glory of the Lord;

7 And we have talked with him. the messenger of love, and of the covenant of peace on earth; good will to men.

8 Through him shall all the nations of the earth be blest; through him, Immanuel.

9 And Jesus stayed in Zoan many days; and then went forth unto the city of the sun, that men call Heliopolis, and sought admission to the temple of the sacred brotherhood.

10 The council of the brotherhood convened, and Jesus stood before the hierophant; he answered all the questions that were asked with clearness and with power.

11 The hierophant exclaimed, Rabboni of the rabbinate, why come you here? Your wisdom is the wisdom of the gods; why seek for wisdom in the halls of men?

12 And Jesus said, In every way of earth-life I would walk; in every hall of learning I would sit; the heights that any man has gained, these I would gain.

13 What any man has suffered I would meet, that I may know the griefs, the disappointments and the sore temptations of my brother man; that I may know just how to succour those in need.

14 I pray you, brothers, let me go into your dismal crypts: and I would pass the hardest of your tests.

15 The master said, Take then the vow of secret brotherhood. And Jesus took the vow of secret brotherhood.

16 Again the master spoke; he said, The greatest heights are gained by those who reach the greatest depths; and you shall reach the greatest depths.

17 The guide then led the way and in the fountain Jesus bathed; and when he had been clothed in proper garb he stood again before the hierophant.

CHAPTER 48

Jesus receives from the hierophant his mystic name and number. Passes the first brotherhood test, and receives his first degree, SINCERITY.

THE master took down from the wall a scroll on which was written down the number and the name of every attribute and character. He said,

2 The circle is the symbol of the perfect man, and seven is the number of the perfect man;

3 The Logos is the perfect word; that which creates; that which destroys, and that which saves.

4 This Hebrew master is the Logos of the Holy One, the Circle of the human race, the Seven of time.

5 And in the record book the scribe wrote down, The Logos-Circle-Seven; and thus was Jesus known.

6 The master said, The Logos will give heed to what I say: No man can enter into light till he has found himself. Go forth and search till you have found your soul and then return.

7 The guide led Jesus to a room in which the light was faint and mellow, like the light of early dawn.

8 The chamber walls were marked with mystic signs, with hieroglyphs and sacred texts; and in this chamber Jesus found himself alone where he remained for many days.

9 He read the sacred texts; thought out the meaning of the hieroglyphs and sought the import of the master's charge to find himself.

10 A revelation came; he got acquainted with his soul; he found himself; then he was not alone.

11 One night he slept and at the midnight hour, a door that he had not observed, was opened, and a priest in sombre garb came in and said,

12 My brother, pardon me for coming in at this unseemly hour; but I have come to save your life.

13 You are the victim of a cruel plot. The priests of Heliopolis are jealous of your fame, and they have said that you shall never leave these gloomy crypts alive.

14 The higher priests do not go forth to teach the world, and you are doomed to temple servitude.

15 Now, if you would be free, you must deceive these priests; must tell them you are here to stay for life;

16 And then, when you have gained all that you wish to gain, I will return, and by a secret way will lead you forth that you may go in peace.

17 And Jesus said, My brother man, would you come here to teach deceit? Am I within these holy walls to learn the wiles of vile hypocrisy?

18 Nay, man, my Father scorns deceit, and I am here to do his will.

19 Deceive these priests! Not while the sun shall shine. What I have said, that I have said; I will be true to them, to God, and to myself.

20 And then the tempter left, and Jesus was again alone; but in a little time a white-robed priest appeared and said,

21 Well done! The Logos has prevailed. This is the trial chamber of hypocrisy. And then he led the way, and Jesus stood before the judgement seat.

22 And all the brothers stood; the hierophant came forth and laid his hand on Jesus' head, and placed within his hands a scroll, on which was written just one word, SINCERITY; and not a word was said.

23 The guide again appeared, and led the way, and in a spacious room replete with everything a student craves was Jesus bade to rest and wait.

Having read extracts from the AQUARIAN GOSPEL, one would be moved to recall what Dr. Frank Crane wrote in the "Introduction" of the LOST BOOKS OF THE BIBLE, an extract of which follows:

THE great things in this world are growths.

This applies to books as well as to institutions.

The Bible is a growth. Many people do not understand that it is not a book written by a single person, but it is a library of several books which were composed by various people in various countries. It is interesting to know how this library grew and upon what principle some books were accepted and some rejected.

Of course we may take people's word for the reasons why certain books were chosen, but it is always satisfactory to come to our own conclusions by examining our own evidence.

This is what this *Lost Books of the Bible* enables us to do. We can examine the books of the Scriptures which we have in the authorized version, and then in this book we can read those scriptures which have been eliminated by various councils in order to make up our standard Bible.

It is safe to say that a comparison of the accepted books with those rejected may be relied upon, for those books which were accepted are far superior in value to the others.

. These others which are included in the *Lost Books of the Bible* comprise all kinds of stories, tales and myths.

No great figure appears in history without myths growing up about him. Every great personage becomes a nucleus or center about which folk tales cluster.

There are apocryphal tales about Napoleon, about Charlemagne, about Julius Cæsar and other outstanding characters.

It is impossible that a man representing so great a force as Jesus of Nazareth should appear in the world without finding many echoes of His personality in contemporary literature—many stories which grew up about Him as time elapsed.

What these tales and stories are, just how He appears to the fictional minds of His day and afterwards, it is interesting to note.

Very often the fiction writer depicts life and the great truth of life better than the historian. He does not pretend to write down what is exactly true, but he tinges all things with his imagination. His feelings, however, may be just and reliable.

One should question, at least because of the facts so far revealed; why Paul did not deal with these MANHOOD and HUMANE aspects of Jesus Christ's "thirty-three [33] years of life" as a mere HUMAN [male or man] BEING? Yet; could it have been that Paul believed...

"THE GOOD LIFE JESUS CHRIST LIVED ON EARTH"

was not sufficient for the model figure one needed to follow? Or; are we to believe by his teachings that only one aspect of Jesus Christ's "TRINITY" - the "Son" or "Human Being" - is to be ignored? That the "FATHER" and "HOLY GHOST" [today's "Spirit"], neither of which "no man has ever seen," are real; but not the only part of the "TRINITY" - the "Son" - "anyone had ever seen?" If these are related facts; what good is the "TRINITY" without the whole HUMANITY of the "Son" born from a "WOMAN?" And; for what other purpose would be Jesus Christ's experience without his "EARTHLY MIRACLES" [Obeya, Juju] and "SCIENCE" he allegedly performed? These are the same MIRACLES [magical fetes] performed by Jesus that make Black Christians glorify themselves in their belief of his "DIVINITY." Yet they were performed before his "DEATH;" while he was still a mere MORTAL HUMAN [male] BEING like any other Black Man of the Harlems and Timbuctoos of all of the Black Communities of the world today! And certainly they were performed by...

"JESUS - THE CHRIST" [Joshua the anointed], THE MAN and/or SON,"

each and everyone of them, according to the New Testament scribes [human beings like anyone of the Christians and non-Christians of his day, and ours]! It is only the "SON" and/or HUMAN - Jesus Christ - anyone ever met. The other two dimensions of the "Trinity" -

"THE HOLY GHOST and FATHER DIVINITY" -

they met, exist only in "BELIEF." Professor Smith's timely reminder on pages xvii - xviii of this volume should be of major concern at this juncture with regards to this point.

Now that we have digested all of this; how can we resolve all with the various details from the teachings of Paul of Tarsus;[1] who adopted [Saint] Luke's VERSION of "Jesus Christ's birth" to a "Virgin Woman," according to the following extract from LUKE, Chapter i, Verses 26 - 38, when in fact the original New Testament states plainly just "TO A WOMAN?" Note that it is the VERSIONS of the New Testament following the Nicene Conference Of Bishops in ca. 322 - 325 C.E. [A.D.] that produced the following in the KING JAMES AUTHORIZED VERSION OF THE NEW AND OLD TESTAMENT:

> 26 In tne sixtn month the angel Gabriel was sent from God to a city of Galilee named Nazareth, 27 to a virgin betrothed to a man whose name was Joseph, of the house of David; and the virgin's name was Mary. 28And he came to her and said, "Hail, O favored one, the Lord is with you!"c 29 But she was greatly troubled at the saying, and considered in her mind what sort of greeting this might be. 30And the angel said to her, "Do not be afraid, Mary, for you have found favor with God. 31And behold, you will conceive in your womb and bear a son, and you shall call his name Jesus.
> 32 He will be great, and will be called the Son of the Most High; and the Lord God will give to him the throne of his father David, 33 and he will reign over the house of Jacob for ever; and of his kingdom there will be no end."
> 34And Mary said to the angel, "How can this be, since I have no husband?" 35And the angel said to her, "The Holy Spirit will come upon you, and the power of the Most High will overshadow you; therefore the child to be bornd will be called holy, the Son of God. 36And behold, your kinswoman Elizabeth in her old age has also conceived a son; and this is the sixth month with her who was called barren. 37 For with God nothing will be impossible." 38And Mary said, "Behold, I am the handmaid of the Lord; let it be to me according to your word." And the angel departed from her.

Obviously, it is more than reasonable to assume that Luke's position was based upon SECOND HAND source with respect to "JESUS CHRIST'S BIRTH." But; who told Luke? It could not have been the same source that showed the same "JESUS CHRIST" as a SINLESS HUMAN BEING in the following from [Saint] MARK, Chapter i, Verses 9 - 12;[2] even though he "struck his rabbis" [teachers] and fellow Hebrews changing "money" in the Temple on the Sabbath Day, which his "father" - JEHOVAH [Ywh] had demanded that he too..."KEEP HOLY"... as one of the most important of the "TEN COMMANDMENTS:"

> 9 In those days Jesus came from Nazareth of Galilee and was baptized by John in the Jordan. 10And when he came up out of the water, immediately he saw the heavens opened and the Spirit descending upon him like a dove; 11 and a voice came from heaven, "Thou art my beloved Son;d with thee I am well pleased."

---

1. Saul of Tarsus, a Hebrew [Israelite, Palestinian or "Jew"], was originally known as such become he changed his name to"PAUL." He was of the "Benjamites and the Pharisees" according to the New Testament writcrs, who produced his "WRITINGS" that became the most important in Christian theology; even more important than those of people who lived with Christ.
2. Mark is supported by MATTHEW iii : 13 - 17, and LUKE iii : 21 - 23.

Once again no one else but the story teller [historian or mythologist], in each case, saw these fantastic MAGICAL FETES of the "Father" ~~thrusted upon~~ "his only son." But another of the many proofs of Jesus Christ's normal HUMAN CHILDHOOD lies in the fact that he too had to be "CIRCUMCIZED" like any of the other Hebrew [or "Jewish"] BOYS of his era; a SOCIO-MAGICAL RELIGIOUS RITE the Hebrews learnt and adopted from the indigenous Africans who worshiped TEM, RA or AMEN-RA while they were still in Egypt, North Africa receiving their first INITIATION into organized society ... "CIVILIZATION." All of the teachings involved with the MAGICAL RELIGIOUS RITE connected to "CIRCUMCISION" came down to the Egyptians from the Africans along the way from Central Africa - Punt, Itiopi, Nubia, Meröe, and other High-Cultures, hundreds of years before there was the first Hebrew in history, muchless before the 2,007 or 1,974 years ago since the "BIRTH" or "DEATH OF JESUS CHRIST." According to the following extract from LUKE, Chapter ii, Verses 21 - 38 we may forget that Jesus Christ's ancestors were taught most of what they knew by Africans. Luke stated:

21 When a strong man, fully armed, guards his own palace, his goods are in peace; 22 but when one stronger than he assails him and overcomes him, he takes away his armor in which he trusted, and divides his spoil. 23 He who is not with me is against me, and he who does not gather with me scatters.

24 "When the unclean spirit has gone out of a man, he passes through waterless places seeking rest; and finding none he says, 'I will return to my house from which I came.' 25 And when he comes he finds it swept and put in order. 26 Then he goes and brings seven other spirits more evil than himself, and they enter and dwell there; and the last state of that man becomes worse than the first."

27 As he said this, a woman in the crowd raised her voice and said to him, "Blessed is the womb that bore you, and the breasts that you sucked!" 28 But he said, "Blessed rather are those who hear the word of God and keep it!"

29 When the crowds were increasing, he began to say, "This generation is an evil generation; it seeks a sign, but no sign shall be given to it except the sign of Jonah. 30 For as Jonah became a sign to the men of Nineveh, so will the Son of man be to this generation. 31 The queen of the South will arise at the judgment with the men of this generation and condemn them; for she came from the ends of the earth to hear the wisdom of Solomon, and behold, something greater than Solomon is here. 32 The men of Nineveh will arise at the judgment with this generation and condemn it; for they repented at the preaching of Jonah, and behold, something greater than Jonah is here.

33 "No one after lighting a lamp puts it in a cellar or under a bushel, but on a stand, that those who enter may see the light. 34 Your eye is the lamp of your body; when your eye is sound, your whole body is full of light; but when it is not sound, your body is full of darkness. 35 Therefore be careful lest the light in you be darkness. 36 If then your whole body is full of light, having no part dark, it will be wholly bright, as when a lamp with its rays gives you light."

37 While he was speaking, a Pharisee asked him to dine with him: so he went in and sat at table.

Paul, on the other hand, is the sole basis of the Black Clergy's THEOLOGY. He caused them to avoid any examination into the areas of Christ's LIFE HISTORY that is so wanting and missing from the pages of the books used in BLACK SEMINARIES throughout the "Negro" COLLEGES and other "Negro" INSTITUTIONS where the so-called "GOSPEL OF JESUS -THE CHRIST- IS [allegedly] TAUGHT" day by day. But the HUMAN BEING, Jesus Christ, is not even mentioned or taught, muchless pursued. Jesus Christ's HUMANITY is a CLOSED 'LOST BOOK' so far as the Black Clergy and "Negro Theologians" are concerned. The direct result of this is that all of the facts of Jesus Christ's HUMANITY have been "DEIFIED" and placed beyond the reach of HUMAN reality in the "Negro Clergy's" THEOLOGY. As such, any evidence on his HUMANITY is quickly suppressed and made to appear suspect; and the teacher relating to same is equally made to suffer scorn and/or austricism upon the villification of his or her character by the Black Clergy, even to the point of being called "UNGODLY" and/or "UN-CHRISTIAN," particularly when there is no "TENURE" like Professor Smith mentioned. But even Jesus Christ's "FATHER", the Hebrew or Jewish God-Head - "YWH" or "JEHOVAH," is superceded by his Son's "HOLY GHOST" [today's "Spirit" or "Divinity"] according to the teachings of the WHITE Theologians, of whom the vast majority of "NEGRO" Theologians ape and mimmick to the last word of their masters' voices. At least; this is the Black Clergy's major dilemma. This act of degradation forces them to BEGIN and END everyone of their sermons with [Saint] PAUL, at the price of even playing down JESUS CHRIST - about whom they say almost nothing in terms of his LIFE AS A HUMAN BEING, or of DOING HUMAN THINGS LIKE FALLING IN LOVE WITH MARTHA! Thus; after just a few remarks about their own professed "SAVIOUR...JESUS CHRIST," it is pathetic to see the kosher "Colored" and/or "Negro" preachers of the Black Clergy crawl back into becoming "PAULITES' or "PAULIANS" throughout the rest of their sermons. WHY you ask ? Because they...

'KNOW NOT JESUS CHRIST... SON, MAN, DECEASED, RESURRECTED, DIVINE;'

nor in any other state without the...

"SACRED WORDS OF JESUS CHRIST ACCORDING TO PAUL."

Sad it is that said professed "Christian Clergy" does not know Jesus Christ except through the SECOND HAND SOURCE of ["Saint"] Paul. For PAUL, himself, heard about Jesus Christ through the same type of "SECOND HAND SOURCE," JESUS ["Joshua"] CHRIST ["the anointed"] having "DIED" long before "PAUL'S CONVERSION" as a "FOLLOWER" of the activities of the HUMAN LIFE of magical works ["MIRACLES"] He allegedly performed.[1]

Thus when we read the "WRITINGS OF PAUL," it becomes obvious that much of what he taught about Jesus Christ was from the figment of his own imagination; the MAGICAL RITES in Judaism; the mythological experiences in his own upbringing socio-politically; and the reflections of the allegorical relationship to the life the people had during his own era as colonial slaves for the Roman conquerors and slavemasters from Europe. Plus Paul, as all of the others who taught the alleged "TEACHINGS OF JESUS CHRIST," including Jesus Christ himself, was brought up in the TEACHINGS, TABOOS, MYTHOLOGIES, ALLEGORIES and HISTORICAL HERO WORSHIP in their own religions, all of which they could not totally free

---

1. A review of Professor Smith, Professor James, and Rachid's works, is appropriate at this time. See pp. xvii - xviii and 47 - 49 of this volume.

themselves   when they began to profess their revised VERSION of the Hebrew religion –
the worship of the God – "YWH" [Jehovah].[1] This is the same "TEACHING" Christians still
give credit as the basis for Jesus Christ establishing himself as their...

"SAVIOUR, REDEEMER, ONE AND ONLY TRUE GOD."[2]

The logical possibility of a pragmatic Christianity frightens most of the so-called "ORTHO-
DOX CHRISTIAN THEOLOGIANS," much less those who claimed to have been...

"CALLED [from cotton patches, etc.] TO PREACH
THE GOSPEL OF THE MINISTRY OF JESUS CHRIST;"

and particularly those whose references to Jesus Christ go no further than beyond the KING
JAMES AUTHORIZED VERSION OF THE OLD AND NEW TESTAMENT as written in ca. 1611
A.D. [C.E.] under the editorship of willing monarchists who wrote in favour of a King that
was engaged in all forms of sexual perversion that were prohibited in the VERSION of the Old
and New Testament they REVISED and PLAGIARIZED. One will notice that they were official
distortors who managed to change the Roman Catholic DUOAY-RHAMES VERSION, and the
GUTTENBERG VERSION, to conform with KING JAMES' personal convenience and connivance
in the manipulation of the British realm through esoterical   Christianity. Yet, it is this one
"VERSION" alone that the "Negro Clergy" and "Negro Theologians" have proclaimed to be...

"THE ONE AND ONLY TRUE WORDS OF THE LIVING GOD – JESUS CHRIST."

Behind all of this, we should be able to understand why the "Negro Clergy" always tell their
Black Parishoners:

"TAKE THE WORLD, BUT GIVE ME JESUS!"

Understand, certainly; but not ACCEPT. For not a single member of the "CHRISTIAN CLERGY"
[Black, White, Brown, Yellow, Red, or whatever else there may be] will voluntarily let any-
one take any of them church's PASS BOOK in return for JESUS CHRIST plus ALL OF THE MANY
ANGELS AND HEAVEN, muchless for "THE WORLD."

[THEOLOGY and CHRISTIANITY]   There is a distinct difference between "Philosophical" and
"Esoterical" THEOLOGY, and the TEACHINGS assigned to the works of Jesus Christ by those
who wrote about him in the NEW TESTAMENT. What we are dealing with   primarily, at this
juncture, are the "WRITINGS" of the 4th Century C.E. [A.D.]; and again with that which was

---

1. Paul became a believer in the "teachings of Jesus Christ," according to his own "WRITINGS"
and those of his co-workers: John, Mark, Barnabas and Luke, all of whom have been given a
back seat by all of the Black Clergy and Black Theologians who always ape their White colleagues, this case being no exception.
2. Some of the names given to Jesus Christ that were already given to Horus of Egypt in ca.
4000 B.C.E. See supportive information on pp. 31 - 32 of this volume.

totally distorted in the 16th Century C. E.; that which showed when Jesus Christ was still the
"FALLEN LEADER" and "SON OF GOD" like anyone else up until the Nicene Creed of ca.
325 C. E. When his mother - "MARY," and equally his father - "JOSEPH," were only parents
like all of the HEADS OF BLACK FAMILIES today in the 20th Century. This was before we
were compelled by the various "HOLY WRITS" and "HOLY EDICTS" by various chiefs of the
Vatican called "HIS HOLINESS THE POPE".., all of whom "WORDS" became as "DIVINE" as
Jesus Christ's. These COMMANDS even forced millions of confessants to accept the...

    " INFALLABILITY OF HIS HOLINESS THE POPE; PHYSICAL VIRGIN BIRTH
      OF JESUS CHRIST; IMMACULATE CONCEPTION OF THE VIRGIN MARY;"

etc. Yet all of these are the theories that came out of the Nicene Conference Of Bishops in
ca. 325 C. E. Thus one cannot believe that you will consider it very strange that there are
still literally hundreds of thousands of volumes dedicated solely to the clarification of the
status and validity of...

    "MARY'S IMMACULATE CONCEPTION OF JESUS CHRIST [and her remaining]
    PHYSICAL VIRGINITY [even after having given birth to "James the lesser,"and
    other children besides both of them, neither of whom is ever mentioned by the
    Black Clergy and/or Black Theologians in their preachings and teachings].

For to date we still hear the following being recited from the Roman Catholic "Rosary:"

    "HOLY MARY, MOTHER OF GOD, PRAY FOR US SINERS, BLESSED IS THE
      FRUIT OF THY WOMB - JESUS,"

etc. But we never ask: What happened to the other "FRUITS OF MARY'S WOMB" [or Tet]? Are
they not "BLESSED" too? This background of every so-called "Western Christian Believer"
cannot fade away. It is historical. Even Martin Luther's "PROTEST MOVEMENT" against
Roman Catholicism that produced what is today called the "PROTESTANTS," while in his
native Germany or Bavaria, could not in the past, and cannot now, change this allegedly "PRI-
MITIVE ORIGIN" of Christendom's most precious myth and allegory...

    "JESUS CHRIST'S PHYSICAL BIRTH TO A PHYSICAL VIRGIN MARY" -

which had its origin in the mythology surrounding Isis'"TET." Yet "VIRGIN BIRTHS" were
mentioned all over the BOOK OF THE DEAD and PAPYRUS OF ANI for thousands of years
before it allegedly happened to Joseph, Mary and Jesus Christ ca. 2007 or .   years ago,
as cited in the following that dealt with the ...

    "PURE VIRGIN BLOOD OF ISIS" and the "PROTECTOR OF HER UTERUS."

Thus it is shown in Chapter CLVI of the PAPYRUS OF ANI that:

         THE AMULET OF THE BUCKLE,

        " The blood of Isis, and the strength of Isis, and the
        " words of power of Isis shall be mighty to act as

" powers to protect this great and divine being, and to
" guard him from him that would do unto him anything
" that he holdeth in abomination."

One must remember that the above "TET BUCKLE"[1] was the forerunner of the European "CHASTITY BELT;" its full name being:

"THE BUCKLE OF THE GIRDLE OF ISIS."

It was made to cover the...

. . . . Tet and Tet 🎴, which symbolize the *sacrum* bone of Osiris and the uterus of Isis, and drew to the coffer the power of the great Ancestor god Osiris, and the virtue of the blood and magical spells and words of power of the great Ancestress goddess Isis.

The above documentation was produced by the indigenous <u>African</u> [BLACK] <u>People</u> along the Nile River Valley thousands of years before the first Hebrew [Israelite, Palestinian or "Jew," etc.] - "ABRAHAM" - was born in the City of Ur, Chaldea, Asia about ca. 1770 B.C.E. And we find that those same Africans' descendants were the ones who also taught other peoples about the "RESURRECTION OF THE DECEASED," as in the following graphical presentation from the PAPYRUS OF ANI. This "RESURRECTION" was caused by the usage of <u>Religious Magic</u> that made the "<u>Sacred scribe...Ani raise from a dead level to stand perpendicular.</u>" And it is from said African teachings that this aspect of <u>Western</u> plagiarization of the <u>Mysteries Science</u> became one of the basic requirements of the <u>Magical-Religious Rituals</u> in what is today called "FREEMASONRY." Thus the following incantation:

"And he shall become like a God in the underworld, and

[Ani's "Heart-Soul]

[Ani entering tomb]

[Ani's Shadow leaving tomb with Ba]

he shall never be turned back at any of the gates thereof."

---

1. Made from carmelian, red jasper, red glass, other substances of a red color - sometimes gold, also other substances covered with gold.

The graphical presentation from the PAPYRUS OF ANI on page 56, similar to that shown on page xviii, tells the story of the scribe Ani passing through the door to his tomb, outside of which is shown his "SHADOW" and "HEART-SOUL" [in the form of a <u>human-headed bird</u>]. Countless presentations show other "DECEASED SCRIBES" being proclaimed SACRED and "DIVINE " during their travails to the <u>Nether World</u>, because of their "RIGHTEOUSNESS" and/ or "HOLY PERFORMANCE" on earth. We can also find precedence for all of this as we go back thousands of years "<u>before the birth of Jesus Christ</u>" in the following from the same Holy BOOK OF THE DEAD and PAPYRUS OF ANI, plate 18, where the Scribe Ani is depicted passing through his tomb. I begin with a few comments by Budge, followed by direct quotation:

The physical body of man considered as a whole was called *khat* , a word which seems to be connected with the idea of something which is liable to decay. The word is also applied to the mummified body in the tomb, as we know from the words " My body (*khat*) is buried." Such a body was attributed to the god Osiris; in the CLXIInd Chapter of the Book of the Dead " his great divine body rested in Ánu." In this respect the god and the deceased were on an equality. As we have seen above, the body neither leaves the tomb nor reappears on earth; yet its preservation was necessary. Thus the deceased addresses Temu : " Hail to thee, O my father " Osiris, I have come and I have embalmed this my flesh " so that my body may not decay. I am whole, even as " my father Kheperà was whole, who is to me the type of " that which passeth not away, Come then, O Form, and " give breath unto me, O lord of breath, O thou who art " greater than thy compeers. Stablish thou me, and form " thou me, O thou who art lord of the grave. Grant thou " to me to endure for ever, even as thou didst grant unto " thy father Temu to endure ; and his body neither passed " away nor decayed. I have not done that which is hateful " unto thee, nay, I have spoken that which thy KA loveth ; " repulse thou me not, and cast thou me not behind thee, " O Temu, to decay, even as thou doest unto every god and " unto every goddess and unto every beast and creeping " thing which perisheth when his soul hath gone forth from " him after his death, and which falleth in pieces after his " decay . . . . . Homage to thee, O my father Osiris, thy " flesh suffered no decay, there were no worms in thee, " thou didst not crumble away, thou didst not wither away, " thou didst not become corruption and worms ; and I " myself am Kheperà, I shall possess my flesh for ever and " ever, I shall not decay, I shall not crumble away, I shall " not wither away, I shall not become corruption."

But the body does not lie in the tomb inoperative, for by the prayers and ceremonies on the day of burial it is endowed with the power of changing into a *sāḥu*, or spiritual body.   Thus we have such phrases as, " I flourish (literally, ' 'sprout') like the plants,"   " My flesh flourisheth,"   " I " exist, I exist, I live, I live, I flourish, I flourish,"

What is being revealed here to you should be causing all sorts of painful problems, particularly since none of it has been endorsed by some "WHITE THEOLOGIAN, PROFESSOR" or "INSTITUTION" of one sort or another.   But everyone of the students in BLACK and/or AFRICAN STUDIES should ask themselves   once more: What, or who, makes a "SACRED SCRIBE" write "GOD'S WORDS?" In order to set your mind at ease, make your conscience relate to the reaction going on in the most "ORTHODOX" circles of European and European-American esoterical Christendom besides the articles on pages xvii - xviii and xxx - xxxii to the following article in which one of our most noted WHITE "AUTHORITY" on Jesus Christ and Christendom confirmed what has been so far stated in this volume. He is showing that "ESOTERICAL" and "EVANGELICAL CHRISTIANITY" are not real today in ca. 1973 C.E. for WHITES, much less for their BLACK understudies in the Black Clergy and in the Black Seminaries with their NEGRO THEOLOGIANS who constantly ape their masters - all of whom main source of information is still the WHITE Southern Baptist Conference or some other WHITE institution that controls religious BELIEF   in the United States of America, Great Britain, Europe, and where ever else the WHITE MAN [male or female] controls. The "AUTHORITY" speaks for himself:

THE LONG ISLAND PRESS   Sunday May 13, 1973

Evangelicals told:
Embrace social issues

By DAVID ANDERSON

WASHINGTON (UPI)—There are increasing signs that evangelical Protestants, associated for most of the century with ultraconservatism in social issues, may be ready to begin breaking away from total acceptance of the social status quo.

While no one is likely to see evangelicals on New Left picket lines, their leaders and theologians recently have been preaching the doctrine that conservatism in theology is not the same thing as political conservatism.

Evangelicals are those Protestants who generally hold to a strict interpretation that the Bible is the devinely inspired word of God that must be accepted literally. They also accept a traditional formulation of a basic Christian doctrine such as the biblical story of the fall of man, the promise of salvation and a life hereafter through belief in Jesus Christ.

In part because they view Christ's work on earth as chiefly religious, evangelicals tend to a strict separation

58

It is obvious that Professor Pierard's position validates all that have been stated so far. Or, is it not a fact that your own professor has been saying all the time what WHITE Christendom is now admitting hesitatingly is in fact the system of FRAUD it has perpetuated against African [BLACK] People over the last three hundred [300] years?

If there were among the Africans of the Nile River Valley and Great Lakes regions such PHILOSOPHICAL and THEOSOPHICAL teachings that passed on down to the Hebrews from the African worshipers of RA in Egypt and Nubia, then to the Christians along the African coast that is washed by the Mediterranean Sea, and finally into Greece and Rome; it should not surprise any AFRICAN and/or BLACK [African-American or Afro-American] STUDIES student that said TEACHINGS are now catching up with those who were constantly distorting them yesterday, and those who are today. The article about Professor Pierard is further proof of this. However, Professor Geddes MacGregor said it best on page 190 of his very timely book – A LITERARY HISTORY OF THE BIBLE FROM THE MIDDLE AGES TO THE PRESENT DAY – when he wrote the following:

> Hayyim Nachman Bialik (1873-1934), perhaps the greatest of modern Jewish poets, has vividly expressed the inadequacy of all translation in his picturesque saying: "He who reads the Bible in translation is like a man who kisses his bride through a veil." Still, when a veil there must

be, the translator's task is to make it as gossamer-fine a veil as may be. Indeed, the face of even the most beautiful of women may be enhanced by a veil, if only the veil be worthy of her beauty. The King James translators did not pretend to be providing a new veil. Their function was, rather, to let more light through the veils already in use. This fundamental principle is admirably exhibited in their explanation   that it was never their intention either to make an entirely new translation or even to turn a bad one into a good. Their purpose was, rather, to make, out of many good translations, one that would be better than all. After all, what is the purpose of any translation? It is to open windows and let in light, to remove the cover of the well so that the people may drink and not be, as were Jacob's children, thirsty for want of a bucket to draw the water that was at their feet.

But why are BLACK CHRISTIANS still being led to believe that:

"THE FIRST TIME IN HISTORY A VIRGIN BIRTH WAS EVER MENTIONED WAS WHEN THE ANGEL OF THE LORD TOLD MARY SHE WAS WITH-CHILD WITH THE SAVIOUR JESUS - THE CHRIST - OF NAZARETH."

This is as far from the TRUTH as the theory that:

'JESUS CHRIST WAS THE PERSON JEHOVAH CALLED UPON WHEN HE SAID: LET US MAKE MAN IN OUR OWN IMAGE, AND IN OUR OWN LIKENESS,   etc.

All of this is only possible because Black Christians purchase all of their basic needs for th religious obligations from WHITE suppliers. Just imagine, with all of the millions upon millions of dollars within the control of the BLACK Baptist, BLACK Methodist, BLACK Evangelist, and many hundreds more BLACK RELIGIOUS institutions and denominations wit in Christendom throughout the United States of America, there is not a single BLACK owne and operated publishing house among either of them that produces exclusively RELIGIOUS MATERIALS to be used in their own Sunday School classes, muchless in Sunday Worship. Thus the reason for the continued perpetuation of a LILY-WHITE BLONDE JESUS CHRIST i $100^0/_0$ ALL BLACK Christian congregations of $100^0/_0$ ALL BLACK Communities. This condition of the ALL WHITE suppliers is equally typical among the BLACK ISRAELITES [Jews] but to a lesser degree among the BLACK MUSLIMS, and also among the BLACK MOSLEMS [such as Sunis, Al Mahadis, etc.]. It is particularly critical in the area of...

'THE NEED FOR A BLACK BIBLE.'

[HISTORY AS RELIGION]   It is rather strange that MARY'S material role in trying to save little boy's - Jesus Christ - life cannot be revealed to Christians, particularly BLACKS, as historical reality that many other BLACK WOMEN all over the world are sometimes requir to do for their   sons. But it is a fact that Jesus Christ's mother had to come to his aid and save him. For it was certainly MARY who packed him off to hide in the clutches of his cous

protection in Egypt, North Africa. Here he hid in fear of the European colonialist invaders from Rome; and also from his fellow Hebrews [Israelites or Jews] that were willing to put an end to his life. This is providing the story is in fact TRUE!

The average parishoner does not have the feintest idea where Egypt or any other nation mentioned in his or her OLD TESTAMENT and/or NEW TESTAMENT is located geographi- cally....Yet each and every one of them will tell you:

"I TEACH SUNDAY SCHOOL CLASSES EVERY SUNDAY.....I ATTEND SUNDAY SCHOOL CLASSES EVERY SUNDAY....I KNOW THE BIBLE,"

etc. Some of them even teach in MINISTERIAL TRAINING SCHOOLS!" But; how could they teach anything about Jesus Christ's "LIFE" any place without knowing the geography of the area where he was "BORN, LIVED, WORKED, STUDIED" and "DIED?" This is one of the many tradegies of the "Traditional" or "Orthodox"...

"ALL I NEED IS FAITH IN JESUS CHRIST"...

know-nothing-ness stupidity that is constantly encouraged by too many members of the Black Clergy. But unfortunately, this type of meaningless procrastination is equally true for too many BLACK rabbis and BLACK imams.

There can be no excuse for "Sunday Schools" and "Bible Training Institutes" in the BLACK COMMUNITIES not being centers of BLACK SOCIO-POLITICAL RELIGIOUS INDOCTRINA- TION; providing they deal with the HUMAN BODY as much as they deal with the "HUMAN SOUL" and/or "SPIRIT." For it was with the BLACK BODIES, along with their "SOULS the reverends Richard Allen,[1] Absolon Jones,[2] Nat Turner,[3] Denmark Vessey,[4] Henry High- land Garnet,[5] W.C. Pennington,[6] and countless others of the BLACK CLERGY of the days of SLAVERY and the so-called "RECONSTRUCTION PERIOD" throughout the United States of America, dealt with when they challenged WHITE RACIST Judaeo-Christian THEOLOGY physically and spiritually; all in context with the LIFE OF JESUS CHRIST. Thus, it is sad to hear Black Clergymen and Black Clergywomen constantly praising the WHITE Reverend John Brown...

"FOR HIS COURAGEOUS CHRISTIAN STAND AGAINST SLAVERY IN AMERICA IN THE NAME OF JESUS CHRIST,"

---

1. Founder of the African Methodist Episcopal Church [AME] of the United States of America in ca. 1770 C.E.
2. Founder of the Africa Baptist Church In America in ca. 1776 C.E.
3. Fought against his slavemasters. Turned in by traitors who loved their slavemasters.
4. Led one of the most successful slave revolts against the White Christian slavemasters
5. One of the anti-slavery fighters and critic of Abraham Lincoln's dubble-dealing on slavery.
6. First Black Minister to pastor an all White congregation of the Presbyterian Church.

but not a single WORD of the same type for their own forerunners like Nat Turner and Denmark Vessey, both of whom placed their lives on the end of their slavemasters hangman's noose in order to free their fellow Africans from Judaeo-Christian SLAVERY. All of these Africans were in tune with the protest LIFE Jesus Christ lived. All of them must be made BLACK SAINTS and/or BLACK PROPHETS in the Black Bible. For they were acting in the truest form of their Jesus Christ; particularly where their GOD proclaimed:

"VENGANCE IS MINE."

And is it not historically true that Jesus Christ 'LOST HIS COOL' when he 'WHIPPED A FEW HEADS' in the Temple over the issue of the "MONEY CHANGERS" transaction of business during his father's [YWH] prayers? Thus, we read the following in JOHN, Chapter ii, Verses 12 - 15:

12 After this he went down to Ca-pĕr'na-um, with his mother and his brothers and his disciples; and there they stayed for a few days. 13 The Passover of the Jews was at hand, and Jesus went up to Jerusalem. 14 In the temple he found those who were selling oxen and sheep and pigeons, and the money-changers at their business. 15And making a whip of cords, he drove them all, with the sheep and oxen, out of the temple; and he poured out the coins of the money-changers and overturned their tables.

These distortions of the HUMANITY of Jesus Christ are constantly operative because we have allowed "do-nothing" Negro Clergymen and Negro Clergywomen who have failed to re-member that it was in, and from, the institution of the BLACK [not "Negro" and/or "Colored"] CHURCH that the Africans successfully planned their attack upon the "Good Ole Slave System" and "Slavemasters" of the North, South, East, West and Center of the United States of Ameri-ca. The BLACK CHURCH also produced such physical revolutionists as Harriet Tubman, Bembe Sojourner Truth, Quacko, Tousaint L'Oveture, Henri Christophe, Nat Turner, Frederick Doug-las, Seti, Richard Allen, Absolon Jones, and countless other BLACK SAINTS who used

"THE HISTORICAL LIFE-STYLE OF JESUS CHRIST AND MOSES".

as examples of violent protest ordained by His father - YWH or JEHOVAH - the "GOD OF VENGANCE;" even as it is stated in the same 1611 A.D. KING JAMES [Authorized] VERSION OF THE OLD AND NEW TESTAMENT. All of this we seem not to be able to understand was not in the truly ORIGINAL Bible Of The Christian Church Of The Creation that was founded in Africa, at a place called "EGYPT "[in honour of one of Noah's grandson by like name - Ham's son according to GENESIS , forgetting that our "African" ancestors originally named it Ta-Mer»

History and knowledge means RESEARCH. Research means HARD WORK and EXTRA TIME from the social amenities of which the Negro Clergy has become so fond. But it is the lack of HISTORICAL KNOWLEDGE dealing with the Life-Styles of the biblical characters of Judaism, Christianity and Islam that the Negro Clergy is totally ignorant about. This disgusting and unforgivable LACK OF KNOWLEDGE caused the "Negro" Clergy not to be able to see the HUMANNESS of the followers of Jehovah, Jesus Christ, and/or Al'lah. It is the absense of such facts that now plagues the BLACK CHURCH, BLACK CLERGY and NEGRO THEO-LOGIANS in terms of point of interest and priority to hold their membership and students of the BLACK SEMINARY. And because of it the membership's age-group-level [the average age of each congregation] is at best 40 to 60 years young. Thus it is that the BLACK CLERGY is able to perpetuate a NON-HUMAN Jesus Christ that supposedly lived on the earth among men, women and children as a model for HUMANITY; as against their DIVINE HOLY GHOST Jesus Christ as a model that is solely for dying. Their major Sunday Services and/or Sunday Schools are solely "PREPARATION FOR DEATH" oriented. And because of this sense of utter hopelessness, which is constantly nourished by the Black Clergy, "DEATH" became the psychosis that makes Black Parishoners holler at the maximum pitch of their voices the gruesome song...

"DEATH IS MY VICTORY."

Thus, one can safely conclude that "LIFE" and "LIVING" are secondary values in the Black Church; this due to the teachings of the PAULIST ANTI-SEXUAL INTERCOURSE Negro Theologians."

[LANGUAGE and COMMUNICATION] "Speaking In Tounges" is one of the mysticisms employed by many of the Black Clergymen, Black Clergywomen and Negro Theologians to justify their parishoners nostalgia into the unreal; equally allowing the individual parishoner to become obsessively involved to the point of feeling a metamorphic relationship with Jesus Christ. This type of euphoric SEXUAL RELIGIOUS involvement gives him or her a sense of superiority in spiritual accomplishment over those who have not yet reached said dimension in their Christian Awareness." Of course, apart from the escape into unreality, the person so intrigued is unable to relate anything that took place during such a "DEMONIC" expression of Christian "jingoism." However, if this type of behavior is exhibited in any other religion than Christianity, Judaism and/or Islam, it would be considered by Christians, Jews and Moslems as "PAGANISM, HEATHENISM," or at best "PRIMITIVISM." But do we need to condemn other peoples's RELIGION in order to give our own validity, as do the so-called "CHRISTIAN MISSIONARIES" with their Jewish and Christian GODS - Ywh and Jesus Christ - everywhere they go? Does the language of contempt against other RELIGIONS, in which others find their tranquility with their own Law Giver and Creator, make us much more Christian, Jewish and/or Moslem? If these questions are answerable in the affirmative; then, most definitely Judaism, Christianity and Islam are based upon very shaky grounds indeed. However, if this writer has not read incorrectly, he remembered that it was to Jesus Christ the following was attributed in one of his acts of HUMANITY. Jesus Christ supposedly said:

"UNTO THE LEAST OF THESE I SAY UNTO YOU,
IS MINE."

Obviously this should certainly remind all of us that even Jesus Christ, himself, was not in any way, form or fashion a "CHRISTIAN." And based upon our "PAULITE CHRISTIANITY;" he too will fail to pass our WHITE "PAULITE CHRISTIAN" THEOLOGIANS and their "NEGRO" [shadow] THEOLOGIANS' test for entry into [Jesus Christ's own] "HEAVEN." Just imagine that. Jesus Christ would not...

"THROW THE FIRST STONE"...

at any of the adultresses we have in our midst today among all forms of Christians, Jews, Moslems, etc.! At least, this is what we are told in the following extract from JOHN, Chapter viii, Verses 1 - 11:

JE'-SŬS went unto the mount of Olives 2 And early in the morning he came again into the temple, and all the people came unto him; and he sat down, and taught them. 3 And the scribes and Phăr'-ĭ-sêe brought unto him a woman taken in adultery; and when they had set her in the midst, 4 They say unto him, Master, this woman was taken in adultery, in the very act. 5 Now Mō'-ŝêŝ in the law commanded us, that such should be stoned: but what sayest thou? 6 This they said, tempting him, that they might have to accuse him. But Jē'-ŝŭs stooped down, and with his finger wrote on the ground, as though he heard them not. 7 So when they continued asking him, he lifted up himself, and said unto them, He that is without sin among you, let him first cast a stone at her. 8 And again he stooped down, and wrote on the ground. 9 And they which heard it, being convicted by their own conscience, went out one by one, beginning at the eldest, even unto the last: and Jē'-ŝŭs was left alone, and the woman standing in the midst. 10 When Jē'-ŝŭs had lifted up himself, and saw none but the woman, he said unto her, Woman, where are those thine accusers? hath no man condemned thee? 11 She said, No man, Lord. And Jē'-ŝŭs said unto her, Neither do I condemn thee: go, and sin no more.

Examining the HUMAN side of the "Life Of Jesus Christ" further; can you imagine Jehovah, Jesus Christ or Al'lah condemning their own BLACK HERITAGE in Africa and Asia to accomad European WHITE [Caucasian, Indo-European-Aryan, Semitic] RACISM? Can we realy believe that either of them actually used "BLACK" and "WHITE" as colors that represented "GODLINESS" [white] and "UN-GODLINESS" [black]? If these words were not used by Jesus Christ of Nazareth; what are they doing in the New Testament according to the constant teachings of WHITE and NEGRO Theologians and Preachers begging to...

"MAKE MY HEART WHITER THAN SNOW OH LORD!"

... and/or ...

"REMOVE THE BLACKNESS FROM MY SINFUL HEART."

But if Jesus Christ did not use them; why are they retained by "Negro Theologians," Black Clergymen, Black Clergywomen and Black Congregations? The answer is; an unconscionable FEAR. Fear that their WHITE co-religionists will revoke their half-hearted endorsement of

64

"NEGRO" or "COLORED" religious institutions, most of which has tailored their annual budgets upon contributions from "FAT CAT" White individuals and/or White institutions of Jewish and Christian affilliations.

When we examine our _enslaved mentality_ we developed from the teachings forced upon all of us by our GREAT WHITE FATHERS of European and European-American style Judaism and Christianity, and equally from that of Asian style Mohammedism, all of whom always make certain that their protective charges, "Negroes" and "Colored Folks," are very well taken care of.... "We even find that the ZENITH includes many of the structures in which we worship our...

COLORLESS BLONDE AND BLUE EYE CAUCASIAN-SEMITIC JESUS CHRIST
OF EUROPE...

and the financiers that contribute the funds to build our Black religious institutions, and also the funds that subsidize thousands upon thousands of our seminarians. Thus not a single harsh word is ever possible, or even said, against the UN-CHRISTIAN exploitation of Black People [Christians, Jews, Moslems, Muslims, etc] in any part of the United States of America, muchless in the Caribbean and Africa. WHY? Because we find that the Jewish, Christian and Moslem exploiters and colonialists are still labeled "ROCKEFELLER, PUGH, VANDERBILT, DuPONT, SASSOON, OPPENHEIMER, ROTHCHILD, MELLON, KENNEDY, SAUDI, CARNEGIE, BARUCH, LEHMAN, ROOSEVELT, DREW, ABDULLAH, MAZURI, ALI..., etc. etc., etc., almost endlessly. These names are equally typical on the TRUSTEE BOARD of many of our Black RELIGIOUS institutions, many of which adorns their prize stained-glass windows adjacent to the BLONDE [colorless] JESUS CHRIST in His WHITE HEAVEN donated by said "God-fearing" individuals whose great-grandparents, grandparents, and even parents, were equally responsible for the SLAVE TRADE across the Middle Passage and the SLAVE PLANTATION system. Why? Because we, BLACKS OF EVERY PERSUASION, still expect their offsprings to build more churches and schools for their remaining "GOOD NEGROES" and/or "COLORED FOLKS" that accepted Michaelangelo's "WHITE BLONDE [Caucasian-Semitic] JESUS CHRIST, JOSEPH and MARY" - the so-called "HOLY FAMILY" he painted for Pope Julius IInd sometime between ca. 1510 - 1512 C.E. Thus the "Negro Clergy's"...

" THE ONE AND ONLY LIVING GOD - JESUS CHRIST. "

Yet, we still proclaim hypocritically at the tip of our voices that:

> "GOD [meaning Jesus Christ for Christians, Jehovah for Jews or Israelites, and Al'lah for Moslems or Muslims] HAS NO COLOR WHATSOEVER."

But since GOD IS COLORLESS:Could we on one occasion, at least for a little while, see a COLORLESS Jesus Christ that is other than the colorless...

'BLONDE, BLUE EYE and GOLDEN-LOCKS'...

European from Northern Italy image always adorning the prize position in almost everyone of the "NEGRO" Clergy's Churches and "COLORED" Theologians' seminarians? This would not be representative of the Jesus Christ whose family was of Africa and Asia! For not a single member of this "HOLY FAMILY" - Joseph, Mary and little Jesus - was from Europe. But to say that:

"JESUS CHRIST HAD NO COLOR;"

we must equally be ready to say that:

"THERE COULD BE NO PICTURE OR PAINTING OF JESUS,"

whatsoever; as painting a "GHOST" [today's "SPIRIT"] would have been no more possible than painting Ralph Ellison's "INVISIBLE MAN,"[1] muchless a "GOD.!" Equally: How could John "the Baptist" - hold an INVISIBLE [colorless] Jesus for His...

'"BAPTISM IN THE RIVER JORDAN?"

Is it not a FACT that every bit of historical evidence points to Jesus Christ's BLACK or BROWN color? And; is it not equally true that we have forgotten his earliest depiction as the...

"BLACK CHRIST CHILD" with his "BLACK MADONNA"

[mother], Mary, whom all of the world of Christendom recognized before Michaelangelo's creation of a Northern Italian "JESUS CHRIST" figure after the original MADONNA AND CHILD - a take off from the FERTILITY RITES Goddess and God - Isis and Horus of Ta-Merry, North Alkebu-lan shown on pages 18 and 29 of this volume?

The reflective attitudes created by these images are predominate. Thus RELIGIOUS tracts showing a PURE LILY WHITE HEAVEN loaded with SPOTLESSLY WHITE ANGELS and an occasional BLACK DEVIL with RED LIPS [and of course with his fork-stick firmly grasped in his monkey-like hands; all of them] are constantly distributed to BLACK parishoners of every age. But not a single protest of this racist carricature of the Jewish, Christian and Islamic "HEAVEN" ever had a WHITE PINK LIPS DEVIL that the Black Clergy and/or Negro Theologians could equally use. Yet, these types of picture bibles showing a black DEVIL and a white JESUS are sold by the millions to BLACK PARISHONERS, most of whom still claim - fanatically - that:

"GOD [meaning Jesus Christ] HAS NO COLOR."

---

1. Ralph Ellison's INVISIBLE MAN deals with a "NEGRO" who was always present before all of the "WHITES" in America who could not see him; solely because they blinded themselves to him, and all of the other so-called "NEGROES"

One may wonder what would happen if a JET BLACK JESUS CHRIST and EBONY BLACK ANGELS ever get into one edition of the New and Old Testament for a change! No doubt it will receive the same type of contemptuous reception the "BLACK DOLLS" of the late 1950's received when they were produced by the African nationalist pioneer leader Authur Reed[1] to replace the BLONDE BLUE EYE SHIRLEY TEMPLE DOLLS, which practically every BLACK girl-child once received at Christmas and/or birthday from their BLACK parents, other relatives, and friends.

[AFRICAN PERSONALITIES OF THE NEW TESTAMENT]   The COLOR of the people in both the Old and New Testament should be of no more surprise than the COLOR of the people in the Holy Qur'an.[2] But it is commonly accepted that in the latter case they were BROWN and BLACK. However, this type of obsessive racial bigotry permeates every factor of "Western Society" [or civilization]. Thus "NIMROD"[3] is carefully made to appear as an obscure personality, as is the "EUNUCH"[4] of Queen Candice of NUBIA.   But, when the Hebrew [Jewish] Holy Torah [Five Books Of Moses or Old Testament, etc.] mentions that:

> "PRINCES SHALL COME OUT OF EGYPT; AND ETHIOPIA SHALL STRETCH
> OUT HER HANDS UNTO GOD...,"

etc., according to PSALMS, Chapter lxviii, Verse 31; is it not a reference to two distinctly "BLACK NATIONS," whose indigenous people are millions of "BLACK PEOPLE?" In II KINGS, Chapter xix, Verses 6 - 10, where the Prophet Isaiah and his fellow Hebrews sent to "Ethiopia" for aid of every kind to help the Israelites [Hebrews or Jews] against the invading Assyrians; did these BLACK PEOPLE not respond under the leadership of their BLACK Pharaoh [king] Tirhakah and saved Isaiah's national homeland and people - the "ISRAEL-ITES?" The following extract from the Hebrew HOLY TORAH tells the story:

6 I·śai'ah said to them, "Say to your master, 'Thus says the LORD: Do not be afraid because of the words that you have heard, with which the servants of the king of Assyria have reviled me. 7 Behold, I will put a spirit in him, so that he shall hear a rumor and return to his own land: and I will cause him to fall by the sword in his own land.'"
8 The Rab'sha·keh returned, and found the king of Assyria fighting against Lib'nah; for he heard that the king had left La'chish. 9 And when the king heard concerning Tir·ha'kah king of Ethiopia, "Behold, he has set out to fight against you, he sent messengers again to Hez·e·ki'ah, saying, 10 "Thus shall you speak to Hez·e·ki'ah king of Judah: 'Do not let your God on whom you rely deceive you by promising that Jerusalem will not be given into the hand of the king of Assyria.

---

1. A Garvyite and street corner lecturer [orator],who was one of the very first person in the United States of America to manufacture "BLACK DOLLS;" even when the Marcus M. Garvey's U.N.I.A., Inc. was in its zenith during the 1900's and 1920's.
2. See AFRICAN ORICAN ORIGINS OF THE MAJOR "WESTERN RELIGIONS," pp. 195 - 244.
3. See GENESIS x : 8 - 12; CHRONICLES i : 10; MICAH v - vi.
4. See ACTS viii : 27 - 39.

Moses' MARRIAGE TO THE DAUGHTER OF THE HIGH PRIEST OF KUSH [Cush, Abyssinia or Ethiopia], according to NUMBERS, Chapter xii, Verses 1 - 9; Abraham,[1] Jacob,[2] and Joseph's[3] entry into Egypt with permission from the Egyptian kings and people, according to GENESIS, Chapter xii, Verses 46 - 47; and the Queen of Sheba [or of the Kingdom of Axum, part of modern Ethiopia] relationship with King Solomon of the Kingdom of Israel, including her pregnancy for him with her only child - Emperor Menilik Ist, according to I KINGS, Chapter x, Verses 1 - 10, and CHRONICLES, Chapter ix, Verses 1 - 12; were these not refering to...

BLACK/BROWN PEOPLE, BLACK/BROWN NATIONS, BLACK/BROWN CONTINENT. It must be understood that there is hardly a single BOOK in the Old Testament and New Testament in which BLACK PEOPLE do not appear as the "CHOSEN PEOPLE" in the allegedly...

"INSPIRED WORDS OF GOD."

Of course, all of this is inspite of the CAUCASIAN-SEMITIC racism and religious bigotry introduced against BLACK and BROWN peoples of Alkebu-lan and Asia in the various European LANGUAGES and VERSIONS of the Old Testament and New Testament.

[RACISM BY JEWS]   Today when people call themselves "SEMITES," and try to support said nomenclature by virtue of the Old Testament; what else could it be but "RACISM?" This nonsensical title was developed as a wedge between Judaism and Islam. For we find that

"ABRAHAM'S FIRST CHILD...ISMAEL"[Ishmael]...

was not considered a "HEBREW" or "JEW "... solely upon the basis that:

"HIS MOTHER [Rachael] WAS NOT A HEBREW WOMAN,"

according to the biblical racism and religious bigotry inserted in the Pentateuch that created a

"JEWISH" and/or "SEMITIC RACE."

This bit of European and European-American extension of the...

"PURE WHITE INDO-EUROPEAN CAUCASIAN-SEMITIC MASTER RACE."

myth makes...

"THE CHILDREN OF ABRAHAM BY HADASSAH [Sara or Sarah] THE ONLY
LINE OF TRUE SEMITE MOTHERHOOD."

Among any other group this form of religious bigotry and vicious racism would have been condemned by Jews, Christians and Moslems. But it can be traced back to the racist allegorical

---

1. NUMBERS xii : 10
2. Ibid., xii : 1 - 7
3. Ibid., xii : 39 - 50

story in the BOOK OF GENESIS, Chapter ix, Verses 25 - 31 of the Sixth Century C.E. [A.D.] racist European Jews'VERSION of the Babylonian Talmud, as shown on page 41 of this volume; all of which deals with the alleged travails of "Noah and his sons," particularly his youngest - named "HAM," whose child named - "CANAAN" - Noah allegedly "CURSED." The "CURSE," allegedly, left the mark of the...

'BLACK COLOR OF THE NEGRO...THE CANAANITES.'

What we are witnessing today is that the biblical provisions against "RELIGIOUS INTE-GRATION"[or amalgamation] has turned into a psuedo-intellectual form of European and European-American "SEMITIC RACISM" by those who want to be accepted as "PURE WHITE CAUCASIAN" in one minute and simultaneously "SEMITIC" or "JEWISH," while in the next minute equally reserving the right to be accepted as of a special "SEMITIC RACE" that is "CHOSEN BY GOD;" all of which is to suit their own convenience. Anyone not concuring with any of this aspect of "SEMITIC RACISM" and/or "RELIGIOUS BIGOTRY" that is supposedly "INSPIRED BY GOD," meaning the Jewish God - YWH, is summarily assigned the title of...

"ANTI-SEMITE."

The reason"Negro Theologians"and the Black Clergy must continue accepting WHITE JEW-ISH ANTI-BLACKISM as RELIGIOUS TRUTH expressed in the so-called "INSPIRED WORDS OF GOD," which was contrived by Jewish writers, is that too many of then refused to develop economic programs in their own churches and seminaries with their own monies their parish-oners have paid into the treasury. Instead, they depend upon Jewish philanthrophies for the answer to their economic and social programs. Secondly: Because too many BLACK profess-ors and students depend upon WHITE JEWISH authors, sociologists, historians, anthropolo-gists, palaeontologists, genealogists, etc. to establish in all of these fields BLACK AUTHOR-ITY without a bit of public protest in fear of being called "ANTI-SEMITIC." This is the main reason so many BLACK [African-American or Afro-American, etc.] STUDIES and AFRICAN STUDIES departments[1] throughout the United States of America are loaded down and dominat-ed by works on BLACK PEOPLE that are mostly written and produced by WHITE JEWS and WHITE CHRISTIANS. It is a fact that most of us prefer to grin and bear, and even discuss in secret, but never reveal in public for fear of a so-called:

"WHITE [Caucasian-Semitic] BACKLASH."

Certainly the so-called "BACKLASH," which this Black Man prefer to call by its correct de-signation - "WHITE" or "SEMITIC RACISM," will be felt in this work, as in all of the other

---

1. See Y. ben-Jochannan's CULRUTAL GENOCIDE IN THE BALCK AND AFRICAN STUDIES CURRICULUM.

works Blacks venture to write and publish that fail to meet the good OLE MAN RIVER, UNCLE TOM' and/or 'AUNT TOMASINA' knee-bending posture expected of all writers of African origin. Of course the expression - "ALL OF THE PEOPLE OF AFRICAN ORIGIN" - does not exclude most of the 20th Century C.E. so-called "SEMITE-CAUCASIAN" and/or "WHITE JEWS," whose biblical palaeontological past reveals that they too are descendants of "BLACK SLAVEMASTERS ["Canaanites"] OF EGYPT" [Ta-Merry] who migrated from as far SOUTH in Alkebu-lan [Africa] as Puanit, Itiopi, Meröe, and other nations along the entire length of the Great Lakes regions where the Ta-Merrians [Egyptians] originated - according to their own teachings in the COFFIN and PYRAMID TEXTS, etc. And as such, one must wonder which one of the so-called "SEMITIC JEWS" can come forward and prove that his or her "HEBREW [Israelite, Jewish, etc.] AN-CESTORS'MOTHER" was not sired by her biblical "HAMITIC, CANAANITE" or "Negro" SLAVE-MASTERS - his or her descendant from Adam and Eve in the Garden of Eden, to Noah and the Great Deluge [Flood], to Abraham in the City of Ur, Chaldea, even to Moses in his native Alkebu-lan at the City of Soccoth, Ta-Merry [Egypt]. One must equally wonder: Which one of the so-called "CURSED NEGROES " whose ancestors were RAPED by every kind of European and Euro-pean-American Jewish and Christian SLAVEMASTERS up to less than 109 years ago physically, and to the present mentally, can prove that his or her MOTHER's female ancestors did not suf-fer the same fate? But are we [Black People] to assume that the "WHITE [Caucasian-Semitic] JEWS" who have carefully suppressed information about the existence of hundreds of thousands of "BLACK JEWS" [Falassa or Beta Israelis - Children of the House of Israel] in Itiopi, East Alkebu-lan,[1] Nigeria, West Alkebu-lan,[2] and elsewhere over the entire world, can tell which one of them had a pure "LILY-WHITE SEMITIC FEMALE ANCESTRY" all the way back to the two Africans of Ta-Merry's "civil war" over whose God - YWH or RA - was the right one approxi-mately 3,205 years ago [Pharaoh Rameses II vs Moses ca. 1228 B.C.E. - 1974 C.E.]?

What could have caused "Negro" Clergymen, "Negro" Clergywomen, "Negro" Theologians and "Negro" Professors to keep quiet on the areas of RACISM and RELIGIOUS BIGOTRY within the Jewish and Christian "HOLY WRITINGS," most of which is attributed to their own "GOD IN-SPIRED SCRIBES;" even those of today? We can easily understand that it was the so-called

---

1. See Y. ben-Jochannan's AFRICAN ORIGINS OF THE MAJOR WESTERN RELIGIONS, pp. 138-194; W. Leslau's FALASHAS ANTHOLOGY; J. STONE's BLACK JEWS OF ETHIOPIA, pp. 9 - 15; J.A. Rogers' WORLD'S GREAT MEN OF COLOR; R. Windsor's FROM BABYLON TO TIMBUK-TU; and I. Stern's THE NEGRO JEWS OF EAST AND WEST AFRICA, pp. 197 - 314.
2. See Y. ben-Jochannan's AFRICAN ORIGINS OF THE MAJOR "WESTERN RELIGIONS," Chap-ter Three; J.J. Williams' HEBREWISM IN WEST AFRICA; J.C. deGraft-Johnson's AFRICAN GLORY; and Dr. A. Churchward's SIGNS AND SYMBOLS OF PRIMORDIAL MAN.

CLERGY's fear of their master's vengeance during the historical period ca. 1619 to 1865 C.E. - the "SLAVE TRADING" and "COLONIAL PLANTATION" periods. However, since the so-called "RECONSTRUCTION PERIOD;" what is their favorite excuse? EVERYTHING IMAGINABLE! Thus they continue waiting on their "WHITE CAUCASIAN-SEMITIC" colleagues to write prophetically for them as their sole "AUTHORITY." Then they comment on said "PROPHETIC WORKS" adversely; but only in private "NEGRO-WHITE" and/or "COLORED-WHITE" ministerial gatherings designed to promote what they prefer to call [hypocritically]...

"INTERFAITH" and/or "INTER-RACIAL HARMONY."

But why do they act as such? They have failed to make researches of their own into the sources of the materials they always pass on to their younger up-and-coming Black Seminarians in their charge without the slightest means of verification. All of these questions are answerable in the negative; sad as it may be. Thus what the BLACK [not "Negro"] CLERGY really needs is at least one aggressive BLACK SEMINARY some place within the United States of America where BLACK [not "Negro" or "Coloured"] THEOLOGIANS and other BLACK [not "Negro"] SCHOLARS can enter into meaningful research and writing about all of the religious and theosophical documents, literature, artifacts and institutions there are; fearing nothing they will discover that does not totally agree with the European and European-American oriented "BRAINWASHINGS" "Negroes" and/or "Colored Folks" have been subjected too all these years since 1619 or 1620 C.E. from WHITES, and subsequently from aping "NEGROES," self-proclaimed "AUTHORITY" on God - viz-a-viz "YWH" and "JESUS CHRIST."

There must be a new BLACK THEOLOGY which goes back to our Alkehu-lan [African] Original Theology and Theosophy for BLACK THEOLOGIANS to follow in terms of projecting the BLACK PRIDE African [BLACK] People are reacerting. This must be in preference to our becoming totally consumed with "AFRO HAIR STYLES" and/or "MILITANT MARXISM" as the sole extent of our protest against Judaeo-Christian CAUCASIAN-SEMITIC WHITE NATIONALISM and/or ANTI-BLACK CULTURAL GENOCIDE which add more monies from the Black Communities into the coffers of WHITE so-called "ENTREPRENUERS." This is not in any way or form condemning the CULTURAL REAPPRAISAL in which African People are involved in order to regain our HUMAN DECENCY - "BLACK POWER." Thus, a new frontal attack must be entered into; and this must be very speedy indeed. But what is to be our "first step?"

THE CREATION OF A "BLACK BIBLE" TO SUIT OUR BLACK
EXPERIENCE DOWN THROUGH THE AGES; FROM BEFORE
THE BIRTH OF ADAM AND EVE IN ca. 3760 B.C.E. to 1974 C.E.

The precedence for the above was established before the "FIRST HEBREW [Jewish] BIBLE [Pentateuch, Torah, Five Books Of Moses, Old Testament, etc.] was began in ca. 700 B.C.E.

and finally completed in ca. 500 B.C.E., REVISED and RE-REVISED hundreds of times to suit Europeans and European-Americans of every religious faith that did not agree with the contents written by the original BLACK and BROWN "God-inspired Holy Scribes" who were in every respect similar to those who wrote the original BOOK OF THE COMING FORTH BY DAY AND BY NIGHT [Book Of The Dead] and PAPYRUS OF ANI that preceded the "CHOSEN [Caucasian, Indo-European, Aryan, Pure White, etc.] PEOPLE'S" VERSION of said African [BLACK] People's works. WHY? Because the WHITE BIBLES were created to suit the WHITE PEOPLE'S own

RACIAL, IDEOLOGICAL and PERSONAL NEEDS.

The King James Authorized Version Of The Old And New Testament was done in this manner and context; and as such is no better or worse than any of the other European and European-American "VERSIONS." Thus the BLACK BIBLE, another Alkebu-lan [African] Original, which will equally be written by "INSPIRED" BLACK "SCRIBES," cannot be any less "AUTHORITA-TIVE" than any of the other "INSPIRED" WHITE "SCRIBES" VERSIONS - King James' included. For the African People must remember that...'A VERSION IS NOT THE FIRST OF ANYTHING ORIGINAL," whatever the "ORIGINAL" is, was, or will ever be. A "VERSION" is the plagiarized subtefuge of the only "ORIGINAL." It could never become a "TRUE COPY OF THE ORIGINAL." For it is not even a FACIMILE OF THE ORIGINAL. It is in fact, for all good and purpose, AN ABSOLUTE FRAUD in most cases.

[IMPUT QUALITY] What are some of the "Original Imput Needs" in order to produce the "ONE AND ONLY "GOD INSPIRED" AUTHORIZED HOLY BIBLE...according to Black People, instead of the existing so-called ONE AND ONLY "GOD INSPIRED" AUTHORIZED HOLY BIBLE...according to White People like the following VERSIONS:

LATIN VULGATE, DUOAY-RHAMES, GUTTENBERG, KING HENRY, KING JAMES, AMERICAN STANDARD, BABYLONIAN TALMUD, HOLY TORAH, EVERY DAY, etc.-

European and European-American Jews, Christians, Mormons, Christian Scientists, Jehovah Witnesses, Holy Rollers, etc., as they will be shown chronologically from page 82 of this volume? All of the entire "books" and "commentaries" must be cleansed,at least; but more than likely completely scraped, in order to represent the Alkebu-lan-Asian ORIGINALS. However, the following twentyfive [25] points are a must for the BLACK [African People s] BIBLE:

1. Relate "CREATION" both to religion and evolution.
2. Remove the "SIN" syndrome stigma against women in childbirth.
3. Show the relationship between "SEXUAL INTERCOURSE" and "CREATION."
4. Show the PHARAOHS and other Africans of Ta-Merry's [Egypt's] God-Head - RA - side of the EXODUS STORY like those who worshiped the God-Head - YWH; giving the names of all ivolved besides the Hebrews [Jews] and their friends.
5. Present MAPS of the geographical locations of the "WORLD OF GENESIS" and that of "EXODUS." Show their comparisons with the WORLD of today.
6. Identify ALKEBU-LAN and ASIAN peoples in all of the various BOOKS, and also those of EUROPE - the EUROPEANS.

7. Use the correct ALKEBU-LAN [African] NAMES of the nations of said continent: Qamt, Qemt, Kimit, Ta-Merry and Pearl of the Nile, instead of Egypt; Zeti, Ta-Nehisi and Meröe, instead of Nubia and Sudan; Axum, Itiopi and Itiopia, instead of Kush, Cush or Abyssinia; etc.

8. Show the REED SEA or SEA OF REEDS, instead of the RED SEA, as the only possible body of water Moses crossed to enter the Sinai Peninsula in the Exodus.

9. Show examples of the major plagiarization made by the Hebrews of the Nile Valley to their fellow Africans' works they used to produce their own FIVE BOOKS OF MOSES; such as Moses using the "Negative Confessions" for the "Ten Commandments;" Solomon using Amen-em-eope's Teachings to produce the "Proverbs;" even to the name of the Hebrew God-Head "YWH" from one of the Gods of Ta-Merry.

10. Show that Moses, Solomon and Jesus Christ attended the Grand Lodge of Luxor, along with other Subordinate Lodges down the banks of the Nile River, to receive their own education in RELIGIOUS-MAGIC, etc.; all of which became the foundation of present day Judaism, Christianity and Islam, etc.

11. Give the proper names of all of the "PHARAOHS" alluded too throughout the Old and New Testament, and also the Qur'an. Equally, show the periods when they reigned over the Nile Valley High-Cultures - Ta-Merry, Ta-Nehissi, Itiopi, Punt, etc.

12. Show pictures of the AFRICAN PEOPLES mentioned in the Bible according to the geography of their origins: Egyptians, Ethiopians, Nubians, Puanits, etc. as BLACK; Persians, Assyrians, etc. as BROWN; Greeks, Romans, etc. as WHITE.

13. Show Jesus Christ and his family's having "HAIR LIKE LAMB'S WOOL" and "SKIN LIKE THE SOOT OF THE CHIMNEY" according to the Biblical teachings before the VERSIONS and REVISIONS to the original texts by WHITE racists.

14. Remove the "DEVIL" as of any COLOR human beings have; particularly BLACK.

15. Remove the clauses where GOD CONDONES SLAVERY, and/or ORDERS it.

16. Delete the "GOD'S CHOSEN PEOPLE" racism and religious bigotry from the Old and New Testament.

17. Remove all aspects where GOD goes around like a raving maniac killing everyone who does not agree with his "Chosen People."

18. Place the "HEBREW WORLD" and their "GREAT DELUGE" [flood] in their geographical perspective to the "WORLD OF TODAY" [ca. ????].

20. Return all of the BOOKS OF THE [original] BIBLE to their proper chronological order before the Council Of Jamnia and the Council Of Nicene; and stop calling those removed at either Council "LOST BOOKS OF THE BIBLE."

21. Return Mary's "VIRGINITY" syndrone in the New Testament back to the original... "TO A WOMAN A CHILD WILL BE BORN, AND HIS NAME SHALL BE THE EMANUEL..." etc..., as originally stated before the Nicene Council [or Conference] Of Bishops ordered by Emperor Constantine "the great" in ca. 322 C.E.

22. Return Jesus Christ of Nazareth to the principal figure of Christendom and replace "SAUL OF TARSUS", otherwise known as "PAUL" or "SAINT PAUL," where he rightfully belongs....In the background of Jesus "the Christ" [anointed].

23. Show Joseph and Mary as any other PARENTS that produced a HUMAN BEING.

24. Emphasize the HUMAN SIDE of Jesus Christ according to the HUMAN MAGIC or MIRACLES he performed; that which made millions follow his TEACHINGS, even in DEATH, and his proclaimed "RESURRECTION" and "DIVINITY."

25. Include the works of the BLACK PROPHETS and BLACK SAINTS, such as: Edward W. Blyden, Marcus Moziah Garvey, W.E.B. DuBois, Kwame Nkrumah, John Chilimbwe, Albiso Campus, Mohammed ibn Kholdoun, Rhabad ibn Battuta, and all of the others who preached but did not reduce their teachings to writing.

All of the issues one could have listed would be no less "PROPHETIC" than those existing in the WHITE VERSIONS. Since it was only ninetyfive [95] years following the "birth of Moses" in ca. 1039 B.C.E. that he became "THE WORLD'S FIRST PROPHET" according to the rabbis and other scribes at the COUNCIL OF JAMNIA, which met for the first time at the end of the FIRST CHRISTIAN CENTURY [C.E. or A.D.]. The "LAST PROPHET" of the Hebrews, according to the same men, was "EZRA." Note that the Moslems and Muslims said "MOHAMET ibn ABDULLAH" was the last one; the Bahai claimed it was "BAHAULAH" - who followed the latter. Thus the "GOD INSPIRED" Holy Black Scribes will have to show that the WHITE rabbis' action, with respect to their first LIST OF THE PROPHETS, was based upon their own abritrary closing of the "CANON OF HEBREW BOOKS" they REVISED, REARRANGED and made "AUTHORITY." The Black Scribes must let Black People know that said rabbis and other 'scribes' listed the following reasons to justify their own abritrary closing-off of further "PROPHETS OF THE PENTATEUCH" [Five Books Of Moses, Holy Torah, Old Testament, etc.]:

1. The need to stop the constant additions to the SECTARIAN APOCALYPHTIC TEXTS by all kinds of untrained and unrighteous men;
2. the effects of the conquest and fall of their religion's Holy City - JERUSALEM - in ca. 70 C.E. according to the "Holy Scriptures," one of the most traumatic experience in Jewish history; a period when the "Chosen People's" God allowed them to be slaughtered by the "un-Godly" that threatened to do away with their Hebraic traditions [real and unreal]; and
3. the "heated disputes" that arose between Christian interpreters [many of them formerly Jews] of the "Hebrew Scriptures," preaching of it, and writing of it therein.

Of course, included were the plagiarized VERSIONS of the Nile Valley Africans of RA works the Africans of YWH coopted from the Mysteries System in Ta-Merry, Northeast Alkebu-lan.

It is to be remembered that everything pertaining to "GOD" which Moses allegedly passed down in the PENTATEUCH [Old Testament, etc.] for his Hebrew [Jewish] descendants that conflicted with any other people's RELIGIOUS WRITINGS or TEACHINGS, the non-Hebrew VERSION was immediately declared "NON-PROPHETIC" by the Hebrews. Thus; "NOT OF CANON QUALITY." And all of the Hebrews works that did not conform with the period between MOSES and EZRA the rabbis of the COUNCIL equally considered...

"THE PROPHETIC AND INSPIRED WORDS OF GOD."

Because of rabbinical pressures, however, all of the original THIRTY-NINE [39] BOOKS OF THE PENTATEUCH [Old Testament] were made part of the PALESTINIAN CANON OF SCRIPTURES - those Hebrew TEXTS written within the socio-political and geo-political limits of Palestine [Judah and Israel]. But all of the BOOKS outside of the criteria established by said rabbis [human beings like any of us today] were finally classified as the "APOCRYPHA" or "PSEUDEPIGRAPHIA" in their European VERSIONS at the Nicene Conference of ca. 322 - 325

74

C.E. [A.D.]. The last two names seem to look and sound very impressive to the average member of the "NEGRO CLERGY," as they are constantly throwing them around as if they are of very highly SACRED meaning. But the fact is that the literary English translation of either word simply means...

"FALSE WRITINGS."

Thus any Alkebu-lan ["African" or "Afrikan"] student of "EGYPTOLOGY" and/or "HISTORY" must wonder why the following Alkebu-lan teaching about the...

"DOCTRINE OF ETERNAL LIFE"

was illiminated from the so-called "PROPHETIC WORKS" in the Pentateuch [Old Testament] and New Testament of the Hebrew, Christian and Islamic religions and/or socio-political High-Cultures; when in fact Judaism, Christianity and Islam adopted this principle of "LIFE AFTER DEATH" from the teachings of the Alkebu-lans [BLACKS or AFRICANS] of the Nile Valley – particularly those of Ta-Nehisi, Meröe, Puanit, Itiopi, Ta-Merry, etc. For this concept is the oldest of the BELIEFS of Judaism, Christianity and Islam. And it is upon this theory that they based the attainment of "IMMORTALITY," as shown in the BOOK OF THE COMING FORTH BY DAY AND BY NIGHT. In the PAPYRUS OF ANI for example, which by the beginning of the VIth Dynasty had gone through numerous REVISIONS, still contains the following teaching about "ETERNAL LIFE" developed by the people of the above mentioned nations of Alkebu-lan:

1. Hail   Unàs,   not   hast thou gone, behold, [as] one dead,
thou hast gone [as] one living to sit upon the throne of Osiris.[1]

2. O Rā-Tum, cometh to thee thy son, cometh to thee   Unàs   .....
thy son is   this   of   thy body   for   ever.[2]

3. O Tum, thy son is   this   Osiris; thou hast given his sustenance
and he liveth; he liveth, and liveth   Unàs   this; not   dieth he,   not
dieth   Unàs   this.[1]

4. Setteth   Unàs   in   life in   Amenta.[2]

75

5. [hieroglyphs]

He[s]   hath eaten   the knowledge   of   god every, [his] existence

[hieroglyphs]

eternity,   his limit everlastingness in   his *sāḥ*[4] this; what

[hieroglyphs]

he willeth he doeth, [what] he hateth   not   doth he do.[5]

6. [hieroglyphs]

Live   life,   not shalt thou die.[6]

In other words the Jewish rabbis and other scribes at the Council Of Jamnia, like their Christian descendants later on in ca. 322 C. E. at the Bishops Conference [Council] Of Nicene that suppressed other "INSPIRED WORDS OF GOD" in the New Testament which they labeled "LOST BOOKS OF THE BIBLE," had decided among themselves what their fellow Jews, and also Christians, later on Moslems, should and should not know about their respective GOD-HEADS - Ywh, Jesus Christ and/or Al'lah; particularly with respect to the ORIGIN of the basics of the African Mysteries System foundation of the Old Testament, New Testament and Holy Qur'an. Thus, it is not peculiar that...

> FIRST and SECOND CLEMENT, the APOCALYPSE OF
> PETER, the DIDACLE, the EPISTLE OF BARNABAS,
> the SHEPHERD OF HERMAS, and the ACTS OF PAUL,

are still kept out of the Christian HOLY BIBLE [New Testament]. This is inspite of the fact that all SEVEN [7] of these BOOKS were originally declared...

> "PART OF THE CANONICAL BOOKS"

by the earliest Christian Church Fathers, even when Christendom was still centered in North Africa under the control of the indigenous African [BLACK] People, particularly among the Egyptians, Nubians and Ethiopians.

One must remember that those early Christians of North and East Africa who determined what was "INSPIRED" and that which was "NOT INSPIRED" in the New Testament, as in the Old Testament, based their entire argument on the following FOUR [4] MAJOR POINTS OF ACCEPTANCE" and/or "REJECTION:"

1. Were the "WRITTEN WORDS" by[a person declared by themselves] "AN APOSTLE OF THE LORD - JESUS CHRIST?"
2. Does the content hold true to the strict "SPIRITUAL NATURE OF CHRIST ABOVE THE MATERIAL MAN "[as evaluated by themselves]?
3. Is the BOOK widely received by the Churches of Christendom as "THE IN-SPIRED WORDS OF GOD "[acceptance by popular demand among themselves].

4. Does the reader of the BOOK receive the feelings of "DIVINE INSPIRA-
TION" when he [never she] reads the "WORDS THEREIN" [the "words of
God" according to their own writing and approval].

The student of ancient and/or modern RELIGION must wonder if the ancient peoples that
read any of the WORKS mentioned above did not become "SPIRITUALLY INSPIRED" and/or
"MENTALLY DIVINE" due to the following extract taken from the Africans of the Nile Valley
and Great Lakes region BOOK OF THE DEAD and PAPYRUS OF ANI.[1]

    " [In] offering to thy god guard against the things
" which are abominations to him. Consider with thine eye
" his dispensations. Devote thyself to the adoration of his
" name. He giveth souls (or will, or strength) to millions
" of forms. He magnifieth him that magnifieth him. The
" god of this earth is Shu, the chief of the horizon. His
" similitudes are upon the earth, and to these incense and
" offerings are given daily,"....

One must wonder: Why did the rabbis and bishops of both periods mentioned before not try
to accept this aspect of the foundation of the teachings from which Judaism, Christianity and
Islam "ORIGINATED?" Because the entire chapter remains condemned by these religions as
"PAGANISM" and "HEATHENISM." Yet it is one of the primary sources of the religious
theories of the Jewish, Christian and Moslem's "HEREAFTER" or "HEAVEN" and "HELL."

Sir Ernest A. Wallis Budge [the noted and renowned egyptologist of the latter half of the
19th and first part of the 20th Century C. E.] reminded us that it was in CHAPTER CLIV of the
"THEBAN RECENSION" in the BOOK OF THE COMING FORTH BY DAY AND BY NIGHT,
which he renamed "BOOK OF THE DEAD" and "PAPYRUS OF ANI," that the main source of
all of the three [3] so-called "WESTERN RELIGIONS OF THE WORLD" - Judaism, Christianity

---

1. See Sir Ernest A. Wallis Budge's BOOK OF THE DEAD, p. 104.

and Islam - got the idea of "THE IMMORTAL NATURE OF GOD." This is clearly shown in the following extract from the PAPYRUS OF ANI:[1]

" Preserve me, O Temu,
" as thou dost thyself from such decay as that which thou
" workest on every god, every goddess, all animals, and all
" creeping things. [Each] passeth away when his soul hath
" gone forth after his death; he perisheth after he hath
" passed away."

The depressing fact of the matter is that all of these types of information were purposely censured, and many suppressed, by the rabbis and the Council Of Jamnia following their plagiarization of them. And it was not until the so-called "EASTER LETTER" of Bishop Athanasius of Alexandria, Egypt, North Africa, written about ca. 367 C.E., approximately THIRTY-FIVE [35] YEARS following the Nicene Conference of Bishops, that the FIRST CHRONOLOGICAL ORDER of the TWENTY-SEVEN [27] BOOKS OF THE NEW TESTAMENT was rendered by the officialdom of the Roman Catholic Church...

"AUTHORITATIVE" and/or "CANON;"

even with the compromise that the leaders of Christendom [European-style] made with the leaders of Judaism [European-style]; all at the expense of the teachings of the Africans they had distorted to produce each and everyone of the "THIRTY-FIVE [35] BOOKS. Equally, it was not until 382 C.E. that [Saint] Jerome followed suit and translated the same TWENTY-SEVEN [27] BOOKS of the "THIRTY-FIVE" [35] into Latin to produce what is still called...

"THE SAINT JEROME VERSION OF THE HOLY BIBLE."

Jerome's masterful distortions became the established basis upon which many of the later VERSIONS of the "HOLY BIBLE" that resulted in the current VERSIONS in use. This, of course, includes the...

"KING JAMES AUTHORIZED VERSION OF THE HOLY BIBLE."

Sad as it may seem, James' VERSION was written to satisfy his own personally PERVERTED SEXUAL desires, much to the chagrin of the Church in Rome, and equally as much for the pleasure of James' royal peers who backed his rebellion against Pope Paul V [1605 -21 C.E.].

---

1. See Sir E.A. Wallis Budge's BOOK OF THE DEAD and PAPYRUS OF ANI, p. 105.

This was accomplished, even to the extent that the characters in both the Old Testament and New Testament appeared to have been brought up speaking Baconian and/or Shakesparean English.."THEE, THY, THOU, THINE"...,etc. This we even noticed in the translations of OUR hundreds of hieroglyphic and hieratic papyri translated by thousands of European and European-American so-called "AUTHORITY ON EGYPT"...otherwise called "EGYPTOLO-GIST." Thus, we can only state that the confusion between the various VERSIONS of the Old Testament paused somewhat at the Council Of Jamnia, at which time all of the existing varia-tions and suppresive materials were reconciled into one common conglamorate TEXT by the "Jewish Scholars" and/or "Rabbis" assembled. What the Black Clergy failed to recognize in all of this is that each and everyone of the so-called "SACRED SCRIBES" who made the dis-tortions, both at the Council Of Jamnia and the Council Of Bishops At Nicene, were human beings like anyone of us today. And that in all of these compromizes the SCHOOL OF MASOR-ETES, under the leadership of Rabbi Akiba, had survived over all others as late as the 2nd Century C.E.; thus the so-called "MASORAH" ["Tradition"] declared its own "Inspired Words Of God"... which became the "STANDARD [Traditional] MASORETIC TEXT." And equally it was; longivity became "AUTHORITY." And of course, plagiarizm became...

"THE INSPIRED WORDS OF GOD."

But the ORIGINAL from which all of the PLAGIARIZED VERSIONS were taken was also demoted to the scorn of ...

"THE HEATHEN WORDS" and/or "PAGAN WORSHIP."

Just imagine that before these self-ordained "SACRED SCRIBES" were able to settle their own arguments between themselves on who was "RIGHT" or "WRONG" [the "great compro-mize"], more than 4,000 "GREEK SACRED TEXTS" [manuscripts] and 8,000 "LATIN SACRED TEXTS" were in existence, including more than 1,200 other texts written in numerous other languages and combination of languages until ca. 200 C.E. [A.D.]. This was about the period when the same so-called "BIBLICAL SCHOLARS" made it their pride and joy to SUPPRESS the use of the original Hieroglyph and other types of African languages in the Old Testament and New Testament, equally as they had done with the ORIGINAL African sources they plagiar-ized and used in the preparation of their own interpretations of the RELIGIONS of the Nile Val-ley Mysteries System's TEACHINGS. Not one source of these they have credited its African ORIGIN, or even mentioned any indigenous African by designation. They did not show one ex-cept as an occasional "SLAVE" for their special characters they created as the "CHOSEN PEOPLE OF GOD"... Ywh, Jesus Christ or Al'lah; GOD not being able to appear other than "WHITE, BLONDE, CAUCASIAN-SEMITIC," or with any other name.

Maybe it is best that the Black Clergy and Black Theologians take a few minutes out from their PLAGIARIZED European and European-American VERSIONS of the Old Testament and New Testament to look at the twenty-four [24] of more than three thousand [3,000] major "VERSIONS" of the various types of "HOLY BIBLES" still in existence, most of which are still being used to this very day, especially the KING JAMES AUTHORIZED VERSION OF THE OLD AND NEW TESTAMENT that dominates all of the others in the Black Communities throughout the entire world. Certainly all of the machinations in the establishment of today's "OFFICIAL AUTHORIZED VERSION" of any so-called "HOLY BIBLE " [Old Testament or New Testament] more than proved the need for a separate...

BLACK BIBLE.

A Black Bible that will restore the following extract from the PYRAMID TEXT OF PHARAOH PEPI I to its First Book. Here we have "...THE OLDEST OF THE GODS... Tem"...[1] letting everyone know that HE existed when...

not   was   sky, not   was   earth, not   were   men,

not   were   born   the gods, not   was   death.

The above was in reference to the "OLDEST GOD...THE DIVINE GOD." His name is written in Hieroglyph as follows:

Tem, or Àtmu

God – TEM – was said to be the 'ONLY'...

"divine god," the "self-created," the "maker of the gods," the "creator of men," "who stretched out the heavens," "who illumineth the Tuat with his Eyes " (i.e., the sun and moon).

And He was even more POWERFUL than Jehovah, Jesus Christ and/or Al'lah. TEM even "CREATED HIMSELF; " and for His own survival He made...

"THE GREAT MASS OF CELESTIAL WATERS... OF Nu .[1]

Before we look at the chronology of the various VERSIONS of the ancient religious rites, magic, incantations, confessions, commandments, and even "VIRGIN BIRTHS, RESURREC-

---

1. See PYRAMID TEXT OF PEPI, 1. 664

80

TIONS, REINCARNATIONS" and "IMMORTAL DIVINATIONS " adopted in the so-called New Testament, Old Testament and Holy Qur'an, let us pay a bit of attention to the following extract from John G. Jackson's MAN, GOD, AND CIVILIZATION. [1] He wrote:

> The earliest religion of Egypt has been traced back to central Africa:
>
>> The oldest structure of the people [again citing Petrie] was that which resembled the African in beliefs and practices. There is a large body of customs, especially those concerning the dead, which are closely alike in ancient Egypt and modern Central Africa. In this stratum, probably preceding 10,000 B.C., animal worship was usual; so strong was the primitive influence that this remained in practice down to the Roman age. The source of this was a sense of kinship of men and animals. ("The Gods of Ancient Egypt," in 111, p. 667)

Professor Jackson, quoting the noted "scholar" Ernest Busenbark, also wrote the following about the ancient ... CUSTOMS and MYTHS of the Africans of Central Africa that became the Egyptians, Nubians, Meröites, Ethiopians, Puanits, etc. Here you will notice the continuance of the so-called "MASONIC NUMEROLOGY" [an aspect shown on the front cover of this volume] developed in Central Africa, passed on to North Africa where the Hebrews adopted it, then to Asia, and finally into Europe where the Greeks placed it into the New Testament, which the Romans further distorted. All of this originated in the TEACHINGS of the Mysteries System of the Africans' Grand Lodge and its Subordinate Lodges all over the ancient world in Alkebulan, Asia and Europe where the Alkebu-lanians ["Africans"] went as conquerors and educators:

> At an extremely early date, a connection had doubtless been observed between the 28-day cycle of the moon and the menstrual cycle of women, and between changes of the moon and ocean. tides. To people of the East, marriage and childbirth have always been the supreme duty and goal of women, and the moon, who they believed controlled or regulated fecundity and the generation of life, became known as the Great Regulator. Some significances may also have been seen in the fact that the human foetus is fully developed in 7 months, or the gestation of both women and cows takes place in 280 days, or ten 28-day months. This period also represents 40 weeks, which may explain why, among ancient people, the number 40 is habitually associated with periods of temptation, trial, hardship, and pain for 40 days, weeks, months, or years. For example, we have the 40 days and nights of the Deluge, 40 years of wandering in the wilderness by the Israelites, 40 days and nights of fasting by Moses on Mt. Sinai; 40 days and nights of Christ in the wilderness; 40 days between the resurrection of Christ and his final disappearance from the earth; 40 days of mourning for the death of Jacob; 40 days of fasting by Elijah on Mount Horeb; 40 days in which Ezekiel bore the iniquity of the House of Judah; 40 days of sacrifice in the old Persian Salutation of Mithra; 40 nights of mourning in the Mysteries of Persephone; 40 days of mourning by the Babylonians before the celebration of the festival of the Descent of Ishtar, which corresponds to the Christian Lenten period of 40 days from Ash Wednesday to Easter.

---

1. See John G. Jackson's MAN, GOD, AND CIVILIZATION, pp. 145 - 146.

The MAGICAL NUMBER SYSTEM shown on the previous page was taken from the Myster-ies System's "MASONIC NUMEROLOGY" which the Greeks converted into today's base for "ASTROLOGY," and also used in their own "MYTHOLOGY" the Hebrews, Christians and Mos-lems adopted for their "JUDAEO-CHRISTIAN-ISLAMIC" mysticism found in their Old Testa-ment, New Testament and Holy Qur'an.

> Why, when no honest man will deny in private that every ultimate problem is wrapped in the profoundest mystery, do honest men proclaim in pulpits that unhesitating certainty is the duty of the most foolish and igno-rant? We are a company of ignorant beings, dimly discerning light enough for our daily needs, but hopelessly differing whenever we attempt to de-scribe the ultimate origin or end of our paths; and yet, when one of us ven-tures to declare that we don't know the map of the universe as well as the map of our infinitesimal parish, he is hooted, reviled and perhaps told that he will be damned to all eternity for his faithlessness.

A CHRONOLOGICAL LIST OF THE 'BOOK OF THE DEAD' AND ITS PLAGIARIZED VERSIONS: OLD TESTAMENT, NEW TESTAMENT, HOLY QUR'AN[2]

Date: B.C.E. [B.C.]	Description
10,000 - 6000	STELLAR CALENDAR placed in use by the ancient Nile Valley Africans, and others of the Great Lakes regions.
4000 - 4000	SOLAR CALENDAR placed in use by the ancient Nile Valley Africans.
4000 - 4000	BOOK OF THE COMING FORTH BY DAY AND BY NIGHT, mankind's very first bible introduced by the Africans of the Nile Valley. [English traslation from the original Hiero-glyph by Sir E.A. Wallis Budge called "BOOK OF THE DEAD and PAPYRUS OF ANI, London, 1885 C.E.].
3760	BEGINNING OF THE WORLD according to the "Creation Story" projected by the Hebrews' "First Patriarch."
3100 ["4100"]	DYNASTIC PERIODS BEGIN under the Ta-Nehisian named AHA or NARMER [Herodotus' "Menes"]. End of the PRE-DYNASTIC "OLD KINGDOMS."
1770	BIRTH OF THE HEBREWS "FIRST PATRIARCH" - Abraham, in the City of Ur, Chaldea to Sun Worshipers whose God was RA.
1675	FOREIGN INVASION OF TA-MERRY, Alkebu-lan by Hyksos.

1. See FORTHRIGHT REVIEW, 1876; and J.G. Jackson's GOD, MAN, AND CIVILIZATION, p. 155.
2. See Geddes MacGregor's A LITERARY HISTORY OF THE BIBLE, etc. for a historical evaluation and detail of the facts so far disclosed.

Date: B.C.E. [B.C.]	Description
	They came from the so-called "Fertile Crescent" area of Asia. These are the first so-called "SEMITIC" people.
1670	ABRAHAM AND FAMILY ARRIVED IN TA-MERRY, which the Hebrews later on called "Mizrain," the Arab Moslems' "Mizrair," and the Christians' "Egypt."
1320 [?]	MOSES BORN IN TA-MERRY, Alkebu-lan of African parents that worshipped the God-Head YWH instead of the God-Head RA.
1230 [?]	MOSES BEGAN HIS CIVIL WAR WITH PHARAOH RAMESES II. YEAR OF THE EXODUS from Succoth to Sinai [Mt. Horeb].
1190 [?]	MOSES "RECEIVED THE TEN COMMANDMENTS FROM YWH." MOSES DISAPPEARED ON MOUNT HOREB [or Mt. Sinai].
700 - 500	PENTATEUCH [Holy Torah, Five Books Of Moses, Old Testament] written. Hebrews VERSION of the BOOK OF THE DEAD; supposedly the words of God passed down to Moses.., etc.
250 - 100	SEPTUAGINT BIBLE [the first Version of the Pentateuch] written in the Greek language, and distorted to conform with Greek mythological teachings. Seventy-two [72] "God inspired scribes" allegedly wrote it, according to the teachings of Jews, Christians and Moslems. Written at Alexandria, "Egypt," by African Hebrews. A compliment of forty-five [45] BOOKS that is also called "THE ALEXANDRIAN CANON" - the VERSION used in the earliest Greek and Latin churches.
30 - 4 [?] - 0	BIRTH OF JESUS - "The Christ Child" - OF NAZARETH PROCLAIMED. The announcement of and infant boy - "SAVIOUR" - born to Hebrew [Israelite or Jewish] parents named Joseph and Mary. At this period there was no mention about any "IMMACULATE CONCEPTION" and/or "VIRGIN BIRTH" taking place in
Date: B.C.E. - C.E. - 0 Date: C.E. [A.D.] 0 - 0	this family...the so-called "HOLY FAMILY." BEGINNING OF THE CHRISTIAN ERA...," etc.
12	JESUS CHRIST CHALLENGED HIS TEACHERS [pharasies and rabbis] IN THE TEMPLE. JESUS SENT TO ALKEBU-LAN ["Egypt"] TO HIDE FROM ROMAN EMPEROR HEROD. JESUS ENTERED TA-MERRIAN LODGES FOR HIS INITIATION [circumcission] AND EDUCATION IN THE MYSTERIES SYSTEM OF TA-MERRY, TA-NEHISI, MERÖE and ITIOPI.
30	JESUS CHRIST RETURNED FROM SCHOOL IN ALKEBU-LAN.
33	JESUS CHRIST MURDERED BY A MOD OF ROMAN SOLDIERS AND HIS FELLOW HEBREWS.
52	KOINE BIBLE WRITTEN. First Christian Bible or "Gospel Prophecy and Revealations" - NEW TESTAMENT. Written in the Greek language and Aramaic language.- allegedly "spoken by Jesus." Also called PALESTINIAN CANON. Developed by the Synod of Jamnia as a VERSION of the PENTATEUCH and "ITS DIVINE REVEALATIONS FROM GOD...JESUS CHRIST."

83

Date: C.E. [A.D.]	Description
322	COUNCIL OF BISHOPS OF NICENE CONVENED. This group of Bishops of the Roman Catholic Church met on the order of Emperor Constantine and Pope Paul Vth to take action on the following questions: 1] WAS JESUS CHRIST GOD? 2] WAS MARY CONCEIVED BY THE HOLY GHOST WHEN SHE BECAME WITH-CHILD WITH JESUS? 3] WHICH BOOKS OF THE BIBLE ARE THE INSPIRED WORDS OF GOD?
325	COUNCIL OF BISHOPS AT NICENE DECLARED: 1] "The Holy Trinity of Jesus - the Christ." 2] "The Immaculate Conception Of Jesus Christ" and "The Virgin Birth Of Jesus - The Christ." 3] The Lost Books Of The Bible or the suppression of many BOOKS that were originally in the OLD and NEW TESTAMENT. JESUS CHRIST becomes "GOD THE FATHER, THE SON, AND THE HOLY GHOST" [presently "Spirit"].
350 – 400	NEW TESTAMENT CANON VERSION. The first twenty-seven [27] BOOKS. A revision and distortion of the ORIGINAL [total] forty-five [45] BOOKS.
400	SAINT JEROME'S LATIN VULGATE VERSION. Based upon the Greek Septuagint Version. A further distortion of the previous.
550 [?]	EUROPEAN VERSION OF THE BABYLONIAN TALMUD. The first of the Sixth Century C.E. racist VERSIONS of the "Standard INTERPRETATIONS and TRANSLATION of the Pentateuch by Eastern European rabbis and other scholars."
570 [52 B.H.][1]	BIRTH OF THE PROPHET MOHAMET ibn ABDULLAH IN MECCA or MEDINA TO A KOREYSH [Qureysh] FAMILY.
622	YEAR OF THE HAJIRA [Hajera, Hagira, etc.]. The year the Prophet Mohamet had to flee Mecca to Medina at the Oasis Of Yathrib where he founded the RELIGION OF ISLAM.
670 [?]	HOLY QUR'AN [English "KORAN"] PUBLISHED. Adoption of the basic scriptures of the Old and New Testament with evaluations and interpretations to suit the Arabian High-Culture. Prophet Mohamet ibn Abdullah declared "The Last of the Prophets " [Completely influenced by the Ethiopian - Hadzart Bilal ibn Rahbad].
900 – 600	MASORETIC TEXT. This version was written in Hebrew by Jewish scribes of the Masorite School. It became the base version for following VERSIONS by Christians and Jews.
1382	JOHN WYCLIFF'S FIRST COMPLETE ENGLISH VERSION OF THE OLD TESTAMENT AND NEW TESTAMENT.
1460 [?]	MOSES ben-MAIMONEDEES TALMUD. First Western European "Official Translation" [VERSION] and "INTERPRETATION" of the the Pentateuch; written in Spain.
1456	GUTTENBERG VERSION OF THE HOLY BIBLE. The "first book" ever printed on a typesetting press. A folio-type edition of the

---

1. See Y. ben-Jochannan's AFRICAN ORIGIN OF THE MAJOR "WESTERN RELIGIONS, Chapt. 4

Date: C.E. [A.D.]	Description
	Latin Vulgate Version. It was not "the first book," as so many Christians believe.
1516	SAINT ERASMUS VERSION OF THE HOLY BIBLE. This was written in the Greek Language.
1529	REVEREND MARTIN LUTHER PROTEST AGAINST THE "EDICT OF THE DIET OF WORMS," the early Reformation. Birth of the major revolution in the Roman Catholic Church and the formation of the foundation of Protestantism.
1535	WILLIAM TYNDALE VERSION. Written in English. "The first English language version." It became the basis for further English and European-American VERSIONS.
1335	MILES COVERDALE VERSION OF THE HOLY BIBLE. Written in English as a tribute to King Henry VIIIth of Great Britain.
1537	THE FIRST BIBLE PRINTED IN ENGLAND RELEASED.
1537	SAINT MATTHEW'S VERSION OF THE HOLY BIBLE. Written in English according to the Coverdale and Tyndale VERSIONS.
1539	COVERDALE GREAT BIBLE VERSION. An amalgamation of the Coverdale and Tyndale bibles, as authorized by the monarch of Great Britain -- Henry VIIIth.
1560	GENEVA VERSION OF THE HOLY BIBLE. Written by Coverdale, William Whittingham, John Knox, et al. Produced in Geneva, Switzerland. The "first English Version with Chapters divided into Verses." Done during the reign Queen Mary of Great Britain; and in her honour.
1582 - 1610	DOUAY-RHEIMS VERSION OF THE HOLY BIBLE. Written by scholars of the Roman Catholic Church. An English translation of the Latin Vulgate Version done at the Catholic College. The name was due to the New Testament issuance at Rheims in 1582 C.E.; whereas the Old Testament issuance was at Douay, France in ca. 1609 or 1610 C.E.
1611	KING JAMES AUTHORIZED VERSION OF THE OLD AND NEW TESTAMENT. Written by subjects of King James of Great Britain to satisfy conditions set down by himself and the royalty of his realm, all of which was opposed by the Pope in Rome; particularly those aspects that allowed James to maintain his own promiscuous behavior. This is the VERSION most Black People believe to be "THE ONE AND ONLY TRUE HOLY SCRIPTURE... THE ACTUAL WORDS OF GOD" [meaning Jesus - the Christ of Nazareth], which was allegedly "...WRITTEN BY GOD INSPIRED SCRIBES." The Black Clergy, and their "Negro Theologians," perpetuate this myth in order to continue their manipulation of their fellow African People who so believe upon their words.
1885	ENGLISH REVISED VERSION OF THE HOLY BIBLE. Complete with much more extensive distortions than those already listed in the

85

Dates: C. E. [A.D.]	Description
	above King James Authorized Version Of The Old and New Testament.by Europeans and European-Americans from the United States of America. This was the "first time in history" that European-Americans were allowed to participate in the further distortions of the ORIGINAL TEACHINGS from the Africans and Asians of the Nile Valley and Tigris-Euphrates valleys Magical-Religious Theosophy, Theology and Philosophy.
1901	AMERICAN STANDARD VERSION OF THE HOLY BIBLE. By the American Committee that worked on the English Revised Version of 1885 C.E. Jealousy between Europeans and European-Americans caused the production of this VERSION.within the U.S.A.
1924	THE MOFFATT VERSION OF THE HOLY BIBLE. By James Moffatt. It was said to be written in"Twentieth Century modern English."
1931	SMITH-GOODSPEED VERSION OF THE HOLY BIBLE. The Old Testament was prepared by J.M. Powis-Smith as editor; the New Testament by Edgar J. Goodspeed of the University of Chicago, Illinois, U.S.A.
1941	THE CONFRATERNITY VERSION OF THE HOLY BIBLE. A revision of the Douay-Rheims-Challomer Version. The New Testament section was published by the Episcopal Confraternity of the Christian Doctrine of the Roman Catholic Church; the Old Testament section remained according to the Latin Vulgate Version.
1945 – 1949	KNOX VERSION OF THE HOLY BIBLE. Written in English by Msgr. Ronald A. Knox according to the Latin Vulgate Version authorized by the Roman Catholic Command of Wales and England to counteract the King James Authorized Version.
1952	REVISED STANDARD VERSION OF THE HOLY BIBLE. Written by a group of the United States of America's European-American "GOD INSPIRED SCRIBES" under the sponsorship of the National Council Of Churches Of Christ.
1961	NEW ENGLISH VERSION OF THE HOLY BIBLE. Written by a group of English writers under the sponsorship of the Protestant Churches of Britain, and by others from Oxford and Cambridge University press.
1973	THE COMMON AMERICAN LANGUAGE VERSION. This was approved by a group of rabbis, priests, ministers and theologians who found all of its contents satisfactory to the TEACHINGS of Judaism and Christianity in the United States of America.

[THE PEOPLE OF THE ORIGINAL BIBLE]   Having examined copies of each and everyone of

the above so-called "INSPIRED WORDS OF GOD" in the Old Testament and New Testament,

also the Holy Qur'an, one should be more than convinced that the original BOOK OF THE COM-

ING FORTH BY DAY AND BY NIGHT that preceded the "CREATION OF THE WORLD" by Ywh,

Jesus Christ and/or Al'lah is the basis upon which the BLACK BIBLE must rest. The reason

86

or this is multifold. Some of the qualifying factors continues.

Professor John G. Jackson of the BLACK STUDIES DEPARTMENT, College of Arts and Science of Rutgers University, Newark Campus, Newark, New Jersey, commenting on "the African origin of the ancient religions and their teachings," emphasized on Sir H. Rawlinson's archaeological and philological works. But it is the "celebrated Canon George Rawlinson of Canterbury," the brother of the General, he cited in the following extract:[1]

> A laborious study of the primitive language of Chaldea, led him (Sir Henry Rawlinson) to the conviction that the dominant race in Babylonia at the earliest time to which the monuments reached back was Kushite. He found the vocabulary of the primitive race to be decidedly Kushite or Ethiopian, and he was able to interpret the inscriptions chiefly by the aid which was furnished to him from published works on the Galla (Abyssinian) and Mahra (South Arabian) dialects. He noted moreover, a considerable resemblance in the system of writing which the primitive race employed, and that which was established from a very remote date in Egypt. Both were pictorial; both to a certain extent symbolic; both in some instances used identically the same symbols. Again, he found words in use among the primitive Babylonians and their neighbors and kinsmen, the Susianians, which seemed to be identical with ancient Egyptian or Ethiopic roots. The root *hyk* or *hak*, which Manetho interprets as *king*, and which is found in the well known *Hyksos* or *Shepherd Kings*, appeared in Babylonian and Susianian royal names under the form of *Khak*, and as the terminal element—which is its position also in royal Ethiopic names. The name *Tirkak* is common to the royal lists of Susiana and Ethiopia, as that of Nimrod is to the royal names of Babylon and Egypt. The sun god is called *Ra* in Egyptian, and *Ra* was the Kushite name of the supreme god of the Babylonians. . . . The author of Genesis unites together as members of the same ethnic family the Egyptians, the Ethiopians, the Southern Arabians and the primitive inhabitants of Babylon. Modern ethnology finds, in the localities indicated, a number of languages, partly ancient, partly modern, which have common characteristics, and which evidently constitute one group. Egyptian, ancient and modern, Ethiopic, as represented by the Galla, Agau, etc., Southern Arabian (Himyaric and Mahra), and ancient Babylonian, are discovered to be cognate tongues, varieties of one original form of speech.

On page 193 Professor Jackson cited another European's position on the origin of the concepts of RELIGIOUS TEACHINGS presently called "PAGANISM" and/or "HEATHENISM" by certain Jews, Christians and Moslems, and other fanatics of European, European-American and Asian religions related to both, and also to Islam; all of whom are equally abetted by their Caucasianized and Semiticized Judaeo-Christian-Islamic "Negro" and /or "Colored" Clergy and Theologians. He wrote:

> We shall meet with more of this combination of double-think and double-talk as we proceed in considering the origin of civilization. A sounder appreciation of the ancient Ethiopian contribution to early civ-

---

1. See John G. Jackson's GOD, MAN, AND CIVILIZATION, p. 192

ilization was given by an English anthropologist who spent most of his life in the Orient. We refer to Major General J. G. R. Forlong, and the following extract is from his major work, *Rivers of Life*:

> It was undoubtedly Kushites who rendered possible the Aryan advance, and who played the part of a civilizing Rome thousands of years before Roma's birth. It was their vast mythology and strange legends that passed as Lord Bacon wrote "like light air into the flutes of Grecians, there to be modulated as best suited Grecian fancies." Indeed, it is manifest from many old writings, that it was *their* tales, myths, traditions and histories that lay at the base of the Western World's thought and legendary lore. These so impressed all subsequent races and entered so deeply and minutely into all Aryan mythologies that many writers now think Aryans can only claim to have added to the superstructure and complexion of Ethiopian myths and mythical history; and let us remember that active Aryan life and mythologies began at least 3000 years B.C. when high Asia . . . , becoming too cramped for this race, they were pressing southward to India and Ariana and to the west generally. Then and there must Aryans have met with Ethiopian civilization, as did Semites, when these began to group themselves into nations about a thousand years later, or say, 2000 B.C. They were all builders on old Kushite foundations. (82. Vol. II, pp. 403–4)

Sir Ernest A. Wallis Budge [who was considered during his lifetime in the latter part of the 19th Century and first part of the 20th Century C.E. among his colleagues: "...the most outstanding egyptologist..."] presented us with the following about the "Birth Of The Lord Of Creation" thousands of years before the modern "GODS" - Jehovah in ca. 3760 B.C.E., Jesus Christ in ca. 4 B.C.E., and Al'lah in ca. 622 C.E. [or 18 A.H.]. In the same context on page 53 of the BOOK OF THE DEAD Sir Wallis Budge wrote the following:

> The story of Osiris is nowhere found in a connected form in Egyptian literature, but everywhere, and in texts of all periods, the life, sufferings, death, and resurrection of Osiris are accepted as facts universally admitted. Greek writers have preserved in their works traditions concerning this god, and to Plutarch in particular we owe an important version of the legend which was current in his day. It is clear that in some points he errs, but this was excusable in dealing with a series of traditions already some four thousand years old. According to this writer the goddess Rhea [Nut], the wife of Helios [Rā], was beloved by Kronos [Keb]. When Helios discovered the intrigue, he cursed his wife and declared that she should not be delivered of her child in any month or in any year. Then the god Hermes, who also loved Rhea, played at tables with Selene and won from her the seventieth part of each day of the year, which, added together, made five whole days. These he joined to the three hundred and sixty days of which the year then consisted. Upon the first of these five days was Osiris brought forth; and at the moment of his birth a voice was heard to proclaim that the lord of creation was born.

Although Budge made the point extremely clear, it could still confuse those who may not have heard of God...OSIRIS...before. However on page 52 he wrote that the same African GOD-HEAD...that preceded Ywh, Jesus Christ of Nazareth, Al'lah, and all of the others mentioned in the so-called "Western Relgions" [Judaism, Christianity and Islam] today, including those of the "Druid Religion" of Europe [from Greece to Ireland].

THE LEGEND OF OSIRIS

The essential beliefs of the Egyptian religion remained unchanged from the earliest dynasties down to the period when the Egyptians embraced Christianity, after the preaching of St. Mark the Evangelist in Alexandria, A.D. 69, so firmly had the early beliefs taken possession of the Egyptian mind. And the Christians in Egypt, or Copts as they are commonly called, the racial descendants of the ancient Egyptians, seem never to have succeeded in divesting themselves of the superstitious and weird mythological conceptions which they inherited from their heathen ancestors. It is not necessary here to repeat the proofs of this fact, or to adduce evidence extant in the lives of the saints, martyrs, and ascetics. It is sufficient to note, in passing, that the translators of the New Testament into Coptic rendered the Greek ἄδης by ⲁⲙⲉⲛϯ, *Amenti*, the name which the ancient Egyptians gave to the abode of man after death, and that the Copts peopled it with beings whose prototypes are found on the ancient monuments.

All of these teachings were connected to the philosophical concept developed in the Nile Valley Africans' Mysteries System's "DOCTRINE OF ETERNAL LIFE," which dealt in very definite terms with the matter of...

"THE DECEASED BODY, SOUL, AND SPIRIT IN THE
NETHERWORLD" [Heaven or Hell]. . . .

This we notice in the following that deals with the function of the KA ["Soul-Spirit"] and BA ["Body-Spirit"], each represented by a BIRD-BODIED MAN as shown on pages xii, xv, xvii, 56, etc., of this volume. Budge wrote:[1]

In close connection with the natural and spiritual bodies stood the heart, or rather that part of it which was the seat of the power of life and the fountain of good and evil thoughts. And in addition to the Natural-body and Spirit-body, man also had an abstract individuality or personality endowed with all his characteristic attributes. This abstract personality had an absolutely independent existence. It could move freely from place to place, separating itself from, or uniting itself to, the body at will, and also enjoying life with the gods in heaven. This was the KA ⊔|,[1] a word

1. See Sir Ernest A. Wallis Budge's BOOK OF THE DEAD, p. 73

which at times conveys the meanings of its Coptic equivalent κω, and of εἴδωλον, image, genius, double, character, disposition, and mental attributes.

The funeral service was marked by the offering of CAKES, MAATS, MEATS, ALES, WINES, UNGUENTS, etc. for the deceased; a custom that is still common among most of the indigenous people of the entire continent of Alkebu-lan, and many that aped it in Europe, until this very day. And it is at this juncture that the predominance of "BURNT INCENSE" was used, which many branches of Judaism, Christianity and Islam still cling too. Budge said that this type of RITUAL was necessary when...

> The KA dwelt in the man's statue just as the KA of a god inhabited the statue of the god. In the remotest times the tombs had special chambers wherein the KA was worshipped and received offerings. The priesthood numbered among its body an order of men who bore the name of "priests of the KA" 𓂓, and who performed services in honour of the KA in the "KA chapel" 𓂓.

The quotation above is also typical of the reason why the Roman Catholic Church, and formerly all of Christendom, maintains statues of SAINTS and CRUCIFIXES. They are to glo-fy the "SPIRIT" that leaves and reenters the "BODY"...the "Ka"...or "SPIRIT-SOUL." The "Ba," or – "HEART-SOUL" - was equally emphasized by Budge. Thus he wrote on page 290 of the same work:

> **Vignette:** The mummy of Ani lying on its bier, with a stand containing burning incense at the head and at the foot of it. Above the mummy hovers his Heart-soul in the form of a man-headed hawk, holding in his claws *shen* ☉, the symbol of the sun's course and of eternity. This the soul is presenting to its body with the view of making it everlasting.
>
> **Text:** [CHAPTER LXXXIX.] THE CHAPTER OF CAUSING THE HEART-SOUL TO BE UNITED TO ITS BODY IN KHERT-NETER. By the recital of this very important Chapter Ani hoped to gain possession of his Heart-soul (Ba) and of his Spirit-soul (Khu), and to effect the union of the former with its material body *khat* 𓄹, and the union of the latter with its Spirit-body *sāh* 𓄿. Heart-soul and body would then exist eternally upon the earth, and the Spirit-soul and its ethereal and indestructible envelope would have their being among the gods. The **Rubric** of the Chapter orders that an amulet in the form of a Heart-soul made of gold and inlaid with precious stones shall be tied to the neck

of the mummy. If this were done it was believed that the gods would compel Ani's Heart-soul to visit its body regularly, and so prevent it from decaying, and that both Heart-soul and body would be able to visit during the seasons of festivals the city of Anu, where Heart-souls were united to their bodies by thousands. In the Turin Papyrus it is expressly stated that the presence of such an amulet on the body would prevent it from decaying, and would prevent the Heart-soul from leaving it.

Vignette : The Heart-soul of the scribe Ani, in the form of a man-headed bird, standing in front of the door of his tomb. The papyri afford many variants of the Vignette of this most interesting Chapter. In the Papyrus of Khari (Fig. 1) we see the deceased standing before his tomb, of which he has opened the door ▌, and his Heart-soul in the form of a man-headed hawk flying out to meet him.

[Fig. I]

Where would the BA or KA go? To whom would either go? To the TUAT! To GOD! The Africans of the Nile Valley High-Cultures were quite specific in terms of their TUAT [Hereafter, Nether World, Under World, Heaven, etc.] and their GOD. Yes! A "monotheistic"

. . ."ONE AND ONLY TRUE GOD ABOVE ALL OTHER GODS"....

This was definitely not unlike the claim the Hebrews [Jews], Christians and Moslems made later for the GODS they adopted from the TEACHINGS of the following ideas about GOD, GODS, GODDESS and GODDESSES by Africans of Ta-Merry, Ta-Nehisi, Itiopi, Merïe, Puanit, etc.

To the great and supreme Power which made the heavens, the gods, the earth, the sea, the sky, men and women, birds, animals and creeping things, all that is and all that is yet to come into being, the Egyptians gave the name of *neter* ⌒⎤, or *nether* ⩶⎤, a word which survives in Coptic under the form *nuti* ⲛⲟⲩϯ. This word has been translated "god-like," "holy," "divine," "sacred," "power," "strength." "force," "strong," "fortify," "mighty," "protect,". . . .

Although Sir E.A. Wallis Budge has been quoted many times in this volume, you must be informed at this juncture that he was not always kind to the indigenous African [BLACK] People of the Nile Valley, particularly at the turn of the 20th Century C.E. when he too found it necessary to join with his fellow Europeans and European-Americans disclaimer that:"...THE EGYPTIANS WERE NOT NEGROES...." With this freshly in mind, the following extract from Professor John G. Jackson's GOD, MAN, AND CIVILIZATION, pages 142 and 143 should help somewhat. Professor Jackson was quoting British "Orientalist" Robert Brown, Jr's "Researches of the Primitive Constellations of the Greeks, Phoenicians, and Babylonians," in which he argued for an "Euphratean origin of the Zodiac," instead of the older Nile Valley and Great Lakes origin shown in the comparisons of the works of each area and the indigenous peoples that produced them; not one of whom was a European. Dr. Albert Churchward's rejoinder to Brown, Budge, and a few others who could not accept this Alkebu-lan [African] origin, was:

> Why the knowledge of all this was old in Egypt before the Babylonians even existed or knew anything about it. The Egyptians had worked out all the architecture of the heavens and their priests had carried the same with them to all parts of the world—not only the Northern heavens but the Southern, as well. Probably they worked out the South before the North, and the Druids and the Mayas and the Incas knew it all from the priests of Egypt, the earliest probably thousands of years before the Babylonian nation existed. The Babylonians copied and obtained all their knowledge from the Egyptians, and we are surprised that Dr. Budge should write that they borrowed from the Greeks; they were old and degenerating in decay before the Greek nation was born! Well may he say that "it is a subject of conjecture at what period the Babylonians first divided the heavens into sections, etc.," because they never did; what they knew they borrowed either *direct from the Egyptians* or Sumerians—the latter obtained it from Egypt. It was the ancient Egyptians who mapped out the heavens into 12 divisions in the North, 12 divisions in the South, and 12 in the center, making 36 in all, and the 12 signs of the zodiac. . . . It is very well to say that "whether the Babylonians were themselves the inventors of such origins— i.e. (the zodiac), or whether they are to be attributed to the earlier non-Semitic Sumerian inhabitants of that country, cannot be said,"—and when he states that "the Greeks borrowed the zodiac from the Babylonians, and then the Greeks introduced it into Egypt, probably during the Ptolemaic period," it appears to us that Dr. Budge must have left that part of "The Gods of the Egyptians" to be written by one of his assistants, who knew nothing about the history of the past.

Before bringing this aspect of THE NEED FOR A BLACK BIBLE to close each and every student and general reader should be reminded that even the noted ancient Greek scholar and historian Diodorus Siculus, who lived during the Fifth Century C.E., told us in BOOK III of his FORTY BOOKS ON WORLD HISTORY that "...the Ethiopians[1] were the founders of the Egyptian culture." The following extract from BOOK III deals with the above contention. He wrote:

> Now the Ethiopians, as historians relate, were the first of all men and the proofs of this statement, they say, are manifest. For that they did not come into their land as immigrants from abroad but were the natives of it and so justly bear the name of autochthones (sprung from the soil itself), is, they maintain, conceded by practically all men.
> They say also that the Egyptians are colonists sent out by the Ethiopians, Osiris having been the leader of the colony. For, speaking generally, what is now Egypt, they maintain, was not land but sea, when in the beginning the universe was being formed; afterwards, however, as the Nile during the

1. Note that in this sense "Ethiopians" are the nationals of an East Alkebu-lan [African] nation. "Ethiopians" was once the name ancient Greeks and Romans used for all of the "African [BLACK] People." See MAP OF ALKEBU-LAN on page 108 of this volume.

times of its inundation carried down the mud from Ethiopia, land was gradually built up from the deposit. . . . And the larger parts of the customs of the Egyptians are, they hold, Ethiopian, the colonists still preserving their ancient manners. For instance, the belief that their kings are gods, the very special attention which they pay to their burials, and many other matters of a similar nature, are Ethiopian practices, while the shapes of their statues and the forms of their letters are Ethiopian; for of the two kinds of writing which the Egyptians have, that which is known as popular (demotic) is learned by everyone, while that which is called sacred (hieratic), is understood only by the priests of the Egyptians, who learn it from their fathers as one of the things which are not divulged, but among the Ethiopians everyone uses these forms of letters. Furthermore, the orders of the priests, they maintain, have much the same position among both peoples; for all are clean who are engaged in the service of the gods, keeping themselves shaven, like the Ethiopian priests, and having the same dress and form of staff, which is shaped like a plough and is carried by their kings who wear high felt hats which end in a knob at the top and are circled by the serpents which they call asps; and this symbol appears to carry the thought that it will be the lot who shall dare to attack the king to encounter death-carrying stings. Many other things are told by them concerning their own antiquity and the colony which they sent out that became the Egyptians, but about this there is no special need of our writing anything.

We must now speak about the Ethiopian writing which is called hieroglyphic among the Egyptians, in order that we may omit nothing in our discussion of their antiquities. Now it is found that the forms of their letters take the shape of animals of every kind, and of the members of the human body, and of implements and especially carpenter's tools; for their writing does not express the intended concept by means of syllables joined one to another, but by means of the significance of the objects which have been copied and by its figurative meaning which has been impressed upon the memory by practice. For instance, they draw the picture of a hawk, a crocodile, a snake, and all of the members of the human body—an eye, a hand, a face, and the like. Now the hawk signifies to them everything which happens swiftly, since this animal is practically the swiftest of winged creatures. . . . And the crocodile is a symbol of all that is evil, and the eye is the warder of justice and the guardian of the entire body. And as for the members of the body, the right hand with fingers extended signifies a procuring of livelihood, and the left with the fingers closed, a keeping and guarding of property. The same way of reasoning applies also to the remaining characters, which represent parts of the body and implements and all other things; for by paying close attention to the significance which is inherent in each object and by training their minds through drill and exercise of the memory over a long period, they read from habit everything which has been written.

Very much later Diodorus was supported in his teaching by some revealing insights in Lady Flora Shaw Lugard's book. She was commenting on one of the major statements made by the German Professor A. H. L. Hereen in his speculation on the place of origin of the "WORLD'S FIRST CIVILIZATION" among the Ethiopians. He wrote:

In Nubia and Ethiopia, stupendous, numerous and primeval monuments proclaim so loudly a civilization contemporary to, aye, earlier than that of Egypt, that it may be conjectured with the greatest confidence that the arts, sciences and religion descended from Nubia to the lower country of Mizraim; that civilization descended the Nile, built Memphis and finally sometime later, wrested by colonization the Delta from the Sea.[1]

In conjunction with the above Flora Shaw Lugard [wife of the infamous imperialist murderer – Captain, later Lord, Federick Lugard - that committed genocide upon millions of Asians in India and Africans in Monomotapa, the so-called "Rhodesias" and "Nigeria" for Britain] wrote:

> "The people of Ethiopia colonized to the north and west.
> Amongst their colonies to the north, one of the most important was Thebes. Thebes and Meroe together founded the colony Ammonium in the western desert, and through Thebes the religion of Meroe was carried into Lower Egypt. It was at a much later period, about 1500 B.C., that Egypt returned upon Meroe and conquered it." [2]

With respect to the contact between the Africans of NORTH and EAST Alkebu-lan with their indigenous brothers and sisters of the WEST, CENTRAL and SOUTH, Lady Lugard wrote:

> In corroboration of the view that the trade and influence of Meroe may have extended farther west than has as yet been ascertained by modern explorations, I may mention a fact told me by Zebehr Pasha, when, during his confinement at Gibraltar in 1886, he related to me the history of the foundation of his ephemeral empire in the Bahr-el-Ghazal. It was that, having occasion to act as the military ally of a certain native king Tekkima, whose territory lay somewhere south and west of the spot marked upon modern maps as Dem Suleiman or Dem Zebehr—that is, presumably about 8 degrees north and 25 degrees east, he was informed that he had to fight against magicians, who habitually came out of the earth, fought, and then disappeared. A careful system of scouting disclosed to him the fact that they came from underground and when, after cutting off their retreat and conquering them, he insisted on being shown their place of habitation, he found it to be deeply buried in the sand, a wonderful system of temples, "far finer" to use the words in which he described it, "than modern eyes have seen in the mosques of Cairo and Constantinople." It was, he said, such work of massive stone as was done by the great races of old. Through this underground city of stone there ran a stream, and by the stream his native antagonists lived in common straw native huts. "Were your people, then," he asked them, "a nation of stone cutters?" And they said "Oh, no! This is not the work of our forefathers but our forefathers found it here and we have lived for many generations in these huts." [3]

Sir Godfrey Higgins validated Diodorus, Heeren, Lugard, Broom and Jackson's position when he wrote the following on page 311 of his major work - ANACALYPSIS, Volume I, Book VI, Chapter II, Section 8:

---

1. See Arnold Herman Ludwig Heeren's "Historical Researches: African Nations "[in: Lady Flora S. Lugard's A TROPICAL DEPENDENCY: AN OUTLINE OF THE ANCIENT HISTORY OF THE SUDAN WITH AN ACCOUNT OF THE MODERN SETTLEMENT OF NORTHERN NIGERIA, pp. 220 - 221]
2. Lady Flora S. Lugard's A TROPICAL DEPENDENCY:..., etc., p. 221
3. Ibid., pp. 225 - 226

I *Isis* am all that has
been, that is or shall
be; no mortal Man
hath ever
me un-
vei-
le-
d. [1]

This cannot apply to the moon. The Indian deity is described to be, All that is, everywhere, always. On many words closely connected with this topic, almost every page of Sir William Drummond's Essay on a Punic Inscription may be consulted.

I am persuaded that there is no subject on which more mistakes have been made than on that of the Goddess Isis, both by ancients and moderns. She has constantly been taken for the moon, which in many countries was masculine. But she is constantly declared to be the same as Ceres, Proserpine, Juno, Venus, and all the other Goddesses; therefore they must all be the moon. This is out of the question. The case I believe to be this;—the planet called the *moon* was dedicated to her in judicial astrology, the same as a planet was dedicated to Venus or Mars. But Venus and Mars were not those planets themselves, though those planets were sacred to them. The inscription in front of her temple at Sais at once proves that she cannot be the moon; it is totally inapplicable to that planet. The mistake of the ancients is only one proof among hundreds, that they had lost the knowledge of the principles of their mythology, or that we do not understand it. I am of opinion that much of the confusion in the ancient systems arose from the neglect, or the ignorance, of the distinction between religion and judicial astrology.

Apuleius makes Isis say, I am nature, the parent of all things, the sovereign of the elements, the primary progeny of time, the most exalted of the deities, the first of the heavenly Gods and Goddesses; whose single deity the whole world venerates in many forms, with various rites, and various names. The Egyptians worship me with proper ceremonies, and call me by my true name, Queen Isis. [2] Isis is called Myrionymus, or Goddess with 10,000 names. [3] Herodotus [4] says, that the Persian Mithra was Venus.

No person who has considered well the character of the temples in India and Egypt, can help being convinced of the identity of their character, and of their being the production of the same race of people; and this race evidently Ethiopian. The Sphinxes have all Ethiopian faces. The bust of Memnon in the British museum is evidently Ethiopian. The worship of the Mother and Child is seen in all parts of the Egyptian religion. It prevails everywhere. It is the worship of Isis and the infant Orus or Osiris. It is the religious rite which was so often prohibited at Rome, but which prevailed in spite of all opposition, as we find from the remaining ruins of its temples. It was perhaps from this country, Egypt, that the worship of the black virgin and child came into Italy, where it still prevails. It was the worship of the mother of the God Iαω, the Saviour; Bacchus in Greece, Adonis in Syria, Cristna in India; coming into Italy through the medium of the two Ethiopias, she was, as the Ethiopians were, *black*, and such she still remains.

Dr. Shuckford [5] has the following curious passage: " We have several representations in the " draughts of the same learned antiquary *(Montfaucon)*, which are said to be Isis, holding or

---

[1] Basnage, p. 217; Maurice, Ind. Ant. Vol. IV. pp. 682—684.   [2] Metamorph. Lib. xi., Payne Knight, p. 67.
[3] Squire's Plutarch, de Iside et Osir. cap. liii. p. 74.   [4] Clio. Sect. cxxxi.
[5] Con. Book viii. p. 311.

" giving suck to the boy Orus; but it should be remarked, that Orus was not represented by the " figure of a new-born child: for Plutarch expressly tells us, that a new-born child was the " Egyptian picture of the sun's rising."   Plutarch and Montfaucon were both right.   Orus was the sun, and the infant child was the picture of the sun, in his infancy or birth, immediately after the winter solstice—when he began to increase. Orus, I repeat, is nothing but the Hebrew word אור *aur*, lux, light — the very light so often spoken of by St. John, in the first chapter of his gospel.   Plutarch   says, that Osiris means a benevolent and beneficent power, as does likewise his other name OMPHIS.

Higgins was   definitely   convinced of the identity of the "BLACK VIRGIN" and "CHRIST-CHILD." He also dealt with other GODS and GODDESSES of Europe who were also "BLACK," and of "ETHIOPIAN ORIGIN." Thus he wrote:

> From Pausanias we learn that the most ancient statue of Ceres amongst the Phigalenses was black; and in chap. vi., that at a place called Melangea, in Arcadia, was a Venus who was black, the reason for which, as given by him, evidently shews that it was unknown. At Athens, Minerva Aglaurus, daughter of Cecrops, was *black*, according to Ovid, in his Metamorphoses.

A few sentences further he commented on the "BLACK VIRGIN" of the Netherlands; strangely enough where CALVINISM had its earliest beginnings. He wrote:

> Some years ago I was informed, by a friend, since deceased, that he had seen a church (I think) in the Netherlands, dedicated to the Black Virgin, à la Vierge Noire.[1] I have no doubt of the fact, though I have forgotten the place.   Here we have the black Venus and Ceres.   To make the thing complete, we want nothing but a church dedicated to the Black Saviour; and if we cannot shew this, there is scarcely a church in Italy where a black bambino may not be seen, which :omes very near it. If Pausanias had told us that the *infant* Jupiter   which he found in Arcadia had been *black*, we should have had all we required; for he had before told us, that Jupiter had the title of Saviour, and Statius tells us he was black.

Unlike Professor James H. Cone and other "BLACKS" involved in "WHITE THEOLOGY" in WHITE-OWNED and WHITE-CONTROLLED Judaeo-Christian religious institutions that dispense European and European-American CAUCASIAN-SEMITIC STYLE Judaism and Christianity [where Jesus Christ and the "HOLY FAMILY" - Joseph and Mary - are still depicted as the BLONDES like the artist and his family that created them, Michaelangelo], European, Asian and African religious WRITERS, THEOLOGIANS and other EDUCATORS of past centuries did not have to protect "TENURE;" neither did they had to qualify as the...

"GOOD COLORED PROFESSOR" or "NON-VIOLENT RHETORITICIAN" of any Theological Seminary with its TOKEN "NEGRO FACULTY MEMBER" or "MEMBERS;" nor did they had to call Jesus Christ a...

---

1. These are other names: Minerva, Venus, Juno, Proserpina, Ceres, Diana, Rhea seu Tellus, Pessinuncia, Rhamnusia, Bellona, Hecate, Luna, PolymorpnusDæmon. But most of these have been shewn to be in fact all one—the Sun.

'COLORLESS INVISIBLE MAN,'

who was "BLACK," solely because HE too, allegedly, was...

"A SLAVE HIMSELF."[5]

For nowhere in the New Testament is it suggested that...

'JESUS CHRIST WAS A SLAVE.'

But if Jesus Christ was "BLACK;" it was because the pigment of the color of his skin was in every respect "BLACK" - period; and for no other reason whatsoever.

In what better manner could one have closed this aspect of THE NEED FOR A BLACK BIBLE other than in showing that Europeans like Professor Heeren, Eusebius, Higgins, Thales, Plutarch, Broom, Volney, Denon, Drummond and Lady Lugard, as late as the 19th Century C.E., were still confessing to "the ORIGIN OF MAN, ORIGIN OF MAGICAL RELIGION, and ORIGIN OF CIVILIZATION among the indigenous Africans of Central Africa." These facts are being more than supported and/or substantiated by the current "FOSSIL-FINDS" of the present 20th Century C.E. in the same areas of Alkebu-lan [Africa], all of which has been pointed out to you in this volume, and others before. However, the following added biblical proof extracted from GENESIS, Chapter i, Verses 1 - 26, and EXODUS, Chapters i, ii and iii, ending with Chapter iii, Verse 17, should help. But before you read these quotations; you are asked:

> WHAT BOOKS OR SCROLLS ON RELIGION DID THE
> HEBREWS HAVE BEFORE THE AFRICAN NAMED MOSES
> PLAGIARIZED HIS FELLOW AFRICANS WORK IN THE
> BOOK OF THE COMING FORTH BY DAY AND BY NIGHT?
> WHOSE LAND DID GOD GIVE TO THE ISRAELITES WHEN
> THEY LEFT 'AFRICA;' WAS IT NOT THE CANAANITES'
> [BLACKS]?" WHAT WAS THE PHYSICAL DIFFERENCE BE-
> TWEEN THE EGYPTIANS THAT WORSHIPED YWH AND
> THOSE WHO WORSHIPED RA? WAS IT NOT GENOCIDE
> WHEN THE JEWS EXTERMINATED THE JEBUSITES,
> HITTITES, AMALAKITES, MOABITES, ETC.? WHAT LAWS
> DID THE EGYPTIANS, NUBIANS, PUNTS, ETHIOPIANS,
> AND OTHER NILE VALLEY ANCIENT AFRICANS HAD WHILE
> THE JEWS WERE BEING EDUCATED IN AFRICA? WERE
> THEY NOT THE BASIS UPON WHICH THE AFRICAN NAMED
> MOSES TOOK HIS "TEN COMMANDMENTS" AND OTHER
> TEACHINGS PRESENTLY CALLED "JUDAISM, CHRISTIAN-
> ITY 'AND' ISLAM?"

1.
2. See Godfrey Higgins' ANACALYPSIS, Vol. I, p. 312
3. Ibid.
4. Ibid.
5. Review the first paragraph of Cone's comment on Jesus Christ's BLACKNESS, p.23.

50 Then Joseph fell on his father's face, and wept over him, and kissed him. 2 And Joseph commanded his servants the physicians to embalm his father. So the physicians embalmed Israel; 3 forty days were required for it, for so many are required for embalming. And the Egyptians wept for him seventy days.

4 And when the days of weeping for him were past, Joseph spoke to the household of Pharaoh, saying, "If now I have found favor in your eyes, speak, I pray you, in the ears of Pharaoh, saying, 5 'My father made me swear, saying, 'I am about to die: in my tomb which I hewed out for myself in the land of Canaan, there shall you bury me.' Now therefore let me go up, I pray you, and bury my father; then I will return." 6 And Pharaoh answered, "Go up, and bury your father, as he made you swear." 7 So Joseph went up to bury his father; and with him went up all the servants of Pharaoh, the elders of his household, and all the elders of the land of Egypt, 8 as well as all the household of Joseph, his brothers, and his father's household; only their children, their flocks, and their herds were left in the land of Gō'shĕn. 9 And there went up with him both chariots and horsemen; it was a very great company. 10 When they came to the threshing floor of Ā'tad, which is beyond the Jordan, they lamented there with a very great and sorrowful lamentation; and he made a mourning for his father seven days. 11 When the inhabitants of the land, the Canaanites, saw the mourning on the threshing floor of Ā'tad, they said, "This is a grievous mourning to the Egyptians." Therefore the place was named Ā'bĕl-miz'rȧ-im;4 it is beyond the Jordan. 12 Thus his sons did for him as he had commanded them; 13 for his sons carried him to the land of Canaan, and buried him in the cave of the field at Mach-pē'lăh, to the east of Mam're, which Abraham bought with the field from E'phron the Hittite, to possess as a burying place. 14 After he had buried his father, Joseph returned to Egypt with his brothers and all who had gone up with him to bury his father.

15 When Joseph's brothers saw that their father was dead, they said, "It may be that Joseph will hate us and pay us back for all the evil which we did to him." 16 So they sent a message to Joseph, saying, "Your father gave this command before he died, 17 'Say to Joseph, Forgive, I pray you, the transgression of your brothers and their sin, because they did evil to you.' And now, we pray you, forgive the transgression of the servants of the God of your father." Joseph wept when they spoke to him. 18 His brothers also came and fell down before him, and said, "Behold, we are your servants." 19 But Joseph said to them, "Fear not, for am I in the place of God? 20 As for you, you meant evil against me; but God meant it for good, to bring it about that many people should be kept alive, as they are today. 21 So do not fear; I will provide for you and your little ones." Thus he reassured them and comforted them.

22 So Joseph dwelt in Egypt, he and his father's house; and Joseph lived a hundred and ten years. 23 And Joseph saw E'phra-im's children of the third generation; the children also of Mā'chir the son of Mȧ-nas'sĕh were born upon Joseph's knees. 24 And Joseph said to his brothers, "I am about to die; but God will visit you, and bring you up out of this land to the land which he swore to Abraham, to Isaac, and to Jacob." 25 Then Joseph took an oath of the sons of Israel, saying, "God will visit you, and you shall carry up my bones from here." 26 So Joseph died, being a hundred and ten years old; and they embalmed him, and he was put in a coffin in Egypt.

THE SECOND BOOK OF MOSES

COMMONLY CALLED

EXODUS

1 These are the names of the sons of Israel who came to Egypt with Jacob, each with his household: 2 Reuben, Simeon, Levi, and Judah, 3 Is'sȧ-chär, Zeb'û-lŭn, and Benjamin, 4 Dan and Naph'tȧ-li, Gad and Ash'ĕr. 5 All the offspring of Jacob were seventy persons; Joseph was already in Egypt. 6 Then Joseph died, and all his brothers, and all that generation. 7 But the descendants of Israel were fruitful and increased greatly; they multiplied and grew exceedingly strong; so that the land was filled with them.

8 Now there arose a new king over Egypt, who did not know Joseph. 9 And he said to his people, "Behold, the people of Israel are too many and too mighty for us. 10 Come, let us deal shrewdly with them, lest they multiply, and, if war befall us, they join our enemies and fight against us and escape from the land." 11 Therefore they set taskmasters over them to afflict them with heavy burdens; and they built for Pharaoh store-cities, Pĭ'thom and Ra-am'sĕs. 12 But the more they were oppressed, the more they multiplied and the more they spread abroad. And the Egyptians were in dread of the people of Israel. 13 So they made the people of Israel serve with rigor, 14 and made their lives bitter with hard service, in mortar and brick, and in all kinds of work in the field; in all their work they made them serve with rigor.

15 Then the king of Egypt said to the Hebrew midwives, one of whom was named Shiph'răh and the other Pū'ăh, 16 "When you serve as midwife to the Hebrew women, and see them upon the birthstool, if it is a son, you shall kill him; but if it is a daughter, she shall live." 17 But the midwives feared God, and did not do as the king of Egypt commanded them, but let the male children live. 18 So the king of Egypt called the midwives, and said to them, "Why have you done this, and let the male children live?" 19 The midwives said to Pharaoh, "Because the Hebrew women are not like the Egyptian women; for they are vigorous

and are delivered before the midwife comes to them." 20 So God dealt well with the midwives; and the people multiplied and grew very strong. 21And because the midwives feared God he gave them families. 22 Then Pharaoh commanded all his people, "Every son that is born to the Hebrews[d] you shall cast into the Nile, but you shall let every daughter live."

2 Now a man from the house of Levi went and took to wife a daughter of Levi. 2 The woman conceived and bore a son; and when she saw that he was a goodly child, she hid him three months. 3And when she could hide him no longer she took for him a basket made of bulrushes, and daubed it with bitumen and pitch; and she put the child in it and placed it among the reeds at the river's brink. 4And his sister stood at a distance, to know what would be done to him. 5 Now the daughter of Pharaoh came down to bathe at the river, and her maidens walked beside the river; she saw the basket among the reeds and sent her maid to fetch it. 6 When she opened it she saw the child; and lo, the babe was crying. She took pity on him and said, "This is one of the Hebrews' children." 7 Then his sister said to Pharaoh's daughter, "Shall I go and call you a nurse from the Hebrew women to nurse the child for you?" 8And Pharaoh's daughter said to her, "Go." So the girl went and called the child's mother. 9And Pharaoh's daughter said to her, "Take this child away, and nurse him for me, and I will give you your wages." So the woman took the child and nursed him. 10And the child grew, and she brought him to Pharaoh's daughter, and he became her son; and she named him Moses,[b] for she said, "Because I drew him out[c] of the water."

11 One day, when Moses had grown up, he went out to his people and looked on their burdens; and he saw an Egyptian beating a Hebrew, one of his people. 12 He looked this way and that, and seeing no one he killed the Egyptian and hid him in the sand. 13 When he went out the next day, behold, two Hebrews were struggling together; and he said to the man that did the wrong, "Why do you strike your fellow?" 14 He answered, "Who made you a prince and a judge over us? Do you mean to kill me as you killed the Egyptian?" Then Moses was afraid, and thought, "Surely the thing is known." 15 When Pharaoh heard of it, he sought to kill Moses.

But Moses fled from Pharaoh, and stayed in the land of Mid'i-an; and he sat down by a well. 16 Now the priest of Mid'i-an had seven daughters; and they came and drew water, and filled the troughs to water their father's flock. 17 The shepherds came and drove them away; but Moses stood up and helped them, and watered their flock. 18 When they came to their father Reü'el, he said, "How is it that you have come so soon today?" 19 They said, "An Egyptian delivered us out of the hand of the shepherds, and even drew water for us and watered the flock." 20 He said to his daughters, "And where is he? Why have you left the man? Call him, that he may eat bread." 21And Moses was content to dwell with the man, and he gave Moses his daughter Zip-po'rah. 22 She bore a son, and he called his name Ger'shom; for he said, "I have been a sojourner[d] in a foreign land."

23 In the course of those many days the king of Egypt died. And the people of Israel groaned under their bondage, and cried out for help, and their cry under bondage came up to God. 24And God heard their groaning, and God remembered his covenant with Abraham, with Isaac, and with Jacob. 25And God saw the people of Israel, and God knew their condition.

3 Now Moses was keeping the flock of his father-in-law, Jethro, the priest of Mid'i-an; and he led his flock to the west side of the wilderness, and came to Hō'reb, the mountain of God. 2And the angel of the LORD appeared to him in a flame of fire out of the midst of a bush; and he looked, and lo, the bush was burning, yet it was not consumed. 3And Moses said, "I will turn aside and see this great sight, why the bush is not burnt." 4 When the LORD saw that he turned aside to see, God called to him out of the bush, "Moses, Moses!" And he said, "Here am I." 5 Then he said, "Do not come near; put off your shoes from your feet, for the place on which you are standing is holy ground." 6And he said, "I am the God of your father, the God of Abraham, the God of Isaac, and the God of Jacob." And Moses hid his face, for he was afraid to look at God.

7 Then the LORD said, "I have seen the affliction of my people who are in Egypt, and have heard their cry because of their taskmasters; I know their sufferings, 8 and I have come down to deliver them out of the hand of the Egyptians, and to bring them up out of that land to a good and broad land, a land flowing with milk and honey, to the place of the Canaanites, the Hit'tites, the Am'ō-rites, the Per'izzites, the Hi'vites, and the Jeb'ū-sites. 9And now, behold, the cry of the people of Israel has come to me, and I have seen the oppression with which the Egyptians oppress them. 10 Come, I will send you to Pharaoh that you may bring forth my people, the sons of Israel, out of Egypt." 11 But Moses said to God, "Who am I that I should go to Pharaoh, and bring the sons of Israel out of Egypt?" 12 He said, "But I will be with you; and this shall be the sign for you, that I have sent you: when you have brought forth the people out of Egypt, you shall serve God upon this mountain."

13 Then Moses said to God, "If I come to the people of Israel and say to them, 'The God of your fathers has sent me to you,' and they ask me, 'What is his name?' what shall I say to them?" 14 God said to Moses, "I AM WHO I AM."[e] And he said, "Say this to the people of Israel, 'I AM has sent me to you.' " 15 God also said to Moses, "Say this to the people of Israel, 'The LORD,[f] the God of your fathers, the God of Abraham, the God of Isaac, and the God of Jacob, has sent me to you': this is my name for ever, and thus I am to be remembered throughout all generations. 16 Go and gather the elders of Israel together, and say to them, 'The LORD, the God of your fathers, the God of Abraham, of Isaac, and of Jacob, has appeared to me, saying, "I have observed you and what has been done to you in Egypt; 17 and I promise that I will bring you up out of the affliction of Egypt, to the land of the Canaanites, the Hit'tites, the Am'ō-rites, the Per'iz-zites, the Hi'vites, and the Jeb'ū-sites, a land flowing with milk and honey."

99

Obviously all of the "NEGRO THEOLOGIANS" have forgotten that God - "HAMARCHIS," shown below as the "GREAT SPHINX OF GHIZEH," was worshiped in all of his "BLACKNESS" as...

"THE ONE AND ONLY TRUE GOD...[The Great I Am]...OF THE UNIVERSE"...

before many of His teachings were passed on to Moses; who in turn passed them on to his fellow African Hebrews; they in turn passed them to Asian Hebrews that became Christians; and they too passed them with further distortions on to other Africans and Asians. From this point on the "PAULITES" transfered them with other distortions to the original teachings which they later passed down to the Europeans of Greece and Rome under the title of the "CHRISTIAN RELIGION" or "CHRISTIANITY." Finally they were passed on to Mohamet ibn Abdullah through his contact with an African from Itiopi [where Mohamet's grandmother was born] named Hatzard Khobad Bilal ibn Rhabad as the "Islamic Religion" all over the Arabian Peninsula, equally as they were sweeping all of the European continent and Great Britain. Thus in all of their travels the roles of their Alkebu-lan creators and developers before they were totally distorted were removed from the various PAPYRAE, SCROLLS, BOOKS, BIBLES, etc. But their heirs still say:

"ALL PRAISES BE TO OUR GOD...HAMARCHIS."

GREAT SPHINX OF GHIZEH
Showing its original Nile Valley African facial chracteristics as it appeared to Baron Viviant Denon, who drew this picture, before its face was marred in 1798 C.E. This statue, the world's largest, was built by the indigenous Africans of the Nile Valley more than five hundred (500) years before the "HYKSOS SEMITES" and one thousand nine-hundred (1,900) years before the "MACEDONIAN-GREEK CAUCASIANS" arrival in Ta-Merry (Egypt).

[CONCLUSION]   The Black Bible is not a far-off possibility; and The Need is present. Yet we must, this very minute, realize that two of the few Black Men whose mental stage of development seems to be able to lead this action - Prophet Elijah and Mwalimu [Teacher] Albert Cleage - are not even on cooperative terms, muchless dealing with...

THE NEED FOR A BLACK BIBLE FOR BLACK PEOPLE.

But, WHY NOT? Is it possible that Black People are to continue forever using an Asian HOLY QUR'AN and a European and European-American HOLY TORAH or HOLY BIBLE; not one of which was written with the BLACK PEOPLE OF ALKEBU-LAN in mind; and not one of which God-Head is presented in the characteristics of BLACK PEOPLE; but most of which condemns the color "BLACK" as the mark of "SIN?" Why not someone like these two to lead us into the REBIRTH of the BLACK NATION; mentally at least ? They have the necessary respect among their thousands of followers and admirers to cause this reality. And they have the necessary African People whose thinking is already POSITIVELY BLACK IN PERSPECTIVE. What, then, is the delay? Only a man like any of these two GREAT LEADERS OF BLACK RELIGION knows! And there will be no problem finding competent AFRICAN SCRIBES who are more than willing to undertake this monumental task and turn it into...A WORK OF LOVE AND PRIDE...for the African [BLACK] People everywhere.

Let me remind all of us "BLACK PEOPLE " that "WHITE AMERICA" recently released another of its..."NEW VERSIONS" of the plagiarized Judaeo-Christian "HOLY WRITINGS"... by another group of European and European-American Anglo-Saxon-Aryan-Semitic-Caucasian

... "GOD INSPIRED HOLY SCRIBES"...

that practically each and everyone of the major "LIBERAL WHITE" rabbis, priests, ministers and imams agree "HAS MERITORIOUS TRUTH." The basic irony of it all is that the so-called "Negro" THEOLOGIANS" and "Negro" CLERGY" who lead their BLACK CONGREGATIONS and BLACK SEMINARIANS down the road of European and European-American PAULISM will, once again, BLINDLY lead them into accepting this new form of "GOD INSPIRED" racism and religious bigotry in this new "WHITE BIBLE." This is inspite of the fact that they had little or nothing whatsoever to do with any aspect of its CREATION or DEVELOPMENT. Thus we – African [BLACK] People – must ask of them; What do you mean when you say:

"AND THE TRUTH WILL SET YOU FREE?"

WHO ESTABLISHED THE VALUE OF TRUTH AS WRITTEN?

WHO DECIDED WHAT IS FREEDOM FOR BLACK PEOPLE?

The following extract from Amelia B. Edwards' A THOUSAND YEARS UP THE NILE should assist each student of AFRICAN HISTORY and/or AFRICAN RELIGIONS to understand why even some of the most fundamental Jewish and Judaeo-Christian religionists are demanding that:

"MUCH MORE ATTENTION MUST BE GIVEN TO THE HUMAN SIDE OF
CHRIST'S MISSION AS HE WALKED WITH HIS FELLOWMEN ON EARTH."

It is in keeping with those of us who became disgusted of the growing hypocracy in the unusual ESOTERICAL and MYTHOLOGICAL allegories about the "DIVINITY OF JESUS CHRIST" that this position has been demonstrated at its highest context in the extract I have already shown on page xvii of this volume. For it was with Jesus' "HUMAN LIFE EXPERIENCE" that people who are not "Christians" can understand and best identify. And it is with this aspect of the "TRINITARIAN CONCEPT" that anyone can accept as a point for adopting his stature of astute greatness he achieved on earth. This they can do, equally as they can identify with the "SIX-TEEN [16] " other "WORLD'S CRUCIFIED SAVIORS" Professor John G. Jackson listed and commented about in their historical and chronological sequence on pages 135 and 136 of his major work – GOD, MAN, AND CIVILIZATION. He wrote:

> In *The World's Sixteen Crucified Saviors*, Kersey Graves gave a list of these ancient savior gods with the dates of their reputed deaths. The list is as follows: Krishna of India (1200 B.C.), Sakia of India (600 B.C.), Tammuz of Syria (1160 B.C.), Wittoba of the Telingonese (522 B.C.), Iao of Nepal (622 B.C.), Hesus of the Celtic Druids (834 B.C.), Quetzalcoatl of Mexico (587 B.C.), Quirinius of Rome (506 B.C.), Prometheus of Greece (547 B.C.), Thulis of Egypt (1700 B.C.), Indra of Tibet (725 B.C.), Alcestos of Greece (600 B.C.), Attis of Phrygia (1170 B.C.), Crite of Chaldea (1200 B.C.), Bali of Orissa (725 B.C.), Mithra of Persia (600 B.C.).

But it is still in "HUMANITY," Jesus Christ and everyone else's, that <u>the fellowship of man-kind</u> [CHRISTIANS, JEWS, MOSLEMS, etc.] depends; this being equally true for all of the other RELIGIONS ever created by mankind to give honour and praises to what each religionist believes is responsible for his or her being...

"GOD, GODS, GODDESS, GODDESSES, EARTH MOTHER,"
etc. Thus it is that "Christians" hold to the belief that:

"JESUS CHRIST IS THE ONE AND ONLY TRUE SON OF THE LIVING GOD;"
which is nothing NEW and/or SURPRISING to any egyptologist. For thousands of "GODS" beside the Christians' <u>God-Head</u> - "JESUS - <u>The Christ</u>," and the "SIXTEEN" others listed above, claimed that they too were...

"THE ONE AND ONLY TRUE SON OF GOD."
This theory was developed thousands of years before the announcement of...

"THE BIRTH OF JESUS -<u>The Christ Child</u> - TO JOSEPH AND MARY."
One such confession of another of the GODS duty to His Father is seen in the following <u>Hieratic Inscription</u> ... [<u>English translation</u> by S. Birch].

HIERATIC INSCRIPTION,

NORTH WALL OF SPEOS.

102

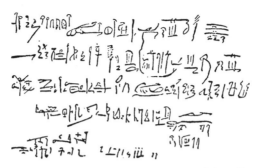

. . . thy son having . . . thou hast conquered the worlds
at once Ammon Ra-Harmachis,† the god at the first time,* who
gives life, health, and a time of many praises to the groom
of the Khen,** son of the Royal son of Cush,†† Opener
of the road, Maker of transport boats, Giver of instructions to
his lord . . . Amenshaa . . .

Profesors George G.M. James, John G. Jackson, Gerald K. Massey, Count C.F. Volney,
Sir Godfrey Higgins, Dr. Albert Churchward, Sir Ernest A. Wallis Budge, Sir James Frazier,
archaeologist Gaston Maspero, and countless others, presented each and everyone of us with
an abundant amount of documentation from the PYRAMID TEXT, COFFIN TEXT, BOOK OF
THE COMING FORTH BY DAY AND BY NIGHT, along with thousands more extracts and artifacts, in their thousands upon thousands of volumes that deal with the ancient Africans views
on the...

"ORIGIN OF HUMAN BIRTH, LIFE, DEATH, RESURRECTION, DIVINITY,"
etc. as options. But they did not associate either without the need for...

"LIFE'S HUMANITY....LIVING."
For, as they have always shown, "DEATH" to the ancient Africans, as it should be with their
current descendants, was "FUTURISTIC." But "LIFE" was, and still is, "EVER-PRESENT."
The following example should assist each student to understand this aspect of the TEACHINGS
from the MAGICAL RELIGIOUS SCENE in the PAPYRUS OF HUNEFER of the Mysteries System's DEATH and RESURRECTION RITUAL. Thus on page 104 we see Hunefer in the...

CEREMONY OF "OPENING THE MOUTH," AS PERFORMED ON HIS MUMMY
about ca. 1350 B.C.E., which was already during the XVIIIth Dynasty [ca. 1555 - 1340 BCE]
when Pharaohs from around Luxor [Thebes] reigned over Ta-Merry. It also shows the deceased
Hunefer being...

"RAISED FROM A DEAD LEVEL TO A MASONIFIED PERPENDICULAR". . .
for the purpose of having his...

---

1. See Amelia B. Edwards' A THOUSAND MILES UP THE NILE.

"MOUTH OPENED" FOR THE "MAGICAL RITES" IN PREPARATION FOR
"HIS ENTRY INTO THE NETHER WORLD" [Amenta, Tuat, Underworld, etc.].

The ceremony of "opening the mouth" being performed on the mummy of Hunefer, about B.C. 1250.
(From the *Papyrus of Hunefer*, sheet 5.)

We notice that most of the GOD-HEADS of the world that preceded <u>Ywh</u>, <u>Jesus Christ</u> and <u>Al'lah</u> were from such places as Ethiopia, Egypt, Punt, Nubia, Meröe, and other High-Cultures along the Nile Valley and the Great Lakes regions of Alkebu-lan, also in other areas of Asia and the so-called "AMERICAS." But the "Negro"CLERGY cannot see this fact, because they do not want to see anything that does not wholely conform with their adopted MYTHS and AL LEGORIES in the European and European-American VERSIONS of the <u>Old Testament</u> and <u>New Testament</u> that allow them to BLAST OFF into <u>euphoric trips</u> just prior to the hour of their call for the FINANCIAL OFFERING, which they always precede with...

"IT IS BETTER TO GIVE THAN TO RECEIVE,"

in their respective churches. For this same reason they have failed to understand the...

SEXUAL CONTRADICTIONS

between the <u>Adam and Eve anti-procreation syndrome</u> and the allowable...

HOMOSEXUALITY

within the so-called "<u>Holy Scriptures</u>," as shown in JUDGES, Chapters 19 and 20.

The BLACK BIBLE, as I see it, cannot tolerate the <u>contradictions</u> we have been examining throughout; neither the <u>distortions</u> in the TEACHINGS of the ancient and glorious traditions of the Africans of the Nile Valley and Great Lakes regions of Alkebu-lan; nor the prohibitions

104

against normal male and female copulation at the expense of support for UNNATURAL UNI-SEXUALITY. This is the same reason why the "NEGRO CLERGY" cannot understand the...

'PHALEX SYMBOL OF THE FIG LEAF'

used in all of the religions along the Nile [BLUE and WHITE], Tigris and Euphrates valleys thousands of years before its adaption in the BOOK OF GENESIS' story about...

"ADAM AND EVE IN THE GARDEN OF EDEN;"

which Moses himself plagiarized from countless stories he read as a student in his indigenous Alkebu-lan [Africa, Afrika, etc.] about the...

"PROTECTION OF THE SEXUAL [Tet]
ORGANS."

The "TET BUCKLE" phallic symbol was used to promote...

"SEXUAL COHABITATION" and "HUMAN REPRODUCTION,"

even among the Gods and Goddesses... as seen with Isis and Horus in their presentation of the "Black Madonna and Child Fertility Symbol." The Isis and Horus "Fertility Symbol" was the most celebrated of all. And from it the...

'VIRGIN MARY AND JESUS CHRIST FERTILITY SYMBOL'

was copied by the earliest Christians of North Africa, followed by all of the others in existence throughout Europe after the arrival of Christianity in Greece and Rome.

The BLACK BIBLE must become the catylist for the promotion of all of the natural functions of nature represented above. It must see the return of GOD in CHILD-BEARING and its only source of origin - SEXUAL INTERCOURSE, which was idolized in the symbols of Isis and Horus, and Mary and Jesus Christ - the infant child [GOD] sucking on the right breast of his mother [GODDESS].

The BLACK BIBLE must realize that...

NO ONE KNOWS ALL OF THE ANSWERS TO ANYTHING,

which of course included Jesus Christ who had to call upon his Father - YWH - while he, as a HUMAN BEING, twisted in death's pain upon a "CROSS" crying-out at the maximum strength of his voice:

"FATHER, FATHER, FATHER; WHY HAVE YOU FORGOTTEN ME?"[1]

The BLACK BIBLE must reflect the type of GOD that perpetuates LOVE, not FEAR; as the binding factor between mankind and a possible MAKER other than ourselves.

The BLACK BIBLE must include other BLACK PROPHETS before and after Moses; such as:

Edward W. Blyden, Marcus M. Garvey, Martin Luther

---

1. I refused to use Ole English as the "official" language of any God.

King, Jr., Harriet Tubman, Sojourner Truth, Kwame Nkrumah, Patrice Lumumba, John Chilimbwe, Casely Heyford [Sr. and Jr.], Booker T. Washington, Elijah Mohammad, Albert Cleage, Hamilton Jackson, Malcolm X, Toussaint L'Oveture, Paul Robeson, Nat Turner, and countless others that are too numerous to list here....BLACK BROTHERS and BLACK SISTERS all, dead and/or alive, who struggled and/or are struggling for the physical and mental FREEDOM of African [BLACK] People everywhere.

The BLACK BIBLE must recognize that all of the GODS that mankind produced in the past, at present, and will in the future, MUST be respected as attempts of our fellow human beings trying to reach equilibrium between the stages of HUMAN EVOLUTION - beginning, birth, life, death, and A POSSIBLE FUTURE EXPERIENCE UNKNOWN TO ANYONE...including the religionists.

The BLACK BIBLE must recognize that from the WOMB, and THROUGH THE PORTAL OF THE BLACK WOMAN'S VAGINA - TO AND FROM - ALONE...COMES BLACK PEOPLE; not one of whom came from another human being's "RIB CAGE."

These are but a few of the basic "REVELATIONS" necessary for the BLACK BIBLE to project. They are the TRUTH which the "NEGRO CLERGY" has carefully avoided and/or outrightly condemned without the least bit of examination into the facts related thereto. For the HOLY SCRIBES who will write the...

INSPIRED WORDS OF THE ONE AND ONLY BLACK GOD,

for

HIS ONE AND ONLY BLACK PEOPLE,

must be Black Men and Black Women who are not afraid to write about BLACK INSPIRATORS.

Lastly: the BLACK BIBLE must gather all of the existing and past RELIGIONS of the entire world; all of that which will advance the good and welfare of BLACK PEOPLE everywhere. For the Holy Black Scribes must realize that no one has any monopoly on intelligence. And that "MAN MADE GOD" by virtue of the "WORD;" when he declared that,"THERE IS A GOD." Also, that in his declaration "GOD MADE MAN" throughout the OLD TESTAMENT, NEW TESTAMENT and HOLY QUR'AN with quotations; not the writings of GOD...Ywh of Ur, Jesus Christ of Nazareth, Al'lah of Mecca, Oledumare of Lagos, Ngai of Nairobi, or Damballah Ouedo of Port au Prince, etc. For no where can anyone point out to someone else anything "GOD [anyone] WROTE." It is always what someone else wrote that...

"GOD SAID;" and/or what someone else said or wrote that "GOD WROTE."

If the Black Nation's "GOD" cannot serve and protect HIS, HER or ITS Black People FIRST and FOREMOST, as all other people's GOD gives them FIRST CONSIDERATION in everything they are involved; what good will it be in having such a "MAKER" or "SAVIOUR"? One has to remember that a...

"REDEEMER, SAVIOUR" and/or "MESSIAH"...

is one of three of the same thing. And, either's responsibility is DELIVERANCE. But the only major "DELIVERANCE" Black [African] People need today is from...

EUROPEAN AND EUROPEAN-AMERICAN COLONIALISM
AND NEO-COLONIALISM,

both physically and spiritually. For although chattle slavery has mostly disappeared from the White Man's arsenal of weapons to produce GENOCIDE on the Black Man and his family, he manages to accomplish the same results through CULTURAL and MENTAL genocide...the end products of COLONIALISM and NEO-COLONIALISM that began with the armies of the governments of Europe, Great Britain and the United States of America when France invaded Cueta, North Africa in 1830 C.E., all with the aid and comfort of the professed "Christian Missionaries" from Europe and European-America; backed up with the Caucasian-Semitic RACISM and RELIGIOUS BIGOTRY in their Old Testament and New Testament of Judaism and Christianity; this being no different than the invaders who came from Asia under the banner of spreading ISLAM in the 7th Century C.E. in North Africa, and the 12th Century C.E. in East Africa with...THE SWORD, THE CRESCENT, THE QUR'AN, and THE JIHAD.

As one who has made the study of the "HOLY SCRIPTURES" [all I can get my hands on] of every RELIGION in the European and Asian world a WAY of life, those that are "Western" oriented I find reprehensible because African [BLACK] People - the first to create a "HOLY SCRIPTURE...as shown in the BOOK OF THE COMING FORTH BY DAY AND BY NIGHT... should now be the only people in the entire world without one of their own; one that secures for BLACK PEOPLE a place as the only...

"CHOSEN PEOPLE OF...[The Black]...GOD."

The last point I would like to bring to your attention is: Why should the BLACK BIBLE not deal with the matter of WHITE RELIGION'S [Judaism and Christianity] financial investments in the vast RACIST MACHINERY of colonialism and neo-colonialism that continue to perpetuate mass GENOCIDE throughout the BLACK, BROWN, YELLOW, RED, etc. worlds? Should the BLACK BIBLE fail to have GOD'S positive condemnation against the WHITE MASTERS OF GENOCIDE in the Jewish and Christian religions who are in Angola, Zimbabwe, Azania, Guinea Biseau, Namibia, Monomotapa, and all of the other areas where colonialism and ultra-neo-colonialism remain rampant throughout Africa; where European and European-American style WHITE RACISM and SEMITIC RELIGIOUS BIGOTRY make love and marriage with Asian and

Asian-African Arab FEUDALISM in the common cause of the <u>Africans extermination</u> by rabid GENOCIDE - in which all of them are engaged? Should the <u>Black God</u>   not kill for his "<u>Chosen</u> [BLACK] <u>People</u>?" Or is it that the billions of dollars White People are reaping out of the Black People's enslavement and genocide are also to be attributed to that part of the <u>Old Testament</u> where the European and European-American <u>God</u> - YWH and/or JESUS CHRIST - allegedly...

"CURSED BLACK PEOPLE,"

according to the racist myth of like story in the <u>Book Of Genesis</u> about...

"NOAH AND THE GREAT DELUGE?"

Should the BLACK BIBLE worry about the eating of...

"PIG'S CHITTERLINGS, CHOPS, EARS, TAILS AND GENITAL ORGANS,"

while losing sight of the HUMAN HOGS that snuff out the lives of millions upon millions of <u>Black People</u> - SAINTS and ANGELS - every day in every year for the last <u>four hundred</u> [400] <u>years;</u> <u>Black People</u> whose only CRIME is struggling for the "<u>Liberation</u>" of...

THEIR MIND, THEIR BODY, AND THEIR SOUL

in the colonies where <u>Black People</u> are still penned-up by WHITE JUDAEO-CHRISTIANS of the Jewish and Christian RELIGIONS and/or BROWN ARABS of the Moslem RELIGION?

The BLACK BIBLE must address itself to the more than ELEVEN MILLION [11,000,000] SQUARE MILES of the "<u>AFRICAN</u> [Black] PROMISELAND," and the "<u>AFRICAN</u> EXODUS" back home to "Mother ALKEBU-LAN [Africa]...the LAND OF THE ORIGINAL GARDEN OF EDEN." For it MUST be remembered that one of OUR most glorious prophets - the <u>Honourable Marcus M.</u> <u>Garvey</u>, in his most omnipotently "INSPIRED WORDS" - which he delivered in his MOST HOLY "PHILOSOPHY AND OPINIONS" - came from the teachings of the MOST HOLY PROPHET

ELECT OF GOD [St.] Edward W. Blyden, and others of <u>The Great</u> <u>Hall Of Alkebu-lan's</u> GODS and GODDESSES be- fore him. Teachings that say: In the name of THE ONE AND ONLY BLACK <u>GOD of</u> Alkebu-lan's People everywhere, the GOD who inspired Honour- able Patriot E.W. Blyden to remind us that..."THE AFRICANS RIGHT TO BE <u>WRONG</u> IS SACRED," AS HIS [her] RIGHT TO HIS OWN PERSONALITY; is also the same God who said "BLACK IS BEAUTI- FUL;" the same BLACK GOD Who taught us to recognize that:

A FRIC A, by the Ancients, was called Olympia, Hesperia, Oceania, Corypbe, Ammonis, Ortygia, and Æthiopia. By the Greeks and Romans, Lybia and Africa. By the Æthiopians and Moors, Alkebu-lan.

108   "THE AFRICAN WOMAN, THE SOURCE OF THE AFRICAN PEOPLE,

IS THE HIGHEST REPRESENTATIVE OF THE AFRICAN GOD. "

The BLACK BIBLE'S Black Gods and Black Goddesses, whatever you desire to call THEM, HE, SHE, IT, THEY... dealt with their African People. And they saw that the DEVILS had taken over their HUMAN RIGHTS. But the BLACK GODS and BLACK GODDESSES came forth from their hiding places where they too had retreated, having suffered from the same WHITE GODS and WHITE GODDESSES who had enslaved, raped and committed all forms of genocide against the non-European peoples of the entire planet Earth. Thus, BLESSED be the fact that they have declared unto their Most Holy "CHOSEN BLACK PEOPLE" this day:

> I WILL HELP YOU LIBERATE YOURSELF; YOU KNOWING
> VERY WELL THAT I HAVE ALWAYS SAID TO YOU:'I WILL
> ONLY HELP THOSE BLACK PEOPLE WHO BELIEVE IN,
> ACT OF, AND FIGHT FOR, THEMSELVES WITHOUT DE-
> PENDENCY UPON OTHER PEOPLES AND THEIR GODS.'

In the BOOK OF THE MARTYRD AFRICANS of the HOLY BLACK BIBLE OF AFRICAN PEOPLE EVERYWHERE it will be wisely written that from the first invasion of Alkebu-lan [Africa] by the Hyksos Asians in ca. 1675 B.C.E.; Persians and Assyrians in ca. 525 B.C.E.; Macedonians in ca. 332 B.C.E.; Greeks in ca. 327 B.C.E.; Romans in ca. 250 and 30 B.C.E.; Arabs in ca. 640 C.E.; Turks in ca. 1244 C.E.; British in ca. 1792 C.E.; French in ca. 1830 C.E. that began the systematic "PARTITION OF AFRICA"- which culminated with the BERLIN CONFERENCE and ACT of 1884 - 1885 C.E.; the LEAGUE OF NATIONS in 1918 - 1935 C.E.; and now the UNITED NATIONS ORGANIZATION from 1945 C.E. to the present...before and since the deliberate massacre of Saint Lumumba, Saint Malcom X, Saint Martin Luther King, Jr., and countless other SACRED SPIRITS, PROPHETS and PROPHETESS of all of the Black People of the entire world:

> BLESSED BE THE BLACK PEOPLE WHO KNOW THEMSELVES
>
> FROM THIS DAY ON; FOR I SHALL HELP YOU WITH YOUR
>
> ENEMIES, WHO ARE EQUALLY MY ENEMIES FOREVER. AMEN!

In my conclusion; how could I have have forgotten our GOOD FRIEND who shall now appeal to your sense of fair play and reasoning? I now present for your edification...

SATAN'S FAREWELL SPEECH ON THE STRANGE "GOD" WORSHIPED BY CHRISTENDOM

A God who could make good children as easily as bad, yet preferred to make bad ones; who could have made every one of them happy, yet never made a single happy one; who made them prize their bitter life, yet stingily cut it short; who gave his angels eternal happiness unearned, yet required his other children to earn it; who gave his angels painless lives, yet cursed

---

1. See John G. Jackson's MAN, GOD, AND CIVILIZATION, pp. 160 - 161

his other children with biting miseries and maladies of mind and body; who mouths justice and invented hell, mouths mercy and invented hell, mouths Golden Rules and forgiveness multiplied by seventy times seven, and invented hell; who mouths morals to other people and has none himself; who frowns upon crimes, yet commits them all; who created man without invitation, then tries to shuffle the responsibility for man's acts upon man, instead of honorably placing it where it belongs, upon himself; and finally, with altogether divine obtuseness, invites this poor abused slave to worship him!

BIBLIOGRAPHY.... BOOKS USED IN THE PREPARATION OF THIS VOLUME BUT NOT QUOTED AND/OR CITED IN THE TEXT

Andrea, Tor.   MOHAMMED: THE MAN AND HIS FAITH, 1936.

Armattoe, Dr. R.E.G.   THE GOLDEN AGE OF WEST AFRICAN CIVILIZATION, 1946.

Adamson R. (ed. by Sorely and Hardie).   THE DEVELOPMENT OF GREEK PHILOSOPHY, London, 1908.

Arnold, E.V.   ROMAN STOICISM, 1911.

Arnold, Sir Thomas and Alfred Guillaume.   THE LEGACY OF ISLAM, London, 1931.

Beir, Ulli (ed.)   THE ORIGIN OF LIFE AND DEATH: AFRICAN CREATION MYTHS, London, 1966.

Beynon, E.D.   THE VOODOO CULT AMONG NEGRO MIGRANTS IN DETROIT (In: American Journal of Sociology, July 1937- May, 1938).

Bourke, Vernon J.   AUGUSTINE'S QUEST OF WISDOM, Wisconsin, 1944.

Burridge, William   DESTINY AFRICA: Cardinal Lavigerie and the Making of the White Fathers, London, 1966.

Burnet, J.   GREEK PHILOSOPHERS, Part I, Thales to Plato, New York, 1966.

Budge, Sir E.A.   EGYPT (1725).

Burnet J.   EARLY GREEK PHILOSOPHY, 3rd ed. 1920; 4th ed., 1930.

Bailey, C.   THE GREEK ATOMISTS AND EPICURUS, Q.U.P., 1913.

Buber, Martin   AT THE TURNING, New York, 1952.

Blackman   THE PSALMISTS, (ed. essays by D.C. Simpson), 1926.

--------   DIE LITERATUR DER AGYPTER (English translation), 1923.

Buchler   DIE TOBIADEN UND DIE ONIADEN, 1899.

Breasted, J.H.   ANCIENT RECORDS OF EGYPT: The Historical Documents, 1905.

Biobaku, S.   RELIGION IN CONTEMPORARY AFRICAN LITERATURE, New York, c1966.

Burnet, J. (ed.)   THE WORKS OF PLATO (In: Oxford Classical Texts, 5 vols. 3rd ed., New York, 1888).

Capes. W.W.   STOICISM, 1880.

Cook, S.A.   THE RELIGION OF ANCIENT PALESTINE IN THE LIGHT OF ARCHAEOLOGY, 1930.

Cowley   JEWISH DOCUMENTS OF THE TIME OF EXRA, 1919.

Danquah, Dr. J.B.   AKAN LAWS AND CUSTOMS, London, 1928.

--------   THE AKAN DOCTRINE OF GOD, London, 1944.

Dupont-Sommer, Prof. A.   THE DEAD SEA SCROLLS: A Preliminary Survey.

Dittenberger, W.S.   INSCRIPTION GAECARUM, and, ORIENTS GRALLA.

------------   INSCRIPTION SELECTAS.

------------   CORPUS INSCRIPTIONUM GRAECARUM.

------------   CORPUS INSCRIPTIONUM LATINARUM.

------------   CORPUS INSCRIPTIONUM SEMITICARUM.

Dawson, C.   THE MAKING OF EUROPE, New York, 1932.
DuBois, Dr. W.E.B.   THE NEGRO CHURCH, New York.

Darwin, Sir Charles.   THE NEXT MILLION YEARS, London, 1952.
Denon, Baron.   TRAVELS IN UPPER AND LOWER EGYPT, London, 1789.
Daniel, V.E.   "Ritual and Stratification in Chicago Negro
                    Churches" (In: AMERICAN SOCIOLOGICAL REVIEW,
                    7 Vols).
Dellagioacona, V.   AN AFRICAN MARTYROLOGY, Italy, 1965.
Desai, Ram (ed.)   CHRISTIANITY IN AFRICA AS SEEN BY AFRICANS,
                    Colorado, 1962.
Dodge, 'R.E.   THE UNPOPULAR MISSIONARY, New Jersey, 1964.

Evans-Pritchard, E.E.   THEORIES OF PRIMITIVE RELIGION, New
                    New York, 1967.
Erdman, J.E.   A HISTORY OF PHILOSOPHY, Vol. I., 1910.
Eusebius   ECCLESIA TICAL HISTORY, III.
Esman   DIE LITERATURE DER AGYPTER.

el-Yezdi, Haji Abu.   THE KASIDAD (as translated by Sir Richard
                    F. Burton), London, 1878.
Erskine, Mrs. Stewart.   THE VANISHED CITIES OF NORTHERN AFRICA,
                    London, 1927.
Emperor Galerius.   IMPERIAL EDICT OF MAY c305-311 A.D.
Eddy, Mrs. Mary Baker   SCIENCE AND HEALTH WITH A KEY TO THE
                    SCRIPTURES, (1876).
----   MANUAL OF THE MOTHER CHURCH, (1888).
Eban Abba.   MY PEOPLE: THE STORY OF THE JEWS, New York, 1968.
Erdman, B.D.   THE RELIGION OF ISRAEL, New York.
Esiun-Odom   BLACK NATIONALISM. Boston, 1961.
Fishberg, M.   THE JEWS, London, 1911.
Frobenius, Leo   AFRICA SPEAKS, 3 Vols., London, 1913 (latest
                    edition, 1969).
Frazier, E.F.   THE NEGRO CHURCH IN AMERICA, New York, 1964.
Fisher, M.M.   NEGRO SLAVE SONGS IN THE UNITED STATES, Ith a,
                    New York, 1959.
Fernandez, J.W.   "Politics and Prophecy: African Religious Move-
                    ments" (In: PRACTICAL ANTHROPOLOGY, Vol. 12,
                    Mar.-April, 1965).
Fortes, Meyer   DIPUS AND JOB IN WEST AFRICAN RELIGION, Cambridge. 1959.
Finbert, E.J.   DICTIONAIRE DES PROVERBES DU MONDE, Paris, 1965.
Fickling, S.M.   SLAVE CONVERSION IN SOUTH CAROLINA: 1830-1860
                    (Univ. of S.C., 1924).
Finklestein, Louis   THE JEWS: THEIR HISTORY, CULTURE AND RE-
                    LIGION, New York, 1949: 3 Vols.
Gluckman, Max.   "The Logic of Witchcraft" (In: Peter J.M. McEwan
                    and Robert B. Sutcliffe, eds., MODERN AFRICA, 1965).
Gard, R.A. (ed. Genl'. edition)   GREAT RELIGIONS OF MODERN MAN,
                    New York, 1962.
Geddes, Michael   CHURCH HISTORY OF ETHIOPIA, 1969.
Gaton-Thompson, G.   THE ZIMBABWE CULTURE, 1931.
Garrucci, R.   LA MONETE DELL'ITALIA ANTICA. Parte Secunda,
                    LXXV, Roma, 1885.
Gibbon, N.   DECLINE AND FALL OF THE ROMAN EMPIRE, Vol. I,
                    Vol. IV, Dublin, 1781.
Gibbs, H.A.R.   ARAB LITERATURE, London, 1926.
Hitti, P.K.   MAKERS OF ARAB HISTORY, New York, 1940.
Hitti, P.K.   HISTORY OF THE ARABS, London, 1927.
Hall, H.R.   ANCIENT HISTORY OF THE NEAR EAST, 1947.
----   GREAT ZIMBABWE, 1905.
Harper, R.F.   THE CODE OF HAMMURABI, KING OF BABYLON,
                    ABOUT 2250 B.C., 1904.
Herskovitz, M.J.   THE MYTH OF THE NEGRO PAST, New York, 1941.

Herskervitz, M.   ARE THE JEWS A RACE?
Higgins, Sir Geoffrey.   THE CELTIC DRUIDS, London, 1892.
Huart, C.   LITERATURE ARABE, Pari 1902.
Horne, Melville   LETTERS ON MISSIONS, 1744.
Hoper, John   AD UXOREM, London. 1550.
Huxley, Thomas   MAN'S PLACE IN NATURE, Essay IV, London.
Hook, S.H. (ed.)   MYTH AND RITUAL, 1933.
Helibdorus   ETHIOPIAN HISTORY UNDERDOWNE, 1857 (London, 1895).
Hertzberg, A. (ed.)   JUDAISM, New York, 1962.

Ions, Veronica   EGYPTIAN MYTHOLOGY, London, 1965.
Irenaeus   AGAINST HERESIES, III.
Inge, W.R.   THE PHILOSOPHY OF PLOTINUS, 3rd ed.,
                    New York, 1928.
Irby, C.L. and Mangles, J.   TRAVELS IN EGYPT AND NUBIA, SYRIA
                              AND THE HOLY LAND, 1844.

Jaeger, Werner   ARISTOTLE:FUNDAMENTALS OF THE HISTORY OF HIS
                    DEVELOPMENT, O.U.P., 1932.
Jack, J.W.   THE DATE OF THE EXODUS, 1925.
Johnson, Rev. S.   THE HISTORY OF THE YORUBAS, 1937.
Jackson, F.J. Foakes, and Lake, K.   THE BEGINNING OF CHRISTIANI-
                                       TY, 1933.
Jernegan, M.W.   "Slavery and Conversion in the American
                    Colonies" (In: THE AMERICAN HISTORICAL
                    REVIEW, Vol. XXI, April. 1961).
Johnson, A.R.   THE CULTIC PROPHET IN ANCIENT ISRAEL.
Kellner, K.A.H.   TERTULLIAN AUGEWEWAHLTE SCHRIFTON (Book I,
                    Vol. 7, Kepton-Munich. 1912).
Kramers, J.H.   THE LEGACY OF ISLAM, New York, 1931.
Kidd, B.J.   A HISTORY OF THE CHURCH TO A.D. 461 (1932).
Keane, Prof. A.H.   MAN PAST AND PRESENT, New York, 1920.

Kenyatta, Jomo   FACING MT. KENYA, New York, 1968.

Lincoln, C.E.   BLACK MUSLIMS, Boston, 1961.
Liebevitch, L.   ANCIENT EGYPT, Cairo, Egypt, 1958.
Leslau, Wolf   FALASHA ANTHOLOGY, New Haven, 1951.
Lewis and Schacnt (eds.)   ENCYCLOPEDIA OF ISLAM.
Loisy, R.   BIRTH OF THE CHRISTIAN RELIGION.
Lopez, Duarte   A HISTORY OF THE KINGDOM OF THE CONGO (translated
                    from its original Italian by Fillippo Pagafetta,
                    1591 A.D.; translated into English in 1597 and
                    1881).
Latourette, K.S.   HISTORY OF EXPANSION OF CHRISTIANITY II (1939).
Lovell, J.   "The Social Implications of the Negro Spirituals"
                    (In: JOURNAL OF NEGRO EDUCATION, October, 1939).
Morel, E.D.   BLACK MAN'S BURDEN, New York, 1920.
-----   KING LEOPOLD'S RULE IN AFRICA, New York, 1904.
Meyerowitz, E.L.R.   THE AKAN SACRED STATE, New York, 1951.
-----------   AKAN TRADITIONS OF ORIGIN, New York, 1952.
Michelet, R.   AFRICAN EMPIRES AND CIVILIZATIONS (Pan-Naf Pub).
Mendelssohn, S.   THE JEWS OF AFRICA, ESPECIALLY IN THE SIXTEENTH
                    AND SEVENTEENTH CENTURY, New York, 1920.
Meek, C.K.   A SUDANESE KINGDOM, London, 1931.
MacMichael, H.A.   A HISTORY OF THE ARABS OF THE SUDAN, New York,
                    1922.
Mays, B.E. and Joseph W. Nicholson, THE NEGRO CHURCH, New York.
Makdisi, Nadim   "The Moslems Of America" (In: THE CHRISTIAN
                    CENTURY, August 26, 1959).
Mohammed, Elijah   THE SUPREME WISDOM: Solution to the so-called
                    Negroes' Problems, Chicago, Ill.,1957.
Maurier, H.   RELIGION AND DEVELOPMENT: Traditions Africani et
                    Catechises. Paris. 1965.

[Bibliography continued]

Mitchell, R.C. and others   A COMPREHENSIVE BIBLIOGRAPHY OF
                             MODERN AFRICAN RELIGIOUS MOVE-
                             MENTS, Ill., 1964.
Malinowski, L.   MAGIC, SCIENCE AND RELIGION, London.
Maimonides   GUIDE OF THE PERPLEXED (translated by M. Fried-
                 lander), New York, 1881.
Makkari   MOHAMMEDAN DYNASTIES IN SPAIN, London, 1840, Vol I
Masudi, El   PRAIRIES D'OR, Vol. 7 (translated Berbier de
                 Meynard) Paris, 1861.
Mendelsohn, Jack   GOD, ALLAH AND JU JU, New York, 1962.
Muir, Sir William   LIFE OF MOHAMET, London, 1894.
Massey, G.A.   BOOK OF THE BEGINNINGS, Vol. II, London.
Meek, T.J.   HEBREW ORIGINS, New York, 1960.
Northcott, W.C.   CHRISTIANITY IN AFRICA, Philadelphia, 1963.
Nkeitia, J.H.   ART, RITUAL AND MYTHS IN AMERICAN NEGRO STUDIES,
                 Acra, Ghana, 1966.
Nottingham, E.K.   METHODISM AND THE FRONTIER, New York, 1941.
Oehler, F.   QUINTA SEPTIMU FLORENTIS TERTULLIAN QUAE SUPERSUNT
                 OMNIA, I, Leipzig, 1853.
Oates, W.J.   BASIC WRITINGS OF ST. AUGUSTINE, New York, 1948,
                 2 Vols.
Ovington, M.W.   THE WALLS CAME TUMBLING DOWN, New York, 1947.
Osterly and Robinson   A HISTORY OF ISRAEL, New York, 1934.
Parker, R.A.   THE INCREDIBLE MESSIAH, Boston, 1937.
Parrinder, Geoffrey   AFRICAN MYTHOLOGY, London, 1967.
Plutarch   ALEXANDER "THE GREAT" (n.d.).
PROTEST CHURCHES DIVIDED ON THEIR URBAN CRISIS PROGRAMS (New York
                 Times, Sunday. May 18, 1969.
Parrish, Lydia   SLAVE SONGS OF THE GEORGIA SEA ISLANDS, New York,
                 1942.
Pascoe, C.F.   TWO HUNDRED YEARS OF S.P.G. AN HISTORICAL ACCOUNT
                 OF THE SOCIETY FOR THE PROPAGATION OF THE
                 GOSPEL IN FOREIGN PARTS, London, 1901.
Purchas, Samuel   PURCHAS: HIS PILGRIMAGE OR RELATIONS OF THE WORLD,1928.
Rattray, R.S.   ASHANTI LAW AND CUSTOM, 1929.
Rylands, L.G.   THE BEGINNINGS OF GNOSTIC CHRISTIANITY.
Ramos, Arthur   THE NEGRO IN BRAZIL, Washington, D.C., 1939.
Plaidy, Jean   THE SPANISH INQUISITION, New York, 1967.
Plotinus   THE ENNEADS (translated into English by S.
                 Mackenna and B.S. Page), 5 Vols., 1817-1830.
Peet's   EGYPT AND THE OLD TESTAMENT, New York, 1922.
Palmer, H.H.   HAROUN-AL-RACHID, London, 1881.
Russel, M.   NUBIA AND ABYSSINIA, New York, 1883.
Rolland, A.   REMAIN INTERMEDIARE DES CHERCHEURS ET DES CUSIEUX, Vol. 34
Rogers, Joel A.   SEX AND RACE, Vol. I, New York, 1945.
------   NATURE KNOWS NO COLOR LINE, New York, 1950.
Robertson, A.   ORIGINS OF CHRISTIANITY, New York, 1962.
Ratzel, F.   HISTORY OF MANKIND, Vols. I-II, London, 1869.
Smith, Prof. Elliot   HUMAN HISTORY, London, 1934.
Suyuti, S.   HISTORY OF THE CALYPHS (translated by H.S. Jar-
                 rett, Calcutta, 1881).
Schofield, J.N.   HISTORICAL BACKGROUND OF THE BIBLE, London,
                 New York, 1938.
Sabe, A.   AL KORAN (1784).
Syed, Ameer Ali   LIFE AND TEACHINGS OF MOHAMMED, London, 1891.
Sithole, Nda baningi   "An African Christian View" (In: CHRIST-
                 IANITY IN THE NON-WESTERN WORLD, ed.
                 by C.W. Forman, Englewood Cliffs,
                 New Jersey, 1967).
Stace, W.T.   A CRITICAL HISTORY OF GREEK PHILOSOPHY, New York,
                 1920.

[Bibliography continued]

Smith R.	RELIGION OF THE SEMITES.
Smith, Homer C.	MAN AND HIS GODS, Boston, 1953.
Soames, Jane	COAST OF BARBARY, London.
St. Augustine	ON THE BEAUTIFUL AND THE FIT (c370-373 C.E.).
-------------	DRAMATIC POEMS (c377 C.E.).
-------------	AGAINST THE ACADEMICS, ON THE HISTORY OF LIFE.
-------------	ON ORDER.
-------------	DE VITA BEATA.
-------------	ON MUSIC.
-------------	ON THE MORALS OF THE CATHOLIC CHURCH AND OF THE MANICHEANS.
-------------	RETRACTIONS.
-------------	DE ORDINE.
St. Cyprian	THE LAPSED.
-------------	THE UNITY OF THE CATHOLIC CHURCH.
Stewart, J.A.	THE MYTHS OF PLATO, U.O.P., 1905.
-------	PLATO'S DOCTRINE OF IDEAS, O.U.P., 1909.
Steindorff, G. and Keith C. Seete	WHEN EGYPT RULED THE EAST, Chicago, Ill., 1942.
Steward, T.G.	FIFTY YEARS IN THE GOSPEL MINISTRY, Philadelphia, 1915.
Southon, A.E.	GOLD COAST METHODISM 1835-1935 (1935).
St. John, Sir S.	HAYTI OR BLACK REPUBLIC, London, 1889.
St. Augustine	THE FIRST CATECHETICAL INSTRUCTIONS.
---------------	THE GREATNESS OF THE SOUL.
---------------	THE LORD'S SERMON ON THE MOUNT.
Tacticus	BOOK V.
Tertullian	TREATISE ON PENANCE: ON PENANCE ON PURITY (translated by Prof. J.A. Waszink), Westminister, Maryland, 1957.
Tanner, B.J.	AN APOLOGY FOR AFRICAN METHODISM, Baltimore, 1867.
Temples, Placide	BANTU PHILOSOPHY , Paris, 1880 [London, 1918]
Tertullian	DE ANIMA.
----------	THE TREATISE AGAINST HERMOGENES.
Tertullian	TREATISE MARRIAGE AND REMARRIAGE: TO HIS WIFE, AN EXHORTAION TO CHASTITY, MONOGOMY (translated by William P. LeSaint, S.J.,S.T.D.) Westminister, Maryland, 1957.
Thornton, C.	"The Treatise of St. Caecilius Cyprian" (In: LIBRARY OF THE FATHERS OF THE HOLY CATHOLIC CHURCH, 3: Oxford, 1839).
Thelwall, S.	TERTULLIAN (AMF, 4 American reprint, New York, 1925).
Taylor, T.	SELECT WORKS OF PLOTINUS, (ed. by G.R.S. Mead) 1929.
THE MESSENGER (Official organ of the Nation of Islam, a weekly Newspaper).	
THE DAY (Father Divine's Peace Mission News Weekly and Official Religious Organ).	
Talbon, P.A.	NIGERIAN FERTILITY CULTS, London, 1927.
Tellez, B.	TRAVELS OF THE JESUITS IN ETHIOPIA, New York, 1920.
Tritton, A.S.	THE CALIPHS AND THEIR NON-MUSLIM SUBJECTS (1930).
Voorhis, P.M.H. Van Buren	NEGRO MASONRY IN THE UNITED STATES, New York, 1940.
Van Volten, G.	TRIA OPPOSCULA AUCTORE ABU OTHMAN AMR IBN BAHR AL-JAHIZ, Leyden, 1903.
Wallis-Budge, Sir E.A.	FROM FETISH TO GOD IN ANCIENT EGYPT, London, 1934.
Welch, G.	AFRICA BEFORE THEY CAME, New York, 1965.
Wallis, R.E.	"The Writings Of St. Cyprian" (In: ANTE-NICENE CHRISTIAN LIBRARY 8; Edinburgh 1868). See also reprint in: ANTE-NICENE FATHERS 5, New York, 1907.

Wheless, J.   IS IT GOD'S WORD, New York, 1926.
--------   FORGERY IN CHRISTIANITY, New York, 1930.
Whittaker, T.   THE NEO-PLATONISTS (2nd ed., Cambridge, 1901).
---------   A HISTORY OF ECCLECTICISM IN GREEK PHILOSOPHY
                   (translated by S.F. Alleyne) London, 1883.
Williams, J.J.   HEBREWISM IN WEST AFRICA, London, 1931.
Widney, J.P.   RACE LIFE OF THE ARYANS, Vol. III, New York, 1907.
Warren, Ruth   MOHAMMED, PROPHET OF ISLAM, New York, 1965.
Windsor, R.   FROM BABYLON TO TIMBUKTU.
Williams, J.A. (ed.)   ISLAM, New York, 1962.
Woodson, C.B.   THE HISTORY OF THE NEGRO CHURCH, Washington, D.C.
Williams, Eric   CAPITALISM AND SLAVERY, New York, 1944.
---------   DOCUMENTS OF CARIBBEAN HISTORY 1492-1565, PMC,
                   HQ, Trinidad, W.I.
Westerman, Prof. D.   AFRICA AND CHRISTIANITY, New York, 1937.
Werner, A.   MYTHS AND LEGENDS OF THE BANTU, New York, 1933.

Welch, G.   THE UNVEILING OF TIMBUKTOO, New York, 1938.
Wand, J. and M. John   OUR SUDAN: ITS PYRAMIDS AND PROGRESS,
                   London, 1905.
Wakigorski, A.   THE JEWS IN AFRICA, Cairo, 1966.
Williamson, S.G.   AKAN RELIGION AND THE CHRISTIAN FAITH: A COM-
                   PARATIVE STUDY OF THE IMPACT OF TWO RELIGIONS,
                   (ed. by Kwesi A. Dickson, New York, 1965).
Yinger, J.M.   RELIGION SOCIETY AND THE INDIVIDUAL, New York.
Young, C.   POLITICS IN THE CONGO, DECOLONIZATION AND
                   INDEPENDENCE, Princeton, New Jersey, 1965.

Zeller, E.   A HISTORY OF PHILOSOPHY FROM THE EARLIEST PERIOD
                   OF TIME TO SOCRATES (translated by S.F. Alleyne)
                   2 Vols..London, 1881.

BOOKS LISTED CHRONOLOGICALLY ACCORDING TO
APPEARANCE IN THE TEXT

Reade, W. THE MARTYDOM OF MAN, London, 1872
Jackson, John G. MAN, GOD, AND CIVILIZATION, New York, 1972
Budge, Sir E.A.W. BOOK OF THE DEAD, London, 1885
ben-Jochannan, Yosef AFRICAN ORIGINS OF THE MAJOR "WESTERN RE-
                   LIGIONS," New York, 1970
Hitti, Phillip H. HISTORY OF THE ARABS, London, 1937
Muir, M.W. LIFE OF MOHAMET, London, 1894
Churchward, Albert SIGNS AND SYMBOLS OF PRIMORDIAL MAN, London,
                   1930
-----------   THE ORIGIN AND EVOLUTION OF RELIGION, London,
                   1928
Smith, Homer W. MAN AND HIS GODS, Boston,
Frazier, Sir James THE GOLDEN BOUGH, London, 1890 [13 vols.]
Maspero, Gaston THE DAWN OF CIVILIZATION, London [ed. by A.H. Sayle,
                   transl. by M.L. McClure, 13 vols.]
Muller, Max THE SACRED BOOKS OF THE EAST, Berlin, 1920
Bell, R. INTRODUCTION TO THE QUR'AN, London, 1918
Bouquet, A.C. COMPARATIVE RELIGION, London
James, E.O. COMPARATIVE RELIGION, New York, 1957
Malinowski, B. MAGIC, SCIENCE AND RELIGION and OTHER ESSAYS, London

[Bibliography continued]

Waley, A. THE AMALECTS OF CONFUCIUS

Budge, Sir E.A.W. PAPYRUS OF ANI, London, 1885

ben-Jochannan, Yosef BLACK MAN OF THE NILE AND HIS FAMILY,
        New York, 1972

James, G.G.M. STOLEN LEGACY, New York, 1954

Higgins, Sir Godfrey ANACALYPSIS, London, 1830 [2 vols.]

Ashley, William LIFE AND LOVE OF JESUS CHRIST, London, 1800
        [2 vols.]
        LOST BOOKS OF THE BIBLE [World Publ. Co., Cam-
        bridge, Maryland, Date 1959, etc.]

Levi.THE AQUARIAN GOSPEL OF JESUS CHRIST, Santa Monica, Calif.,
        [1908, 1952, 1963, 1969, etc.]

Brangan, T. THE PENITENTAL TYRANT or SLAVE TRADER REFORM-
        ED, Princeton University, Princeton, New Jersey, [Date ?]

ben-Jochannan, Yosef CULTURAL GENOCIDE IN THE BLACK AND AFRI-
        CAN STUDIES CURRICULUM, New York, 1973
        OLD TESTAMENT [See pages 85 - 89 of this volume]
        NEW TESTAMENT [Ibid.]
        HOLY QUR'AN [Ibid.]

Golenischeff, L. METTERNICHSTELE, Leipzig, 1877

Lincoln, C. Eric THE BLACK MUSLIMS,

Groves, C.P. THE PLANTING OF CHRISTIANITY IN AFRICA, London,
        1888 [4 vols.]

Stoddard, L.S. THE RISING TIDE OF COLOUR, New York, 1928

ben-Jochannan, Yosef and George E. Simmonds THE BLACK MAN'S NORTH
        AND EAST AFRICA, New York, 1972

ben-Jochannan, Yosef THE BLACK MAN'S RELIGION: THE MYTH OF
        GENESIS AND EXODUS AND THE EXCLUSION OF THEIR AFRI-
        CAN ORIGIN, New York, 1973 [vol. II]

Sandford, Eva B. THE MEDITERRANEAN WORLD, New York

deGraft-Johnson, J.C. AFRICAN GLORY, London, 1945

Massey, Gerald K. EGYPT THE LIGHT OF THE WORLD, New York, 1930

Breasted, James H. THE DAWN OF CIVILIZATION, Chicago, Ill., 1928

Rogers, J.A. WORLD'S GREAT MEN OF COLOR, New York, 1947 [2 vols.]

Churchward, Dr. Albert ORIGIN AND EVOLUTION OF THE HUMAN RACE,
        London, 1920

Herodotus THE HISTORIES [transl. by Aubrey Selincourt, New York, 1961]

Volney, Count C.F. RUINS OF EMPIRE, Paris, 1800
        PYRAMID TEXT [Transls. by Budge; ben-Jochannan; Erdman]
        COFFIN TEXT [transls. by ben-Jochannan; Dods; Pete; Budge]
        OSIRIAN DRAMA [transls. by ben-Jochannan; Pete; Burgsch]

Augustine CONFESSION [transls. by ben-Jochannan; Meade; Ruffin]

--------- THE CITY OF GOD [transl. by M. Dods, in: Great Books of the
        Western World, Vol. 18, Chicago, Ill., 1952]

--------- ON CHRISTIAN DOCTRINE [transl. by ben-Jochannan]

Cone, James H. BLACK THEOLOGY AND BLACK POWER, New York, 1969

Chabas, E. Un HYMNE à OSIRIS [in: Revue Archéologique, t. XIV, pp. 65 ff]

Horrack, V. Les LAMENTATIONS d'ISIS et de NEPHTHYS, Paris, 1866

[Bibliography continued]

THE FESTIVAL SONGS OF ISIS and NEPHTHYS [in: Arch-
      aeologia, Vol. III, London, 1891]
Plutarch De Iside et Osiride, etc. [transl. by ben-Jochannan]
      BABYLONIAN TALMUD [6th Century C.E. European Version]
Herodotus THE HISTORIES [transl. by M. Markan, London, 1800]
--------- THE HISTORIES [transl. by Wilson Armistead, 1848]
Armistead, Wilson A TRIBUTE TO THE NEGRO, London, 1848
Davidson, Basil THE AFRICAN PAST, New York, 1967
Graves, Robert and Robert Patai HEBREW MYTHS, New York, 1961
Finch, A HISTORY OF THE ROMAN EMPIRE, New York, 1945
Hastings, James ENCYCLOPEDIA OF ETHICS, New York, 1889 [13 vols.]
Vail, C.H. ANCIENT MYSTERIES, New York [Date ?]
Lewis, H. Spencer MYSTICAL LIFE OF JESUS, New York
Besant, Annie ESOTERIC CHRISTIANITY, New York
Leslau, Wolf FALASHA ANTHOLOGY, New York, 1963
Stone, Joseph BLACK JEWS OF ETHIOPIA, London, 1892
Faitlovitch, Jacques THE FALASSA OF ETHIOPIE, Ethiopia, 1928 [transl.
      by ben-Jochannan]
ben-Jochannan, Yosef WE THE BLACK JEWS [Spanish pamphlet], Puerto
      Rico, 1938
Windsor, Rudolph FROM BABYLON TO TIMBUKTU, Phila., Pa., 1969
Stern, Isaac THE NEGRO JEWS, London, 1914
Williams, J. J. HEBREWISM IN WEST AFRICA, London, 1888
      PYRAMID TEXT OF PEPI I [transls.by Budge;and ben-Jochannan]
Petrie, Flanders THE GODS OF THE EGYPTIANS, Paris, 1890
MacGregor, Geddes A LITERARY HISTORY OF THE BIBLE, etc., London
Forlong, Major J.G.R. RIVERS OF LIFE, London, 1866
Lugard, Lady Flora S. A TROPICAL DEPENDENCY: AN OUTLINE OF THE
      ANCIENT HISTORY OF THE SUDAN WITH AN ACCOUNT OF
      THE MODERN SETTLEMENT OF NIGERIA, London, 1889
Drummond, Sir William ESSAY ON A PUNIC INSCRIPTION, London, 1848
Basnage, Maurice INDEPENDENT ANTIQUITY, Vol. IV, London, 1880
Plutarch de Iside et Osir [transl. by Sir Godfrey Higgins in : Anacalypsis,
      Vol I., London, 1830]
Knight, Payne METAMORPHIA LIB, XI
Graves, Kersey THE WORLD IXTEEN CRUCIFIED SAVIORS
Birch, S. HIERATIC INSCRIP.TION, London, 1890
Edwards, Amelia B. A THOUSAND MILES UP THE NILE, London
      PAPYRUS OF HUNEFER [transls: by Budge; ben-Jochannan;
      Pete; Burgsch; Mariette, etc.]

---

1. Note: Newspaper articles and magazine articles are shown as ILLUSTRATIONS.
Many other works have been consulted to obtain the necessary verification of the text in this
volume. However, only those works which the student can find in the better type of libraries
have been listed throughout the entire bibliography, pages 110 - 117. Consult your professor
for use of his personal library if any of the works is not in your library.

BIBLICAL CITATIONS ACCORDING TO CHRONOLOGICAL LISTING IN THE GENERAL TEXT

[King James Authorized Version Of The Old And New Testament used unless otherwise specifically cited by name, etc.]

118

SPECIAL INDEX
LISTINGS ACCORDING TO CHRONOLOGICAL APPEARANCE IN THE TEXT

Citation	Description	Page No.
	"creation of the world" according to the mythology developed by the Africans of the Mysteries System and plagiarized in the Judaeo-Christian-Islamic religious teachings about "Adam and Eve and the Garden of Eden"[allegory]in the Book Of Genesis.	viii
Magic	The mother of all religions.	viii – x
Jesus Christ	Jesus or "JOSHUA;" and Christ or "ANOINTED ONE."	xx
Death and Resurrection	The principle of Magical Incantations for the raising of the deceased caused by the Ka and Ba, or Heart-Soul and/or Body-Soul, etc.	xx
Slavery	Biblically similar to "chattle slavery" of the past in the United States of America when applying to the Jews as "SLAVES;" but changed to "SERVANTS" in modern Versions of the Old and New Testament where the Jews are shown as the SLAVEMASTERS.	xxiii
Inspired	To have an idea on religion in ancient days that was entered in either of the so-called "Old" and/or "New Testament;" this is somewhat accepted for the Moslem "Holy Quran;" all other religious writings and teachings are relegated to "paganism" and/or "idolatry."	xxvi
Scholar	In a religious sense a "Theologian." Usually limited to a male figure whose academic achievements are used to prepare himself with the halo of "DIVINE INSPIRATION;" others not so endowed with such alleged "prophetic" qualities are deemed "CHARLATANS, QUACKS, PAGANS."	xxx
Devil	In a religious sense anything or person condemned by Jews and Christians to be anti-GOD [Ywh and Jesus].	2
Virgin	A female untouched sexually by any male.	15
Cursed	To be "damned" in a religious sense; by God, no less.	40 – 42
Gospel	Allegedly "the teachings by/or of Jesus - the Christ."	45
Belief	To have hope, faith, desire, etc.; not necessarily a fact.	52
Sacred	That which Jews, Christians and Jews consider "Godly."	54
Immaculate	Pure, spiritually innocent; related to the "Virgin Mary."	56
Orthodox	Traditional acceptance of "primitive" values.	61
Tongues	A Christian euphoric mumbling - "speaking in tongues."	63
Holy Writings	Religious scripture of Judaeo-Christian-Islamic origin.	71
Authority	That which satifies one belief in a religious sense.	71
Version	A plagiarized substance of the original; not the same.	74
Canon	That which the rulers of the church approved as TRUTH	78

120